Trickster Tales of Southeastern Native Americans

D1570572

ALSO BY TERRY L. NORTON
AND FROM MCFARLAND

*Cherokee Myths and Legends:
Thirty Tales Retold* (2015)

Trickster Tales of Southeastern Native Americans

Stories from the Creek, Natchez, Seminole, Catawba, Cherokee and Other Nations

TERRY L. NORTON

McFarland & Company, Inc., Publishers
Jefferson, North Carolina

LIBRARY OF CONGRESS CATALOGUING-IN-PUBLICATION DATA

Names: Norton, Terry L., 1952– author.
Title: Trickster tales of southeastern Native Americans :
stories from the Creek, Natchez, Seminole, Catawba, Cherokee
and other nations / [adapted by] Terry L. Norton.
Other titles: Stories from the Creek, Natchez, Seminole, Catawba,
Cherokee and other nations
Description: Jefferson, North Carolina : McFarland & Company, Inc., Publishers,
2023 | Includes bibliographical references and index.
Identifiers: LCCN 2023006555 | ISBN 9781476691305 (print) ∞
ISBN 9781476649399 (ebook)
Subjects: LCSH: Indians of North America—Folklore. |
Tales—Southern States. | Tricksters.
Classification: LCC E98.F6 N67 2023 | DDC 398.2089/97—dc23/eng/20230221
LC record available at https://lccn.loc.gov/2023006555

BRITISH LIBRARY CATALOGUING DATA ARE AVAILABLE

ISBN (print) 978-1-4766-9130-5
ISBN (ebook) 978-1-4766-4939-9

Front cover image of rabbit painting © Valery Rybakow/Shutterstock

Printed in the United States of America

*McFarland & Company, Inc., Publishers
Box 611, Jefferson, North Carolina 28640
www.mcfarlandpub.com*

Whenever travelers carry stories from place to place, there will be re-imaginings, translations, appropriations, and impurities. Only the new versions won't be described with those words; artfully told, they will be known as "the truth."

—From Lewis Hyde,
Trickster Makes This World, p. 69

Contents

Contents

Contents

Preface

Purpose

Welcome to the world of the trickster. Here you will meet mischievous pranksters whose clever deceit often creates chaos but sometimes brings benefits. This character takes many forms and comprises a large portion of the traditional tales of Native Americans. Grounded in research and best practice in presenting their folklore and in storytelling, this book focuses on the trickster as he appears in the stories of several indigenous populations of the Southeastern United States.

Scattered among collections made by anthropologists, folklorists, and ethnologists, these stories are here brought together in a single book. Its aim is to introduce today's readers to neglected trickster tales told for generations by the Creek and some of the associated members of what in the eighteenth and nineteenth centuries was the powerful Creek Confederacy: the Hitchiti, Alabama, and Koasati (Coushatta). Also included are Southeastern trickster tales from the Natchez, Seminole, Catawba, and Cherokee. As adaptations from these indigenous peoples, the retellings maintain the culturally authentic plot and character content of the original sources (insofar as these sources preserved them) and are not rewritten to reflect current values and beliefs of what some critics deem appropriate moral and ethical behavior.

In *Books, Children, and Men*, a work as fresh today as when it appeared in 1944, famed member of the French Academy Paul Hazard describes such moralizing individuals as having "good intentions that seldom achieve their purposes."[1] Therefore, in retelling these trickster tales, I have refrained from softening their sporadic harshness or occasional earthy qualities because a character behaves in unsuitable ways in the judgment of contemporary audiences.

After all, to be a trickster is to be a rogue who acts outside conventional norms. In the words of nationally recognized folklore scholar

1

George E. Lankford, the trickster is "the dark side of all of us, freed from the social and personal rules that direct our normal behavior."[2] Little surprise then that he is often a wandering outcast who is frequently banned from settled habitations, lives on their fringes, or dwells far from them yet enters to disrupt them.

And yet, as this book's **Introduction to the Trickster** reveals, the trickster is more than the dark side of humanity, or what Carl Jung terms "the shadow"[3] and defines as the "inferior part of everybody's personality"[4] which expresses itself through "primitivity, violence, and cruelty."[5] No, as we shall see, the trickster is too multifaceted a figure to be confined to the dark side.[6] **Chart 1** and **Chart 2** in the **Introduction** serve as ready references to the trickster's many characteristics in world folklore and give examples of these traits in the retellings here.

Origins and Organization of the Selections

I have grouped the stories in this book based on the cultural and geographical native populations of the Southeast from which they were derived. Although their tricksters are sometimes people or a variety of animals, the foremost representative of the archetype and most often encountered is Rabbit. Based on John R. Swanton's 1929 *Myths and Tales of the Southeastern Indians*, I have placed three retellings about Rabbit at the beginning of the present collection. The reason for this arrangement is that "The Way of Rabbit," "Why Rabbit Steals," and "The People Discover Rabbit's Ways" are *pourquoi* tales that introduce and explain the how's and why's of Rabbit's roguish nature as an indigenous trickster. Other retellings from the Creek, whether the trickster is animal or human, follow.

Again, based on Swanton's groupings, stories derived from other members of the Creek alliance come next—that is, the Hitchiti, Alabama, and Koasati (Coushatta). After these are trickster selections from the Natchez who were not associated with the Creek but whose tales conclude Swanton's text. Because of some historical connections to the Creek, adaptations from the Florida Seminole comprise the next group. Robert F. Greenlee's field research, published in 1945 in *The Journal of American Folklore*, is the foundation for these stories.

Publications of anthropologist Frank Speck's research among the Catawba of the Carolinas serve as two sources for several additional trickster renderings. The first source is Speck's 1934 *Catawba Texts.* In this monograph, Speck supplies the stories in the original Siouan language of the Catawba with an English translation beneath the lines. The English, however, reads as fragmentary with disjointed syntax. To compensate for this drawback to comprehension of the narratives, Speck follows each story with a freer translation into English for easier reading. For the tales I judged to be trickster selections, I based my adaptations on these latter versions in his book. In addition to *Catawba Texts*, Speck's later research on Catawba folklore with Chief Sam Blue led to a second publication in 1947. With co-author L.G. Carr, nine stories appeared in *The Journal of American Folklore*, three of which are trickster tales and adapted here.

Sequenced last are narratives derived from James Mooney's *Myths of the Cherokee* (1900). The reason for assembling these selections after those of the other native groups is that one of the stories ("What Happened to Rabbit") explains how the preeminent trickster of Southeast vanished from the current world of animals and people. Consequently, I have placed this piece as the concluding tale. According to this account, today's animals are now diminished versions of their larger-than-life counterparts of old. Anthropologist Charles Hudson describes this world view as part of the native concept of "ancient time" as opposed "recent time." The beings of ancient time were not constrained by the limitations of recent time. For example, humans and animals could speak the same language.[7]

Mooney further clarifies the idea of ancient time when he says that the animals of long ago "were larger and of more perfect type than their present representatives" and "mingled with human kind upon terms of perfect equality and spoke the same language" before they eventually departed from the present world "for the world above, where they still exist."[8] The Cherokee story "What Happened to Rabbit," therefore, comes last and serves as an elegy to the passing of the mighty legendary character of Rabbit, even if he was for the most part a creator of chaos as a devious, lying rascal.

Issues of Authentication and Sovereignty

Authentication and *sovereignty* are important considerations in adapting literature that originates from Native Americans. **Appendices A, B, and C** address various aspects of these concerns.

Preface

Regarding authentic adherence to native cultures and traditions, **Appendix A: Story Adaptations and Authentication of Sources** provides additional information about the original print versions of the tales, all of which are in the public domain. This appendix also discusses in greater detail the men who collected and helped to preserve the stories—the major ones being John R. Swanton, Frank P. Speck, and James Mooney—along with some of their native informants as well as antecedent written sources such as the collection made by William O. Tuggle who served as a lawyer for the Creek and who in the 1880s traveled to Oklahoma Territory to record their folklore. Swanton derived a sizable portion of the first part of his collection from Tuggle.

Chart 3: Original Written Sources for the Adaptations accompanies **Appendix A**. Having access to this information allows readers to judge for themselves the accuracy and authenticity of my retellings when compared to the sources used, although the degree of these qualities in the sources is a matter of some question. One further consideration explored in **Appendix A** relates to controversies on adapting indigenous stories and my approach to presenting the selected trickster tales.

Appendix B: Sovereignty and Appropriation discusses the controversy of ownership of Native American folktales. The issue is one of on-going debate and will likely remain unresolved, but the main points of contention involve who may legitimately present traditional indigenous stories, whether orally or in print. That is, should only today's members of native groups have exclusive control over the presentation of their culture, or may informed individuals outside these populations render material that relates to indigenous folk narratives? **Appendix B** explores some of the key facets and limitations of this question, especially those surrounding oversimplified perspectives on appropriation.

Appendix C: Social Climate and Swanton's Use of Latin is an essay that delves into a unique issue of authenticity related to Swanton's collection besides his reliance on Tuggle's manuscript—namely, Swanton's shift in language from English to Latin whenever part of an indigenous trickster tale becomes off-color or sexually suggestive. Providing an overview of the restrictive social climate that prevailed in the United States between the middle of the nineteenth century though that of the twentieth, the essay surveys how definitions of obscenity and pornography developed in Western culture and were applied to both literary works of art and even to scholarly studies. This climate may have prompted Swanton to use Latin as a less accessible language than English to present parts of stories that in his day might have been considered offensive or having a *corrupting* influence.

Additional Information

Appendix D: Historical Sketches of Southeastern Native Groups and Comments on Selected Variants provides brief histories of the indigenous nations from which researchers compiled their selections. To illustrate similarities that sometimes occur across folktales, this appendix also examines parallel components among a few variants of the same story from different Southeastern nations. The appendix further discusses certain narratives that are derived from African and European sources or that contain parallel features with them.

Acknowledgments

The following members of the York County Chapter of the South Carolina Writers' Association read and offered comments on ways to improve the organization and content of this book: Chuck Brite, Joe Creech, Bobbie Harrison, Reggie Kee, Brodie Lowe, Daniel McGregor, Evelyn Eickmeyer-Quinones, and Donna Wiley. Retired Winthrop University professor of social studies education Jane White also read portions of the manuscript and provided valuable insights and suggestions from her knowledge of Native Americans of the Southeast. A big thank you also goes to the staffs of the Winthrop University Library and to the York County Library for help in my obtaining some of the sources consulted in writing this book.

Introduction to the Trickster

A Ubiquitous Character

The trickster abounds throughout the folk literature of the world and is perhaps its oldest character type. Rarely female, he may be a god, a person, or an animal with human traits. Among the gods are the Greeks' Hermes, the Norse's Loki, the Yorubas' Eshu or Legba of West Africa, the Chinese Monkey King, and the Indian subcontinent's young Krishna. Human tricksters include the sly Greek warrior Odysseus of Homer's epics and the German peasant Till Eulenspiegel of folktales from Middle Ages.

As a mark of the trickster's popularity, numerous folktales about the character have been adapted for school-age readers. Reviewing many of these adaptations for *School Library Journal*, Daryl Grabarek attests to the plethora of such selections, whether as picture books for early elementary grades or as anthologies for older ages.[1]

Among the fecund sources for trickster narratives are indigenous stories from North America. Animals are the primary tricksters of these tales. Folktales from Africa and from the African American tradition are also rife with animal tricksters. Native American narratives include figures like Raven of the Northwest, Coyote of the Southwest, and Rabbit of the Southeast. Among characters from Africa are not only Zomo the Rabbit but also the clever spider Anansi. Included in African American tales is, of course, Brer Rabbit. Perhaps not as well-known to a wider audience is the Signifying Monkey. Scholar Louis Henry Gates finds that this character from African American folklore has parallels in the West African deities Eshu and Legba.[2]

In the Southeastern United States, the trickster Brer Rabbit represents a cross-cultural merging of the indigenous Rabbit and tricksters brought to the New World by African slaves.[3] Professor of folklore David Elton Gay has noted that the blending of such stories from African American and Native American traditions is so interwoven that the tales cannot "be attributed to independent invention" by either group. As Gay observes, this cross-cultural fusion attests to "the long-term interaction" between these societies through which a new set of narratives common to both emerged.[4] He concludes that attempts to establish original sources, whether Native American or African American, is "of limited use" and detracts from "the study of cultural interactions" between the two traditions.[5]

Whatever may be the origins of stories about Brer Rabbit, the previously mentioned tricksters from world folklore reflect but a sampling of trickster manifestations, for a list of these figures could be written upon a long scroll. In the assessment of social philosopher Paul Mattick, Jr., the sweeping diversity of tales about tricksters has caused some anthropologists to question whether there is a universal type whose features can be defined.[6] While there is great variety among tricksters, such that some of them have cultural traits belonging to specific societies, religion professors William J. Hynes and William G. Doty argue that there are enough correspondences among different tricksters to warrant an overall portrait of the figure.[7]

Paul Radin's 1956 seminal study of the Winnebago cycle of myths finds credible evidence for the character's constancy across cultures. Radin describes the trickster as a figure of "special and permanent appeal and an unusual attraction for mankind from the beginnings of civilization." In the same passage, Radin also states that the "earliest and most archaic form" of the trickster is to be "found among North American Indians."[8]

Key Attributes

Yet who is the trickster? Salient features of his character, whether as found in folktales or older myths, emerge not only from Radin but also from additional descriptions by David Russell, Sheldon Cashdan, William J. Hynes, Carl Jung, Lewis Hyde, and Marilyn Jurich. Among the defining attributes of this archetype, Radin says that he is

at one and the same time creator and destroyer, giver and negator, he who dupes others and who is always duped himself. He wills nothing consciously. At all times he is constrained to behave as he does from impulses over which he has no control. He knows neither good nor evil, yet he is responsible for both. He possesses no values, moral or social, is at the mercy of his passions and appetites, yet through his actions all values come into being. But not only he, so our myth tells us, possesses these traits. So, likewise, do the other figures of the plot connected with him: the animals, the various supernatural beings and monsters, and man.[9]

Radin's depiction of the trickster invites comparison with what psychologist Sheldon Cashdan has said about the behavior of other characters found in traditional European fairy tales, even though the stories are not about tricksters. While some of these classic narratives may promote conventional ideas of right and wrong and notions of poetic justice, where the good are rewarded and the bad punished, many of the stories do not, according to Cashdan.

In *The Witch Must Die*, Cashdan analyzes such major European tales as "Hansel and Gretel," "Snow White," and "Cinderella." Based on his investigation, he argues that such fairy tales uniquely present "a specific failing or unhealthy predisposition in the self."[10] For example, "Hansel and Gretel" from the Brothers Grimm involves deceit when the father and stepmother lie to get rid of children they cannot feed. However, more central to the plot is the issue of greed when Hansel and Gretel come upon the witch's cottage. Although they satisfy their hunger, they continue to stuff themselves, with Hansel devouring a large piece of the roof and Gretel shoving out an entire windowpane of sugar to gorge herself. As Radin has said of Native American tricksters and their victims, the children in the German folktale cannot control their basic urges and appetites.

Humorously describing such behavior in terms of the "seven deadly sins of childhood," Cashdan proposes that "Hansel and Gretel" addresses gluttony and the ever-present struggle within children of "knowing when enough is enough."[11] Besides deceit, greed, and gluttony, other familiar stories concern themselves with envy, lust, vanity, and sloth.[12] Therefore, while Radin speaks of the trickster's duping others, lack of impulse control, being driven by appetites and passions, and the absence of social and moral values, Cashdan similarly refers to deceit, uncurbed greed and gluttony, and the notion that the familiar European stories teach little about justice and morality.

None of these age-old issues, however, negates the importance of folktales for children or, I might add, for adults. Beyond the appeal of entertainment and adventure, Cashdan contends these inner struggles are a significant reason that classic European folktales have maintained their value because they concentrate on universal conflicts children encounter as they grow and develop. He avers that the claim the stories impart ethical lessons on justice and morality, or on "correct behavior" promoting "how to succeed in life," is a "common misconception" among some folklorists.[13] For such purposes, Cashdan advises that well-meaning adults look to traditional literature like Aesop's fables or to other children's stories with overt didactic aims.[14]

Of course, the inner conflicts mirrored in folk narratives and enumerated by Cashdan occur within adults as well as children. In a similar fashion, the struggles that consume trickster stories are primarily those of inability to control appetite, the same ones Cashdan finds in "Hansel and Gretel"—namely, deceit, greed, and gluttony. Often, the character who is tricked is the one who lacks self-control and falls prey to being baited by the trickster. For instance, in the Catawba story retold here as "How Possum Tricked Deer and Wolf," the ravenous Wolf gulps down so much of the deer meat Possum tosses down from his safe perch that the more powerful, albeit greedy, predator eventually chokes to death on a hefty joint of venison, thus allowing Possum to escape.

Besides Radin, other scholars have traced additional contours of the trickster. Literature professor David L. Russell describes him as "ambivalent," sometimes heroic but also an "exasperating and wily character outwitting his compatriots," a figure who "delights in bringing havoc to the world." He is "often an antihero and troublemaker who makes life interesting and keeps the rest of us on our toes."[15]

In the indigenous folktales I have adapted, the trickster appears in many guises, whether as animals such as Fox, Partridge, Pig, Possum, Skunk, Terrapin, Turkey, Wildcat, or as human beings. As Russell has observed, such characters deceive and play pranks upon other characters. Many of these antics are humorous. Yet, as already noted, they are sometimes vicious and cruel from the perspective of mainstream morality which, at least on the surface, values compassion and fair play. In mapping the generic strands of the trickster, scholar William J. Hynes says this deceptive aspect emanates from the figure's being an "unconscious numbskull" or a "malicious spoiler."[16]

In the indigenous tales of this book, the lies and pranks are almost always the conscious acts of a cunning prankster like Rabbit. In speaking of the Cherokee version of Rabbit, Mooney found him "generally malicious."[17] I can think of none of the Southeastern stories retold here, whether the trickster is animal or human, in which a trick comes from a buffoon unaware of its consequences. Instead, it is a conscious act, often malevolent but sometimes beneficial.

Occasionally, however, the tables are turned, and the trickster is tricked and gets his comeuppance.[18] In several of the Native American narratives of the Southeast, Terrapin, the land tortoise, is a trickster. In "Terrapin Fools Rabbit" and "Terrapin Outwits the Wolves," he uses duplicity to overcome his antagonists. However, in "How Partridge Got His Whistle," Terrapin reluctantly lends Partridge his long-possessed whistle because the latter promises to return it. The swifter bird, though, keeps just out of reach of the slower Terrapin and soon flies onto the branches of a tree to escape with the stolen prize.

Even so, characters like Terrapin are not the most famous version of the trickster found among indigenous people of the Southeast. Appearing in the great majority of their stories in this collection, their supreme prankster is Rabbit, as already noted. Sometimes tricked by another animal like Terrapin, he deceives more than he is deceived and is a forerunner of more celebrated rabbit tricksters. These range from Brer Rabbit of the Uncle Remus tales of Joel Chandler Harris in the nineteenth century to modern figure like the "bardic" El-ahrairah in Richard Adams' 1972 novel *Watership Down* and to cartoon creations like Warner Brothers' Bugs Bunny who appeared around 1940.[19]

Although trickster narratives may stir oppressed peoples, such as slaves of the Old South and younger readers today, to identify with smaller, weaker characters like Brer Rabbit, who uses his brain to overcome larger, brawnier yet sometimes dimwitted antagonists, the Native American Rabbit is hardly a paragon of virtue or model of just behavior as the prior discussion of trickster attributes makes clear. He shares a pernicious nature with others of his type. Those who would question this view will find all doubts quickly evaporate on a perusal of tales about the fourteenth-century prankster Till Eulenspiegel of Germany. Though readers might argue his purpose is to humble the proud and deflate the pompous, a motive which holds true for many of the stories about him, Till often baits his victims based on nothing more than spite and malevolence. Indeed, among the many characteristics of Till enumerated by translator Paul Oppenheimer is that of sadist.[20]

Like the German Eulenspiegel, Rabbit, too, can be wickedly vengeful for no good reason if judged by conventional ethics. In the Creek narrative "Rabbit Fools Alligator," Rabbit's opening gambit appeals to Alligator's false pride in his own bravery, thereby rendering him subject to Rabbit's scheme. Thus, when Rabbit baits Alligator by asking whether he is afraid of the Devil, Alligator boasts that he is not, allowing Rabbit to use fire to torture Alligator, who, at the conclusion of the story, cannot understand such vindictiveness.

Introduction to the Trickster

Researcher Sandra K. Baringer, however, offers a plausible explanation for Rabbit's seemingly cruel behavior. She indicates that a story like "Rabbit Fools Alligator" partakes of a "cross-cultural" narrative pattern known as "raining fire." Found in several indigenous tales about Rabbit, this motif occurs when an ostensibly weaker character like Rabbit gains advantage over a stronger one like Alligator through manipulating a "powerful cosmic force" such as fire.[21] Of course, a reader not having this background information would likely agree with Alligator's conclusion in which he wonders why Rabbit is such a stony-hearted tormentor.

Besides vengefully displaying superior dominance, the trickster also can be a cultural hero as depicted in various indigenous stories concerning a related motif—the "theft of fire." Widely occurring, it is generally considered one of the oldest mythic patterns, and tales containing it often portray how the trickster relies on his own ingenuity to deceive more powerful fire hoarders. Even at the expense of harming himself, he steals fire to improve humankind's existence.[22]

In this anthology, the Catawba story, "Rabbit Steals Fire from Buzzard," is a variant of the "theft of fire" myth. As a buzzard flock jealously guard a fire in the middle of their circle, Rabbit convinces one of them to raise his wings. Rabbit then slips past and takes the precious fire. In the process, Rabbit burns his toes, but his theft provides people warmth and rest against the cold. (The lack of Native American compartmentalization between human and animal world here is also worth noting as it occurs throughout indigenous stories, not just those of the Southeast.)

Whether in manipulating or stealing cosmic forces like fire, Rabbit as trickster partakes of the nature of the Sun, "the most sacred Southeastern deity."[23] As explained by Hudson, fire was considered sacred and was the "earthly representative and ally of the Sun" as well as "the primordial symbol of purity."[24] Thus, when Rabbit rains fire, he has harnessed the power of the Sun, and when he steals fire, he has given a divine gift to earth's creatures. In this role, a trickster like Rabbit has, in the words of Hynes, crossed "the border between the sacred and profane."[25] In the case of the theft of fire, he has crossed a cosmic boundary, entered the divine, then returned from it as the bringer of a gift essential to the advancement of human society.[26]

Applying Radin's research, Jung describes this aspect of the trickster as an advancement over his earliest stage of development. In his first stage, "physical appetites dominate his behavior" and satisfaction of basic needs governs his acts as he "passes from one mischievous exploit to another." In Jung's view, he is at this phase "cruel, cynical, and unfeeling."[27] Yet, when he reaches his second stage, frequently portrayed by Native Americans as Hare or Coyote, the trickster "appears as the founder of human culture." Jung calls him at this stage "the Transformer."[28] Although he has not yet developed as a fully socialized individual, he has left behind his primitive appetitive urges.[29]

In *Trickster Makes This World: Mischief, Myth, and Art*, cultural critic Lewis Hyde enumerates comparable characteristics discussed thus far as well as others that emerge from trickster tales around the world. **Chart 1** below applies key features from Hyde's study of this figure to Southeastern stories and serves as a ready reference for readers interested in such attributes.[30]

Concerning Southeastern tricksters presented here, the last item of **Chart 1** on promiscuity perhaps needs further explanation. Hyde says that the trickster ignores "boundary markers."[31] In the retold Creek story "How Rabbit Won a Second Wife," Rabbit directs his cunning toward the sexual. He ignores the confines of societal sanctions against adultery and multiple partners. To instigate a tryst with his wife's sister, Rabbit becomes what Hynes calls a "lewd bricoleur."[32] As such, he is a fixer who engages in forming a creative solution or construction with whatever is readily available. Rabbit accordingly invents a story about a bear hunt in which the participants must leave their wives at home and take only their sisters-in-law. At the campsite for the hunt, Rabbit and his wife's sister engage in an illicit union. Rabbit tricks the girl into making her bed on an anthill so that she tosses and turns and cannot sleep. Rabbit leaves his bed on the other side of the fire and goes to comfort her. In Swanson's euphemistic rendition, he then begins "his wooing," thus "winning his second bride."[33]

Chart 1: Summary of Salient Trickster Traits from Folktales, Myths, and Legends (based on *Trickster Makes This World: Myth, Mischief, and Art* by Lewis Hyde)

Trickster Trait	Characters	Indigenous Group/ Story
1. Disturbs or crosses settled boundaries, whether physical or social (13)	Rabbit invades Buzzard's circle to steal fire and let others get warm.	Catawba, "Rabbit Steals Fire from Buzzard"

Introduction to the Trickster

Trickster Trait	Characters	Indigenous Group/ Story
2. Creates traps, often through lies, or sets bait for the unwary who cannot curb appetites or desires (20)	A boy persuades a hungry, "bad" woman to find a deer he killed so that he and his mother can escape.	Catawba, "The Woman Who Stole a Boy and Became a Comet"
3. May be trapped and have his wits sharpened (31)	Wolf traps Pig in Pig's house. Pig claims people are coming. Wolf panics, and Pig kills him.	Catawba, "Pig and Wolf"
4. Toys with and overturns rules (22–23)	Partridge breaks his word, refusing to return Terrapin's whistle.	Cherokee, "How Partridge Got His Whistle"
5. Readily adapts to survive (43)	Rabbit creates a dance to keep from being eaten.	Cherokee, "Rabbit Escapes from Wolves"
6. Takes advantage of opportunities (46–47, 96–97, 140)	Possum uses Wolf's greedy cravings for deer meat to kill Wolf.	Catawba, "How Possum Tricked Deer and Wolf"
7. Sometimes uses disguises or may be a shape-shifter (51–52)	Rabbit turns into a squirrel to trick Alligator into being friends with him.	Seminole, "Rabbit Wants a Wife"
8. Uses double meanings against the literal-minded (57)	Rabbit says he's "a treasure" inside a hollow stump and tricks a man into cutting him out.	Cherokee, "Rabbit Hunts Ducks"
9. Is often a wanderer who stands in portals (39, 41, 96, 125)	Rabbit travels deep into the mountains, stands between worlds in gates and doorways, encounters the hated Flint, and invites him for a visit on the outside of the animals' settlement. Rabbit waits until Flint falls asleep, then causes him to explode.	Cherokee, "How Rabbit Got a Split Lip"
10. Encounters a chance meeting, sometimes at a crossroads, where life is disturbed and change results (120)	Terrapin and Turkey meet by chance. Terrapin loses his scalp as a war trophy. The trickster Turkey gains dark breast feathers that look like scalp hair.	Cherokee, "Terrapin Loses His Scalp"

Trickster Trait	Characters	Indigenous Group/ Story
11. Introduces dirt (filth) into society to disturb its orderliness or stasis (185–187)	A warrior kills a monster snake, but Rabbit claims credit by bringing its rotting body into a village. The elders discover his ruse, tie the putrid snake to him, and banish him.	Creek, "The People Discover Rabbit's Ways"
12. Is promiscuous (284–285)	Rabbit has his wife stay home and takes her sister on a bear hunt. He and the sister become intimate.	Creek, "How Rabbit Won a Second Wife"

This last libidinous feature is one of the trickster's common attributes. Among the sources used for the Southeastern stories in this anthology, the retelling "How Rabbit Won His Second Bride" is among several in its depiction of the promiscuous side of the trickster's nature. Margaret Baker's essay argues that Brer Rabbit, as portrayed by Joel Chandler Harris, demonstrates "little that is sexually suggestive" and that, when the character does, it is "very subdued."[34] Baker speculates that this dearth of libidinous behavior occurs because children were the primary audience for the stories and because Harris collected his material toward the end of the nineteenth century and during the early twentieth, "a time of legendary resistance to anything prurient."[35]

Both of Baker's explanations are plausible. And yet another reason for little sexuality in Brer Rabbit tales could be the association of Harris and his fellow Georgian William O. Tuggle. Hudson states that Harris knew the Tuggle family and that he had read Tuggle's manuscript containing Creek narratives. Several of the stories Harris published use Tuggle's wording "almost to the letter."[36] In thus following the source material for Creek tales, Harris had little from Tuggle's work to indicate Rabbit as being a licentious trickster.

These tales from Tuggle also comprise 46 out of 91 selections in the first part of Swanton's collection, "Creek Stories." Only the tale of Rabbit's seduction of his wife's sister suggests the character's overt promiscuity. However, other stories in Swanton, which he derived from groups associated with the Creek Confederacy—for instance, the Hitchiti—and from the independent Natchez, contain a handful of narratives about

Rabbit's concupiscence. **Appendices B** and **C** probe this topic further, particularly Swanton's use of Latin when Rabbit becomes more explicitly lustful.

As an aside, the Creek manner of dealing with adulterous violations of normative behavior is instructive considering the dire consequences that Rabbit and his sister-in law might have faced. The wanton couple are indeed lucky no one caught them. For among the Creek, as recorded by Tuggle in *The Indian Diary*, a Creek man revealed that the "sacredly observed" punishment for infidelity was to beat the adulterous offenders "senseless" and then saw off their ears with a "dull knife." According to this informant, whose wife had been unfaithful, he and a party of about thirty other men invoked this Creek sanction and went to the house where his wife and her lover were. There, the enforcers cut off the ears of both "close to the head."[37] After the infliction of this sort of penalty, according to Hudson's wry comment, generally a "marriage was thereby dissolved."[38]

The Cherokee did not impose severe sanctions against adultery. Whether unattached or married, a Cherokee woman would sleep with a willing partner. She could be as unrestrained sexually as a Cherokee man.[39]

Gender Issues

Part of the scholarly discussion of the trickster concerns the seeming rarity of female versions of the archetype. While the present brief introduction is not intended to review the entirety of the debate, the work of Lewis Hyde and Marilyn Jurich provides a framework for comparing different perspectives. Both their books on tricksters saw publication in 1998.

In a review for the *Los Angeles Times* of *Trickster Makes This World*, Canadian author Margaret Atwood has called Hyde "an illuminationist," or someone who "casts light" as "one of those quirky, eccentric Wise Children" that the United States sometimes produces.[40] In his book on tricksters, Hyde asserts that "All the standard tricksters are male." He acknowledges that a few are "androgynous, or at least of indeterminate sexuality."[41] Yet the characters in these cases—for example, Loki—are originally male. After briefly becoming female, they resume a male identity.[42] As for the dearth of female tricksters, Hyde posits three possible explanations: the archetype may derive from patriarchal societies; there may be female versions that have been disregarded; and trickster tales present attributes of the figure that are essentially male "so that even in a matriarchal setting this figure would be male."[43]

Hyde indicates the first explanation of patriarchal cultures not having female tricksters has some plausibility. The male sky-god mythologies of these cultures may have supplanted earlier cultures in which female deities of the earth had primacy. For instance, as heavenly Zeus became more important than terrestrial Demeter, stories of puissant goddesses, some of whom might be trickster figures, grew ever fainter over time.[44]

This change in religious focus, Hyde says, could account for his second explanation. In other words, there are few female tricksters because authorities in folk literature are not aware of or have ignored traditions in which these characters appear. Although he admits that numerous narratives exist about women who lie, thieve, and engage in other unabashed devices of deceit, since these actions are not solely the province of males, he would omit such females from a definition of the trickster. They might have "pulled a trick or two," but they do not have "an elaborated career of trickery." In Hyde's view, a devious act or two "do not make a trickster."[45]

In contrast to Hyde, rather than on myths, Jurich concentrates more on folktales or literary works having a basis in folklore like *The Taming of the Shrew.* Of course, the different categories are not airtight. Nonetheless, in *Scheherazade's Sisters: Trickster Heroines and Their Stories in World Literature,* she surveys some 185 narratives and variants from around the globe. Citing research analyzing the commonly accepted guides on folklore patterns and subjects (Stith Thompson's six volume *Motif-Index of Folk Literature* and Antti Aarne's *The Types of Folktales*), Jurich finds them "faulty" because of a patriarchal bias that lacks "both inclusiveness and objectivity."[46] Thompson's work, for example, contains motifs that disregard women's roles as tricksters. In Jurich's judgment, earlier scholarly works have been reluctant to accept folk narratives in which a female is capable of hoodwinking men and in which she is patently able to rescue them from difficult situations.[47]

In contrast to past patriarchal neglect, Jurich's study reveals "how women can rescue themselves and others *through tricks,* pursue what they need or desire *through tricks,* transform what they find unworkable or unworthy *through tricks.*"[48] She acknowledges that female tricksters can be ambiguous like male characters. Both can perform bad and good tricks. But Jurich concentrates on the motives behind the trick. Bad tricks may be driven by "cruelty or self-aggrandizement" and cause "harm or distress" to "well-intentioned and trusting" victims.[49] Good tricks, on the other hand, can eliminate perils and persecutions, bring desirable changes with long-lasting beneficial results, and ensure no reprisals against those formerly marginalized or deemed outcasts.[50]

Based on Jurich's analysis of folktales, along with some attention to performers of trickery in mythology, the Bible, and Shakespeare, four categories of male and female tricksters emerge. (Jurich coins the term "trickstar" for the latter group.[51]) Although the categories are not mutually exclusive, her designation of types provides additional insight into trickster/trickstar attributes.[52] A condensed description of Jurich's groupings follows. **Chart 2** features examples of these types and their traits as revealed in Southeastern indigenous tales retold in this collection.

Jurich's first type of trickster/trickstar is the jester or buffoon who uses physical comedy as well as disguises and deception to divert or amuse. A subdivision of this category is the simpleton, who is deceived more than deceiving and who is often admired for honesty and humble ways. There is also the wise fool who ironically sees into the true nature of things unlike those whom the world mistakenly deems wiser.

A second type ranges from the morally questionable to deplorable. This grouping includes demons, betrayers, seducers, and thieves. Among their traits are the pursuit of power and profit, self-aggrandizement, and degradation of victims. Yet, with the thief, robbery may sometimes be a means to rectify an inequity.

The next category embraces conjurors, facilitators, and translators. The first might use magic and illusions to achieve ends. The second exploits current conditions to effect desired aims and has the capability to predict how other characters will react to events. The third subdivision of translators in this category manipulates language in the knowledge that a victim will interpret a phrase one way while there are other interpretations that the translator uses to advantage.

Jurich designates her last grouping of tricksters as culture heroes and heroines. These figures foster positive social outcomes and encompass "all that is worthy" and serve as examples to which others may "aspire."[53] Although Southeaster tricksters like Rabbit and Terrapin, as illustrated in **Chart 2,** are too primitive in their development to qualify as full exemplars of this type, they do occasionally partake of the finer traits of culture heroes and heroines as previously demonstrated in the Catawba theft-of-fire story in which Rabbit brings benefits to society.

Chart 2: Examples of Southeastern Tricksters Based on Jurich's Categories

Trickster Category	Trickster Action	Indigenous Group/ Story
1. Jester/Buffoon who amuses through physical action or slapstick	Rabbit offers food to his friend Coyote but ties his tail to a sleeping colt. The colt wakes up and frantically drags Coyote over the ground.	Creek, "Rabbit Fools Coyote"
2. Morally questionable or deplorable	A village council decides to punish Rabbit for his lies and lock him in a box until he faces trial. Rabbit persuades a little boy to let him out, then locks the child in the box. The box floats down river, and the boy dies.	Creek, "Rabbit Escapes from the Box"
3. Translator/Facilitator who can predict how others will react and uses language meanings to control outcomes.	Wolves capture Terrapin and threaten various ways to kill him. He replies how he will foil each attempt. They then decide to throw him in the deepest hole in the river. He uses reverse psychology and begs them not to. They do and he swims off.	Cherokee, "Terrapin Outwits the Wolves"
4. Culture Hero/Heroine who positively influences society	Lion, or Man-Eater, has been killing and devouring many people. Rabbit tricks him into jumping back and forth over a creek. When Lion lands for a final time on the opposite bank, the creek widens into an ocean and leaves Lion stranded in Africa.	Creek, "Rabbit Gets Lion Stranded Across the Ocean"

Concerning the Southeastern tales adapted here, except for the grandmother in the Catawba tale "The Cherokee Hunter Outwitted," none of the other trickster figures is female, whether animal or human. This circumstance occurs despite the fact that indigenous societies in the Southeast were matrilineal. Hudson has noted that, although their source of descent derived through women and women held esteemed positions, the conclusion does not follow that women controlled these societies. Land, houses, and other property may have been owned by females, but "effective political power lay in the hands of men" who ordinarily made all the significant decisions.[54] This finding comports with research furnished by Hyde on the gender of tricksters in Native Americans stories. Out of hundreds of their trickster tales, research shows that only about twenty concern females and none could be described as culture heroes/heroines.[55] In other words, these figures would not be included in Jurich's last category where *trickstars* may appear.

In an evaluation of Jurich's work, folklorist Margaret A. Mills calls it "a rich tapestry," well-researched in its review of female tricksters across cultures and in its critique of tricksters as primarily male.[56] Nevertheless, Mills offers some important reminders in relying solely on print versions of traditional tales and on literature having them as a core foundation. Such texts are decontextualized from oral presentations which involve both how a potential male storyteller frames his narration and how an audience reacts to it. These features of a story told orally also change over time or are repositioned in how an audience interprets them.[57] In her recording and examination of approximately 500 selections told aloud in the 1970s by Persian speakers in Afghanistan, Mills did not encounter "the pervasive misogyny" found in some written texts and thought by Jurich to be "operating fairly uniformly among male narrators."[58]

Conclusion

In summary, the foregoing discussion demonstrates the many attributes the trickster possesses throughout world folklore and in tales of Southeastern Native Americans. Depending on the behavior of an individual representation of a character in different trickster stories or within same story, these "universal and multifaceted qualities" may be dualistic and reflect "antithesis as an essential part" of humanity.[59]

Julius Lester, the late academic and adapter of Brer Rabbit tales for young readers, framed the contradictions within trickster figures as "not the result of cultural borrowings, but of the universality of what it is to be human."[60]

This antithesis occurs throughout Southeastern trickster narratives. In the Creek selection "Rabbit Gets Lion Across the Ocean," Rabbit saves people from the depredations of Lion, or Man-Eater. Yet, in "The People Discover Rabbit's Ways," Rabbit claims credit for killing a monster snake that has devoured two village girls. The people are so disgusted with his lie, they tie the dead serpent around his neck as a sign of his baseness. In the Catawba tale, "How Possum Tricked Deer and Wolf," Possum in the role of trickster denies his appetitive urges, as he sits atop a meat rack, and uses dried venison to bait Wolf, who ultimately chokes to death from lack of self-control. On the other hand, in the Cherokee Story "Why Possum's Tail Has No Hair," Possum is baited by Rabbit who appeals to Possum's vanity about his bushy tail. Rabbit thereby tricks him into having it sheared by Cricket. In "Terrapin Outwits the Wolves," also a Cherokee narrative, the land turtle cleverly contrives to get the Wolves to throw him into the river so that he may escape his doom. However, in the Cherokee selection "How Partridge Got His Whistle," Terrapin is foolish to trust Partridge and too readily gives up his whistle. Terrapin thus allows the faster-moving bird to steal it. Other instances of the double nature of the trickster are abundant.

In pondering the disposition of this archetypal character, Swiss psychoanalyst Carl Jung also refers to this dualistic quality and suggests the figure embodies the conflict between inward primitiveness in humankind and its outward expression of civilization—that is, the struggle between "the two dimensions of consciousness" which is "dependent on the tension of opposites."[61] Beyond the entertainment value of the narratives, Jung concludes that these contradictory inclinations inherent in the trickster are a fundamental reason the stories have lasted. For us as consumers of the tales today, they mirror a less advanced, more primitive stage of moral and intellectual human development, thereby reminding us of what life was once like while at the same time fostering our hope to abandon and forget it, something which cannot be done.[62]

Creek Tales

The Way of Rabbit

From the outset, Rabbit was not content with his lot in life. So, he went to the Ruler of All and said, "Each animal has a better means of fighting than I have. If I'm attacked, the only thing I can do is run."

The Ruler of All responded, "Do you see yonder Rattlesnake? Bring him to me."

Rabbit looked where the Ruler pointed and saw Rattlesnake sunning himself, coiled up and itching to strike. But Rabbit went over anyway, taking a long stick and a piece of string. "The Ruler of All has commanded me to measure you. If you uncoil, I'll see how long you are."

With the sun in his eyes, Rattlesnake could not see the stick and string. But flattered by Rabbit's attention, he proudly uncoiled and stretched himself out to his complete length.

Rabbit rapidly tied the stick around Rattlesnake's head and tail, then brought him to the Ruler. "You have done well," He said. "Now fetch me yonder host of gnats that sing and swarm."

Rabbit took a sack and hopped beneath the swarm and sat down to watch. He noticed that Chief Gnat was playing ball with his young warriors. "You have a large band of men," he noted. "The Ruler of All has ordered me to count your mighty braves. If you fly into this sack, they will follow you and will be easier for me to number."

Pleased by Rabbit's slick tongue, Chief Gnat instantly vanished into Rabbit's bag with all his young warriors close behind. Rabbit hurried to the Ruler of All and lay the sack before him.

"BEHOLD HOW CRAFTY YOU ARE," thundered the Ruler. "Now go. Use the cunning I have given you, and you will realize your destiny."

23

Why Rabbit Steals

Not long after creation, the animals met and decided each one should pick a tree or other plant. Its fruit would belong to that animal's offspring for all time. The animals let Rabbit go first. He could not decide which one to choose, so he went down to the river and walked along the edge as he looked over the trees one after the other. He finally halted beneath the sycamore tree and looked up. Seeing the big seed balls growing from its branches, he said, "I choose the sycamore for my tree."

The rest of the animals then selected what they wanted. Raccoon picked the muscadine vine, and Possum the persimmon tree, and in that way the animals chose the various fruits to be their own.

After a while, Rabbit became hungry and hopped down to the river where his sycamore towered. He searched and rooted over the ground for seed balls, but not a one was there. Then he gazed into the tree where he saw hundreds in the branches. "I'll just sit here and bide my time," he thought. "Some are bound to drop before long."

Rabbit waited, and he waited, and he waited. Dark came and still no seed balls. At last, he hopped home hungry.

Morning came, and back came Rabbit. He peered here, and he peered there. Still no sycamore balls. So, he plopped down under the tree again and sat there all day. Again, he went home hungry.

The third day came, and Rabbit returned. This time, though, he looked a little thin and his eyes were bigger. He stared into the limbs of the sycamore until he got thinner and thinner and his eyes bulged out even more. He waited there until he thought he would die.

When night fell, Rabbit decided he had best eat something. So, he slipped around to where the other animals lived and stole what they had gathered. That's why Rabbit steals today, and that's why all his kin look like him—skinny and with their big eyes bulged out.

The People Discover Rabbit's Ways

The people soon discovered Rabbit's cunning ways through a mysterious event. One time three pretty girls lived close to a spring. Rabbit saw them, fell in love, and often called on them. Not long after, one of the girls went to fetch water at the spring and disappeared. A search party looked high and low but could find no sign of her. Because of his frequent visits, everyone suspected foul play from Rabbit.

Not too many days later, a second sister disappeared. The last time anybody saw her, she had headed toward the spring, but the search party never found her.

As a reward for learning what happened, the father offered the third sister's hand in marriage to anyone who could shed light on the missing girls. Eager to win a bride, a young warrior decided to watch the spring day and night.

One night, a huge snake slithered out of the water as if searching for prey. The warrior killed the monster, and chopping off its head, he took it to his village as a sign of his conquest. There he would display the trophy the next morning.

Rabbit had heard the young man's struggle with the snake and had hidden in the bushes near the spring. When he saw the warrior leave, he took the serpent's body and dragged it to the settlement early the next morning while everyone still slept.

From the council ground, Rabbit yelled, "Here Is the Monster That Killed the Girls! Come and See the Monster I Destroyed!"

Everyone ran to the center of the village. "Rabbit has killed the monster. He has won his bride."

Shortly thereafter, the beautiful third sister, arrayed in a soft deerskin tunic with fancy beadwork, came forward. Rabbit stepped forth to take her hand. But at that moment, the young warrior entered the council ground. Opening a large pouch, he pulled out a bloody object. He lifted it aloft and proclaimed, "Behold the serpent's head. I killed the monster at the spring and cut off his head. There I left his body still writhing in death. I claim the girl's hand." The wedding took place at once between the brave warrior and the last beautiful sister.

As for Rabbit, the villagers tied the decaying body of the snake around his neck. They drove him away as a rascal who lives by lies and tricks. "Take the dead snake," they said. "Like him, you are rotten."

Rabbit Gets Lion Across the Ocean

Long ago, Lion did not live in Africa but on this side of the ocean. Called Man-Eater, he would kill people and devour them. So, everybody wanted Lion on the other side and begged for Rabbit's help.

One day while he was heading from west to east, Rabbit met Lion traveling from east to west. Acting curious, Rabbit said, "What do you eat during your travels?"

"Why, I eat a lot of things when I travel," Lion growled. "What do you eat?"

"Oh, I eat many things, too. Same as you. Why don't we go along together? I know where we can find droves of people."

As the two made their way, Rabbit said, "There's a place up ahead where we can make camp tonight. It's along a creek called Throwing-Hot-Ashes-on-One."

The idea suited Man-Eater just fine. About nightfall, he and Rabbit got to the creek. They made a warm fire, sat down, and talked for quite a spell. After a time, they started nodding off, and Rabbit asked, "What kind of sound do you make when sleeping?"

Lion let out a deep gruff snore. "And what kind of noise do you make?"

"Oh, I just whimper a little every now and then."

Each then lay down on either side of the fire, and pretty soon Rabbit began to whimper softly, "*Nutz. Nutz. Nutz.*" Man-Eater thought Rabbit was now asleep and not long after started snoring like somebody sawing big old thick logs.

All the time, though, Rabbit kept peeping at him until he was sure Lion was sound asleep. Suddenly, Rabbit shot up, took some cold ashes, and dusted himself all over. He then grabbed a wide flat piece of bark and tossed hot ashes and coals on Lion who reared up with a loud roar and yelled, "WHAT IN TARNATION?"

"Don't you remember this creek's named Throwing-Hot-Ashes-on-One? Here's what we'll have to do. Let's jump over to the other side. HURRY! HURRY!" So, Rabbit jumped, and Lion followed.

"NOW JUMP BACK!" Over the creek went Rabbit with Lion right behind him.

"ONE MORE TIME!" Rabbit yelled.

Lion jumped again, but Rabbit stayed put on the west bank. The creek suddenly widened. It grew wider and wider until an ocean separated the east bank from the west bank. Hoping to cross to the other side, Man-Eater roamed up and down the east bank.

Finally, an enormous crane came along. "Do you know how I can get to the other side?" Lion wondered.

"If you climb on my back," answered the crane, "I'll poke my bill into the far bank, and you can walk across."

Man-Eater did just as the crane said, but when he stepped on the crane's long neck, the bird let out a pained cry. "STOP IT! GET OFF! YOU'RE BREAKING MY NECK!"

Lion tried several more times, but each time the crane moaned and groaned something awful about his neck. Lion never was able to cross the ocean. And that's how Rabbit got rid of Man-Eater.

Rabbit Plays Scratch with Wildcat

As Rabbit hopped down a sandy path one day, he noticed some tracks. He raised one of his forepaws and looked closely at the prints in the soft sand. "Whoever made these tracks doesn't have sharp claws like mine."

Rabbit went on his way. After a while, he saw Wildcat resting a little way down the trail. "Those clawless tracks must be his," thought Rabbit. "Here's a chance for some fun."

Rabbit came closer to Wildcat. "You want to play scratch to see who can get the most fur?"

Wildcat grinned. "Sure. Go ahead. I'll play."

"I'll go first." Rabbit stood beside Wildcat and scratched his back as hard as he could. Thinking his claws would be full of hair, Rabbit turned his paw over. He looked it up and down but not a single hair did he see. "No matter," he said to himself. "He doesn't have any claws and can't scratch me."

"My turn," purred Wildcat. Faster than a bullet covered in bear grease, he lashed out with a forepaw and raked it down Rabbit's back. The fur flew, and off came Rabbit's tail. Since that day, Rabbit has only a little white ball of hair where his tail once was.

Rabbit Challenges Two Tie-Snakes

On the opposite sides of a bend in a river lived two tie-snakes. Like others of their kind, they had once been hunters but had mixed and eaten forbidden food like the brains of a black male squirrel, a turkey gobbler, or a blacksnake. As the hunters slept, they would slowly change into huge water snakes with many coils and with horned heads of different colors—yellow, green, white, but mostly blue.

27

Now these two tie-snakes had never met. Rabbit, though, knew where their dens were. One day he approached one of the snakes and challenged, "Let's take a grapevine and have a contest. We'll play tug-o-war and see who's the strongest."

Thinking he could easily beat Rabbit, the big snake agreed. So, they set a time for the contest. Rabbit then crossed over the river and challenged the other tie-snake to the same contest. He agreed as well.

In the meantime, Rabbit cut a thick grapevine. At the appointed hour, he took one end to one serpent and one end to the other. On a little sandy island in the middle of the bend, Rabbit hid among some brush. "NOW PULL!" he hollered.

Well, the two big snakes started tugging. Back and forth they went. One would pull the other almost over the river. The other would then rally and nearly pull the opposite snake across. They thought they were tugging against Rabbit. Both had never judged him to be this strong.

Back and forth went the tie-snakes for hours. Finally, both slithered around the river bend and saw each other. Boy, were they mad at Rabbit. They were so angry they declared, "Let's not allow Rabbit to drink any water from here. We can each keep watch on our own sides of the river."

But that rule did not bother Rabbit. He changed into a dappled fawn so that the tie-snakes could not see him. As such, he quietly stepped down toward river and drank as much water as he wanted.

Rabbit and the Buffaloes' Tug-o-War

Rabbit once saw two buffaloes. One lay on one side of a hill, and the other lay on the opposite side. He hopped up to one of them. "Everybody is always bragging about how strong you are. Let's have a contest, a tug-o-war. I know I'm small, but I'll pull against you, and you pull against me. That way, we can see which one's stronger. When I let out a whoop, you pull."

The buffalo said, "Why should I bother myself with a little fellow like you?" But Rabbit kept on pestering him until he finally agreed to the contest.

"I need to take care of some business first," said Rabbit, "but you wait right here, and I'll be back before you know it." Rabbit then went to the opposite side of the hill where he talked the other buffalo into the same contest with him. He got a long grapevine and stretched it across the hill so that the two could each hold an end in their mouths.

Unbeknown to the pair, Rabbit placed himself in the center of the grapevine at the top of the hill. He then let out a loud shriek. Well, they tugged and they pulled, and they pulled and they tugged. One buffalo would tug the other nearly to the top, and then that one would do the same to his opponent. Back and forth they went, with Rabbit letting out a whoop every little bit.

After a while, the buffaloes started to think something was wrong. They dropped the grapevine, and each headed to the other side of the hill when they bumped into each other. One said, "That Rabbit has played us for fools." So, they decided, "Let's torment him. We'll guard the creek and not let him have any water." And they did just that.

After a time, Rabbit became so thirsty he thought he would pass out. Lucky for him, though, a handsome buck came along. Rabbit got an idea. "Can I borrow your shoes?" he asked.

The buck agreed. Rabbit put them on and headed for the creek where the buffaloes were resting. Neither knew what to think when he called out, "I heard tell you two won't let Rabbit drink from your creek, but I guess you won't mind if I take a sip."

The buffaloes were baffled. The fellow looked like Rabbit, but the tracks were somebody else's. "Rabbit tried to trick us in tug-o-war. That's why we won't let him drink here. But you, Mr. Deer, may have some water."

So, Rabbit quenched his thirst and went back to the buck. As he pulled off the shoes, he laughed and let out a loud whoop. "THAT'S HOW YOU FOOL THEM!"

Rabbit Fools Alligator

One day Alligator had crawled out of the water to sun himself on a log when along came Rabbit who called out, "Mr. Alligator, have you ever seen the Devil?"

"No, I haven't, Mr. Rabbit, but I wouldn't be scared to see him," Alligator answered.

"You know I've seen the Devil, and he told me you were too scared to look at him."

Alligator smiled. "He doesn't frighten me, and you can tell the Devil I said so."

Rabbit looked down at the ground, then looked back up at Alligator. "Since you're such a brave fellow, would you allow me to show him to you?"

"Why certainly," said Alligator.

"Well, if you come up the hill tomorrow, I'll show you the Devil. You'll likely see smoke rising, but don't worry. That's a sign the Devil's barely started on his way."

"Don't fret about me," Alligator replied. "I'M NOT SCARED."

"Now there'll likely be birds squawking and flying all over the place and deer and other animals hightailing by you. But you won't be afraid like them, will you?"

"Oh, no. Not a bit afraid," Alligator bragged.

"Of course, you'll hear fire start to popping and cracking close by, and you'll see the grass blazing all around. Then the Devil will come traipsing by, and you can get a good look at him. You sure you won't get scared?"

"Listen," said Alligator a little put out. "You needn't be so concerned about me. That Devil doesn't frighten me in the least."

"All right," said Rabbit. "I'll be back tomorrow."

The next day, Rabbit returned and shouted, "GET ON OUT OF THE WATER, ALLIGATOR, AND GO ON UP THE HILL. THE DEVEL'S ON HIS WAY!" Alligator crawled out and went up the hill to wait in the high grass.

When Alligator had gotten to the top of the hill far away from the water, Rabbit grinned and laughed. He took off toward a tree that lightning had hit, snatched a burning branch, and ran back up the hill. He set the grass on fire and watched it blaze in a circle around Alligator. Rabbit then hopped over to a sandy bare patch and sat down under a tree to see what would happen. Smoke soon thickened the air, birds rose in clouds, and the four-footed beasts skedaddled for their lives.

Alligator could barely see as he called out, "MR. RABBIT, WHAT'S GOING ON?"

"Don't worry. Just stay still. It's only the Devil coming. He's just started out."

Sputtering and sizzling, the fire quickly swept through the high grass. "OH, MR. Rabbit, WHAT'S THAT SOUND?" Alligator moaned.

"Calm down. That's nothing but the Devil catching his breath. You'll see him soon enough." Rabbit rolled around in the sand and kicked his hind legs aloft.

By now, the fire had surrounded Alligator and burned nearer and nearer until it lit the grass beneath him. He twisted and flailed this way and that.

"Don't Be Afraid, Mr. Alligator! Try to Stay Still a Liitle Longer! The Devil's Almost There, and You Can Get an Eyeful of Him!" Rabbit shouted as he saw Alligator thrashing around from the heat. But Alligator had had enough. He set off down the hill through the blazing grass and headed toward water, all the while snapping and biting and carrying on from the pain.

"Whoa, Mr. Alligator," Rabbit laughed. "What's the big hurry? You aren't afraid of that old Devil, are you?"

Alligator paid no attention and plopped in the water as fast as he could. As it cooled his scorched hide, he wondered, "How can Rabbit be so lowdown and mean?"

Terrapin Fools Rabbit

One day, Rabbit and Terrapin got to talking. As they chitchatted about this and gossiped about that, Rabbit said, "We ought to have us a race?"

Terrapin hesitated before he slowly replied, "Well, I guess that would be all right. We could race across over the ridge to the bottom of the next valley, but I need a little time to get ready."

"I can whip you easily," Rabbit bragged.

"I doubt it," said Terrapin, and the two began to boast about who could beat the other.

Terrapin finally asked, "Would it be all right if I put a white feather in my hat? I'm so low to the ground I might not be recognized by those who want to watch the contest. A feather might help them see me better."

"Sure," Rabbit answered. "I don't see any harm in a white feather."

Since the race was set for the next day, Terrapin left to prepare. That evening, he went to see his friends and spoke to all the terrapins who had gathered. "I've got to race Rabbit tomorrow, and he's sure to beat me as slow as I am, and I need your help, not just for my sake but for the honor of the whole terrapin clan."

When all agreed to help, Terrapin continued. "Here's what we'll do. Once the race starts, Rabbit will outrun me. But I want one of you with

31

a white feather in your hat to wait about halfway up the ridge. Then another can wait at the top, and a third can wait about halfway down the other side. When you see Rabbit come running, make out like you're racing ahead of him. When he passes you, pull the feather off your head and turn aside into the bushes. That way, Rabbit can't see you if he looks back. Got it?" The other terrapins nodded they understood.

The next morning, Terrapin went to the starting place. As soon as the race began, Rabbit passed him, and he pulled out his white feather and turned off the path. Rabbit kept on running when he suddenly saw Terrapin and his white feather bobbing up the slope ahead of him. "He must be mighty fast," Rabbit said to himself. "I didn't even see him pass by me."

Rabbit streaked past the second terrapin who disappeared the same way the first one had. Rabbit soon saw the next terrapin at the top of the ridge. Rabbit wondered, "How'd he get so far ahead of me? I know I ran by him just a moment ago." *ZIP! ZIP! ZIP!* Rabbit raced past this one, who removed his feather and turned off the trail also.

Rabbit crossed the top of the ridge. He could not believe his eyes. There was Terrapin with his white feather going down the other side toward the valley. And with that, Rabbit gave up and ran off into the bushes rather than face sure defeat.

Raccoon, Panther, and the Deer

As Panther prowled through the woods one day, he met Raccoon. "I'M GOING TO EAT YOU!" Panther threatened.

But before the big cat could pounce, Raccoon replied, "Oh, I'm too small to make a meal for you. Let me get some food to satisfy us both." Convinced by Raccoon's words, Panther agreed.

"Here's what we'll do," Raccoon said. "You lie down and act like you're dead. I'll fetch some dry leaves and rotted wood and stuff your nose and mouth and scatter everything over you to make it look like you're covered with maggots. While you're stretched out, I'll tell the deer you're dead and get them to come and dance around you. I'll sit by your head, beat a tom-tom, and sing. When a fat buck gets close, I'll poke you. You can then jump up and tear his throat out. That way, we'll both have plenty to eat."

"Sounds good to me," said Panther. So, he stretched out on the ground while Raccoon stuffed his ears and nose with rotted wood and scattered more rotted wood along with dead leaves over his body to look like flyblow.

Raccoon then hunched off, running to find the nearest deer. The first one he found was an old doe. "PANTHER'S DEAD!" he hollered. "STRETCHED OUT ON THE GROUND AND COVERED WITH MAGGOTS! COME AND SEE FOR YOURSELF!"

The old doe, however, was timid and answered, "If he's dead, let him lie there."

Raccoon next saw a fawn. "PANTHER'S DEAD! COME AND SEE FOR YOURSELF!" The fawn followed Raccoon back to Panther, took one look, and ran off to tell the deer their foe was dead.

Soon a crowd assembled, and Raccoon waddled up toward Panther's head. "Let's celebrate. I'll beat my drum and sing, and you can dance around the body."

The deer started their victory dance, and Raccoon sang,

> CHING-A-CHING
> CHING-A-CHING
> CHING-A-CHING CHING!
>
> CHING-A-CHING
> CHING-A-CHING
> CHING-A-CHING CHING!

Around the dead Panther, the dancing deer circled. Caught up in the celebration, a big buck strutted near Panther's head. At once, Raccoon poked Panther, who leapt on the buck and killed him. And that's how Raccoon saved himself and had a feast.

Rabbit and the Woman's Only Son

A boy once lived with his mother. He was her only son. From their house, they could see the crests of the mountains. When she would catch him looking toward them, she would always repeat this warning. "Son, you see how close we live to the mountains. You must promise me never to go beyond them."

One day, the boy went hunting and had walked in the mountains for a long time. Before he realized, he had reached their topmost ridge. From there, he peered into the valley below where he saw a beautiful city. It seemed to call to him to visit, and before he was aware, he found himself descending into the valley. As he approached the city, he walked through green meadows, beside crystal waters, and beneath great groves of towering trees. Beautiful maidens appeared everywhere he cast his glance.

After a while, the boy became tired and returned home. He kept to himself that evening, remaining silent and looking lonesome. Sensing her son was not himself, his mother declared, "You have crossed over the mountains, my son. That much is clear."

"I could not help myself," the boy answered with a faraway look in his eyes. "While hunting, I came to the crest of the mountains, and from there, I beheld and entered a world so beautiful I can think of nothing else."

His mother gave a strong sigh. "Now you know why I warned you. Those who see the beautiful city are never happy anywhere else. They act as if under a spell. Once they have passed beyond the mountains, their homes and former lives lose all attraction, and they remain discontented. So, I must help you as best I can."

The next morning, the woman rose early. She fashioned for her son a dazzling costume, and she sent him into the woods to snare songbirds of every kind. From a canebrake, she took a reed and made a flute for the boy, and from other reeds she prepared a headdress on which the songbirds might sit.

On completing her tasks, the mother called to her son. "Play your flute," she urged, and when the boy played, the birds joined in its sweet sound and sang to his music. "Now go to the city over the mountains," she said, "and when you enter the council house, play your music while your songbirds sing. Then ask to speak before the council and the king."

So, the boy left and did exactly as his mother had told him. Hearing his wonderful flute and birds, a crowd soon gathered round him and directed him to their king. In the council house, the people offered him a seat of honor, and his music enchanted everyone, including the king. No gift seemed too good for him, and all treated him with loving-kindness. Word soon spread that the king would offer his daughter as bride to this stranger who had brought such delight to the city.

Time passed quickly. One day, the young man asked the king and his council to follow him to the river that flowed near the city. When they reached the stream, he removed his costume and headdress and dove into the water. He swam beneath the river where he crossed from one bank to the other several times without taking a breath. When he had finished, he rested in the water beside the bank. The fish rose to the surface, and the people shot them with arrows. So many were their numbers the people enjoyed a great feast that evening.

The young man continued to provide fish. Unbeknown to everyone, Rabbit lurked in the woods near the river and observed how the stranger had supplied food for the people. One day, as he rested beside the bank and they shot the fish with their arrows, Rabbit stole his costume and flute, then scampered into the forest. On emerging from the river, the young man could not find his clothes, though he searched all along its bank. No one knew what had happened to his belongings.

The next morning, as soon as the people had gathered, Rabbit strutted into the council house. Dressed in the stranger's costume and headdress, he puffed his checks and blew as hard as he could on the flute. But the music was not pleasant, and the birds refused to sing. Rabbit swatted at them and cried, "SING! SING! SING! WHY WON'T YOU SING?"

Before the king's warriors could seize him, Rabbit announced, "Let us feast once more. Follow me to the river." And off he ran with the king and his council trailing behind him.

Rabbit tossed the stolen clothes and flute on the bank and plunged into the water. Like the young man, he swam across the stream. Back and forth. Back and forth. And though he swam beneath the water four times, not a single fish floated to the surface.

When Rabbit's head finally appeared, the people cried out,

> IT'S THAT LIAR RABBIT!
> IT'S THAT LIAR RABBIT!
> IT'S THAT LIAR RABBIT!
>
> HOLD HIM! HOLD HIM! HOLD HIM!

So, the council seized Rabbit when he came out of the river and put him on trial. They ruled that as a deceitful rascal he could never enter the city again and chased him into the forest.

As for the king's daughter, she married the young stranger. When they joined their hands together, the birds fluttered their wings and began a wild and heartfelt tune.

Rabbit and Wolf

At one time, Rabbit and Wolf were friends and lived near each other. Some pretty girls also lived nearby, and Rabbit decided to visit them. But he first called on Wolf. "Let's you and me go see those pretty girls this afternoon."

"Fine with me," Wolf said. So, they walked over to the girls' place.

When the two got there, the girls invited them to have a seat, and before long, they took a liking to Wolf and chatted more with him than with Rabbit. Since the girls ignored him, he just sat and watched the good time they had with his friend. By and by, though, Rabbit became put out with how things were going and said, "It's getting late. I guess we better be heading back home."

"Oh, let's stay a little longer," Wolf responded, and he and Rabbit ended up remaining late into the evening.

Just as both got up to go, Rabbit spoke to one of the girls alone. "You know the one you talked to and had so much fun with is actually my old saddle horse."

The girl shot back, "I believe you're lying."

"No, I'm not, and to prove it, I'll ride him over here in the morning."

The other girl overheard the conversation and added, "Well, if you ride him by here, we'll believe you." She then said loud enough for Wolf to hear, "NOW YOU COME BACK ANY TIME."

Anxious to visit again, Wolf called on Rabbit early the next day. "You ready to go?" he asked.

Rabbit pretended he had just gotten out of bed. "I don't feel up for a visit. I'm about dead. I was sick the whole night."

Wolf begged and pleaded, trying to pet and humor Rabbit who kept going on about how sick he was. Finally, though, he said, "Maybe we could visit if you let me ride you to the girls' house." Wolf quickly agreed.

"But you know what?" Rabbit added. "I still feel bad. I don't think I can stay on unless I have a saddle to steady me."

Again, Wolf agreed. "All right. Now let's go."

Rabbit paused. "You know what would make me feel even better is if I put a bridle on you." This notion did not set too well with Wolf. "I'd be able to hold on and trust myself not to fall off of you." Eager to see the girls, Wolf consented to the bridle.

Saddled and bridled, Wolf was ready to go, but Rabbit still stood there, then added, "You wouldn't mind if I wore spurs, would you?"

"Oh, Rabbit, I'm too ticklish for spurs."

"Don't worry," reassured Rabbit. "I won't use them, but I would feel more confident if I had them on."

At last, Wolf agreed. "Just remember I'm highly ticklish, so don't spur me."

"You need not fret, my friend. Besides, when we get close to the house, we'll remove everything—saddle, bridle, and spurs—and walk."

So, Wolf and Rabbit headed for the girls. But as soon as they came in sight of the house, Rabbit dug the spurs into Wolf's flanks. *ZIP! ZIP! ZIP!* Wolf ran past the place but not before the girls glimpsed him whiz by.

"Too bad they saw you," Rabbit consoled. "I'll tie you up down here and come back soon. Then you can slip off without any shame."

As Rabbit hopped up to the house, he called out, "You saw my old saddle horse, didn't you?"

"Why, yes," the girls answered. "Now come up on the porch and sit a spell." They talked a while, and Rabbit had the best time with them.

As it was getting toward dark, Rabbit thought he should check on Wolf and left. He realized Wolf would be angry after being tied up a long time, so he wondered how to let him loose and still be safe. Seeing a thin hollow log, Rabbit began beating it like a drum, then hurried to Wolf and shouted, "Did you hear that drum? The soldiers are hunting for you and are on their way."

Wolf's eyes widened with fright as he begged, "Untie me! Let me go!"

Before Rabbit got the knot completely loose, Wolf broke free and took off down the road. *BOGGITY, BOGGITY, BOGGITY, BOGGITY, BOGGITY.* Rabbit heehawed, went back to the house, and acted like he was already married.

Beside the house, there was a peach orchard. One day Rabbit told the girls, "I'll shake some peaches down for you." They all went into the orchard, and Rabbit shinnied up a tree. While up there, he glanced down the road and saw his old friend Wolf heading his way.

"RABBIT," he shouted, almost under the tree, "YOU'RE MINE NOW!"

Rabbit pretended to gaze into the distance and called out as if to somebody. "THAT FELLOW YOU'VE BEEN HUNTING IS IN THIS ORCHARD. HE'S STANDING RIGHT HERE UNDER ME." As before, Wolf took off down the road. *BOGGITY, BOGGITY, BOGGITY, BOGGITY, BOGGITY.*

But Wolf hadn't yet finished with Rabbit. Sometime later, Rabbit was leaning on a tree that bent so far over it looked like it would fall any second. Rabbit happened to cock one eye open, and down the road he saw Wolf coming toward him. He heard Wolf holler, "I GOT YOU NOW!"

Unfazed, Rabbit replied as Wolf got closer, "The girls told me this tree might fall any time. They asked me to hold it up and said they would give me four hogs for my trouble. I don't care for pork, but I know you like hog meat. If you take my place, you can have it."

Wolf was always hungry, and his appetite got the best of him. As he leaned against the tree, Rabbit added, "Hold it tight and push hard because, if you don't, it's sure to fall." Then he sashayed off.

Wolf held on and held on to the tree until his front legs began to hurt and quiver like a leaf shaking in the breeze. Finally, they became so numb he let go and jumped hard to the side to keep from getting crushed. The tree stayed rooted where it stood.

"THAT RABBIT IS NOTHING BUT A LIAR!" exclaimed Wolf. "I should have known better. If I ever catch him, I'll fix him for good." But Wolf never did catch Rabbit.

How Rabbit Married the Widow's Daughter

There was once a widow whose daughter was so beautiful suitors came from miles around to court her. Yet she refused to marry.

Though Rabbit was getting up in years, he had remained single. Well, as fate would have it, he fell in love with the pretty daughter and thought he would ask for her hand in marriage. Since he was small and did not cut much of a figure, he knew his chances were slim to none. So, he devised a plan to get the girl and her mother to agree to a match.

Rabbit went down to the creek, cut a cane, and made a blowgun. Then slipping over to the widow's cabin, he sneaked around to the chimney, bore a hole in it near the ground, and stuck his blowgun through to the fireplace. When dark came the next evening, he went back and put his ear up to the hole in the cane so he could hear what the widow and her daughter said.

"Daughter, you know I'm getting on in years, and you're not getting any younger yourself. You have had many beaus come here but won't consider a one. You ought not turn down everyone who wants to marry you."

"But, Mother, I don't care for any of them. They don't suit me."

"Dear, you are far too particular. Now run to the spring and fetch some water."

The widow's words were hardly out of her mouth when Rabbit skedaddled through the grass and hid in the weeds by the spring. Down the path traipsed the daughter humming a tune. When she dipped her bucket in the water, Rabbit chanted in a low, monotonous voice, "THE GIRL WHO DOES NOT MARRY WILL DIE."

The daughter dropped her bucket, raised up in a flash, and caught her breath. She looked to the left and then to the right. She looked behind, and she looked in front. Hearing nothing, she quickly bent over to fill her bucket. Rabbit now slipped over to the other side of the spring. In the same deep tone, he sang out, "THE GIRL WHO DOES NOT MARRY WILL DIE."

As fast as her legs could carry her, the girl ran back to the cabin and gasped, "Oh, Mother, I heard a terrible voice at the spring, but no one was there." By now, Rabbit was back at the chimney and listening.

"What did the voice say, Daughter?"

"It said, 'THE GIRL WHO DOES NOT MARRY WILL DIE.' I heard it on both sides of the spring and hightailed it back here."

"I knew it," muttered the old lady.

Before she could say another word, Rabbit droned through his blowgun, "THE GIRL WHO DOES NOT MARRY WILL DIE."

The daughter's hair stood on end. "That's the voice," she whispered terrified.

"OH, I HEARD IT!" shrieked the widow. "YOU'LL DIE FOR SURE! YOU BETTER MARRY THE FIRST ONE WHAT COMES a-COURTIN'!"

"Yes! Yes!" the daughter wheezed, trying to catch her breath.

When Rabbit heard the girl agree to marry, he took off home and called his aunt. "The widow's daughter wants to get married, and you've got to go and make my offer."

The aunt tottered to her feet and headed that very night to the widow's cabin. As soon as the old lady darkened the door, the widow blurted out all the strange details of the evening, then added, "I've told my girl she needed to marry, and my mind's made up. She'll take the first one what comes along."

"Well, what a coincidence. That's why I've come. My nephew, Rabbit, wants to offer his hand."

Stunned, the widow said nothing. Then a deep voice from the ashes in the chimney slowly mouthed, "THE GIRL WHO DOES NOT MARRY WILL DIE."

"TAKE HER! SHE'S HIS!" exclaimed the mother.

In this way, Rabbit won his wife, and the widow's beautiful daughter became his bride.

Rabbit Tricks Coyote

Rabbit and Coyote had been good friends for a long time. One day, when Rabbit was out and about, he saw a colt sleeping by the side of the road. He paid it no mind and went on his way. After a while, he met his old friend Coyote and decided to do him a favor.

"I saw something for you to eat a little piece back. If you want, I can drag him somewhere so you can have a feast. Then I'll be on way and find some food for myself."

Rabbit's friendly offer pleased Coyote right much. "That's mighty kind of you," he said and followed Rabbit to the sleeping colt.

Rabbit whispered, "On second thought, I'm not as strong as you, so I'll tie your tail to his and push while you drag."

Careful not to wake the colt, Rabbit tied the two tails together. Pretending he was going to push the colt along, he next lifted it by the ears. Of course, the colt woke with a start, bucked a time or two, kicked up his back feet, and took off down the road with Coyote bouncing along behind. He twisted this way and flopped that way, but all he could do was barely claw the dirt.

Rabbit yelled, "STOP FLOPPING AROUND AND PULL HARD!"

Coyote shouted back, "HOW CAN I PULL WHEN I'M NOT STANDING ANYWHERE?" And off he raced.

After a while, the tails untied, the colt escaped, and Coyote got loose. By then, though, Rabbit had already run for cover.

Rabbit Deceives the Other Animals

For his many lies and tricks, the animals had arrested Rabbit and had gathered for his trial. When his turn came to speak, Rabbit stood and addressed the council. "I have an important warning to give you from God. He appeared to me and announced he plans to destroy everything because the animals have grown too wicked. But he will not punish you if you do as I say. Destruction is coming soon, but you must follow my advice and release me."

Hardly had the words crossed Rabbit's lips when the other animals laughed and ridiculed his story. "IT'S ONE OF HIS TRICKS!" some shouted. "ANOTHER BIG LIE!" yelled others. Jeers and hisses filled the air.

When the ruckus died down, Rabbit solemnly said, "Well, just wait and see."

The animals cried out, "YOUR WORDS DON'T SCARE US!" Then the council adjourned, saying they would return and debate Rabbit's fate over four days.

In the meantime, Rabbit sent for the Partridge King and asked him to pay a visit. Rabbit said, "I can be of great service to you if you help me out of this trouble. As you know, you and your fellow partridges are subject to one type of food and cannot roam freely and eat what you please."

Curious, the king asked, "How can I help?"

"Here's the plan. Gather your partridges into one gigantic flock before the council meets in the morning. Have your people wait out of sight and south of the meeting ground. When I raise my paw in your direction, have your partridges explode into the air, fluttering and beating their wings with a mighty rush and noise like the end of the world." The Partridge King nodded in agreement.

Rabbit continued. "On the second morning, take your flock east of the council ground. Do the same when I signal. On the third morning head north, and on the fourth go west. Just remember to stay out of sight. Each time you take flight, be louder than the time before. Follow my plan, and your flock can eat anywhere." The king consented, and he and Rabbit parted.

The next day the council called Rabbit to their assembly. He flounced in, grinning and bowing and carrying on. "Know that I love each of you and regret how your wickedness will bring you to destruction. But today you will receive a sign from the south. Heed it, free me, and obey me. Three more warnings will appear—from the east, the north, and the west—one each day after the first and each one louder than before. The next day, destruction will follow."

Oh, how the animals laughed Rabbit to scorn. "WHAT A JOKER! WHAT A LIAR! MORE! MORE! TELL US MORE!" they mocked.

After the hullabaloo died down, Rabbit faced south and raised his paw. A loud scratchy *KUT, KUT, KUT* rose from that direction. The animals became silent, peered at one another, and murmured, "Did you hear that?"

"Destruction's warning," Rabbit replied gravely.

A few said, "Let him loose. He's done no harm"

Others protested, "It's one of the rascal's tricks."

The next day Rabbit addressed the council. "Your doom awaits. Hear it in the east." He raised his paw, and a sound like loud thunder *BOOMED AND CRACKED.*

This time more animals shook with fear. "Maybe he's telling the truth. Maybe we are doomed." Still others maintained, "It's another trick. He's with us, and the noise is out yonder." The council now scattered until the next day.

On the third morning, Rabbit marched in and spoke with a severe look. "I cry for justice, and you refuse me. Today the north will announce its warning."

At the sign, the *AIR ROARED*, and the *GROUND SHOOK.* The animals quivered in terror. To their chiefs, many clamored, "FREE RABBIT! FREE RABBIT!" But the head animals resolved to wait for the last warning. If none came, Rabbit must receive his punishment.

The fourth day, the animals slowly entered the council ground and cast timid glances toward the west. Breaking the deep and awful silence, Rabbit declared, "How sad your fate. How miserable your end. If you only had heeded my plea. With my sign, the end now comes." He raised his paw. From the west arose a wild furor of *FLUTTERS, BUZZES, TREMORS, AND ROARS.*

With one voice, the animals gave a mighty shout, "RELEASE HIM! RELEASE HIM!"

So, they set Rabbit free, and off he ran to the Partridge King.

"You may eat where you will," Rabbit announced. And ever since that day, partridges have roamed as they please, eating to their fill wherever they wish.

Rabbit Escapes from the Box

Rabbit continued to lie and deceive, and again had to appear before the council early one summer. If found guilty this time, the council planned to drown him. Meanwhile, the council confined Rabbit to a box, put it by a creek, and left him there awaiting trial. But before it took place, a small child walked down to the creek when no one was around. Hearing a noise inside the box, the child asked, "What are you doing in there?"

Rabbit replied, "I'm listening to the best music there ever was."

"I want to listen, too," the child said. "Let me in."

"Open the box and climb on in," Rabbit urged and told the child how to unfasten the lid. Right after the child got inside, Rabbit jumped out, locked the child inside, and ran into the woods

By now, the council had declared Rabbit guilty, returned to the box, and tossed it into the creek. "We got rid of him this time. He won't trouble us any longer."

As it was early summer, the Festival of the Green Corn soon arrived, and the custom was to allow every criminal who had been exiled to return to the settlements. The people had barely swept clean the dancing ground when Rabbit hopped in, clothed in red. Astonished, the people could only stare as he danced with all the pretty girls.

"Didn't we drown him?" some asked.

Others whispered, "I thought we locked him in a box and threw him in the water."

One called out, "How Did You Get Back Here?"

Rabbit shouted over the sound of the drums, "I'm Glad You Tossed Me in the Creek! I Floated to a Glorious Land with Thousands of Beautiful Girls. They Pressed Me to Stay with Them, and Now I Regret I Came Back."

On hearing about the new country and beautiful girls, the young warriors gathered round, asking Rabbit over and over about his stay. "Show us the way," they begged.

"First, I must warn you I am the only one who has ever returned from that country. Yet I will show you how to go." He then instructed, "Prepare boxes like the one you made for me."

Rabbit next selected the young men he most envied for their strength and handsome faces. "Have your friends shut you inside the boxes, carry you to the creek, and let you float away to the lovely land."

A year passed, and early the next summer the Festival of the Green Corn rolled round. The people had anxiously waited for their young warriors to return home, but none had yet appeared. One day, while searching far down the creek, some of the people found the boxes stranded on a sandbar. Opening them, they saw the bodies of the young men. The people also discovered a small box. Inside were the bones of the little child.

"That Rabbit has cruelly deceived us again," the people complained and questioned him closely.

"I warned you. I am the only one who has ever returned from that land. I told your young warriors. Yet they begged me to point the way. They have no one to blame but themselves."

How Rabbit Won a Second Wife

Rabbit's wife had a younger sister who was very pretty. She lived with Rabbit and his wife. One day, when Rabbit was at home, he lay down and put his head in the lap of his wife. While he rested, she rubbed it gently. Her sister got up and said, "I's going to get some water." She took a bucket and headed down to the spring.

As soon as the girl left, Rabbit jumped up and told his wife, "I have to tend to some business." He went out the door and ran down to the spring where he hid in the nearby bushes.

When the sister arrived, Rabbit called out, disguising his voice, "Is Rabbit at home?"

Not seeing anyone, the girl glanced around, then looking toward the voice, answered, "Yes, he is."

"Well, you tell Rabbit that the people are going on a big bear hunt, and they want Rabbit to be sure and come. They want him to go ahead of the hunters and prepare a camp and get a fire going. The rules are no one can take his wife but must take his wife's sister instead."

The girl hurried back to the house at once. Rabbit, though, ran back by a different path and got there first. When the sister walked in, he was already there, resting as before with his head in his wife's lap.

The girl passed on the message but left out the part about taking only her and not the wife on the hunt. Rabbit lay there and waited. After a spell, he asked, "Is that all?" With that, the girl told everything.

The wife said, "You and my sister go on the hunt. I'll stay home." She stood up and prepared some things for them to take to camp. The two then left.

Just before the sun went down, Rabbit and the sister chose a campsite. He cleared the ground and built a fire. They waited and waited, but none of the hunters showed up.

"Well, if that don't beat all," Rabbit grumbled. He then hopped on a hollow log and looked every which way to see if anyone was coming.

The sun had set, and Rabbit complained, "I can't believe those hunters never showed up."

44

As darkness fell, he added, "There's no use waiting. We might as well turn in for the night. You can sleep on that side of the fire, and I'll make my bed on this side."

Rabbit knew on the sister's side was an anthill. When she stretched out, the ants began to stir. Well, she tossed this way and turned that way, and she scratched here and scratched there.

Rabbit went over and began to comfort her in her distress. And that's how he won his second wife.

The Boy Who Outwitted the Buffaloes

One time a little boy named Tookme and his grandmother lived together. When he grew older, he liked to go hunting with his three dogs. Their names were Simursitty, Jeudawson, and Benboton. Because the boy had killed many buffaloes, the herd went to council to decide what to do.

Two of the buffaloes said, "We'll turn ourselves into beautiful girls, and we'll get rid of Tookme."

So, one evening the two girls traveled to the grandmother's house and tried to sweet talk the old woman. But she did not fall for their flattery and whispered to her grandson to beware of them. Even the dogs did not care for the pair and growled when they got too close.

As it was getting on toward night, the girls invited themselves to stay. They turned toward Tookme and begged, "Won't you tie up those dogs? They might bite us during the night. We won't be able to sleep if they're not chained outside."

The young man fancied the girls and agreed to chain the dogs. The grandmother, though, did not trust them and again whispered, "Something's not right about those two."

Well, the girls spent the night anyway and the next morning said they had to return to their settlement out on the prairie. They looked at Tookme and asked, "Why don't you come with us?"

"No!" the old woman cried out. "HE CANNOT GO WITH YOU!"

After some wrangling, everyone agreed that Tookme would travel part of the way to the prairie. So, he and the girls left and came to a herd of buffaloes. The girls instantly turned into two cows and made a sign for the rest of the herd to surround Tookme.

Alarmed, the young hunter jammed one of his arrows into the dirt, and it changed into a cottonwood tree. In a wink, he shimmied up the tree out of reach of the threatening herd. Not to be outdone, the buffaloes butted the tree and gouged it with their horns until it crashed to the ground. But as it shook and tottered, Tookme jumped from its branches and stuck another arrow into the ground. It, too, became a cottonwood, and up he went.

The buffaloes attacked this tree also, and the same thing happened. Over and over, they would attack each new tree, and Tookme would stick another arrow into the dirt. Before long, he had used up all his arrows. He then tossed his bow down, and from it sprang a tall sycamore. He quickly scooted up it.

High in sycamore limbs, Tookme yelled, "HERE, SIMURSITTY! HERE, JEUDAWSON! HERE, BENBOTON! HERE! HERE! HERE!"

Below, the buffaloes laughed and loudly mocked, "TOOKME! TOOKME! TOOKME!"

Back at her house, the grandmother was asleep and snoring. But the dogs began to bark and howl and carry on something fierce. She woke up and ran outside. The dogs jumped and snapped, slobbering all the while and trying to break their chains.

Then from far off, the grandmother faintly heard, "Here, Simursitty. Here, Jeudawson, Here, Benboton. Here, here, here."

At once the old lady knew her grandson was in danger. She unchained the dogs, and off they flew, yipping and yapping all the way. In a flash, they scared off the buffaloes and saved their master.

The Boy and the Lion

Lion had killed many people and had long terrified the countryside. A poor father who lived in that land had five sons. Because they had nothing to eat, he gave a knife to each of his boys and told them to go and earn a living as best they could.

The boys left and came to where five roads met. They decided each one should pick a road and stick his knife in it. "If somebody takes a knife, we will find out who he is." So, each picked a road, stuck in his blade, and started walking.

With his little dog, the smallest son went down the less traveled road and soon arrived at a pretty house enclosed by a fence. An old lady stuck her head out the door and asked, "Why are you here?"

The boy replied, "My father sent my brothers and me out to find work and earn a living."

The woman answered, "Since I do not have any children, you could live here and work for me." So, the boy stayed with her and worked.

Every day, as he did his chores, he heard gunshots—some in the early morning and some in the late evening. "Ma'am," he asked, "why are those guns being shot?"

"Why, don't you know there's a lion that's been catching and eating people, and the hunters are trying to kill it."

"I'd like to go and see for myself," the boy said.

Somewhat flustered, the old lady told him, "I don't think that's a good idea. That lion's killed many men, and he would surely tear apart a little fellow like you."

"Well, I'd still like to go."

The boy kept on and on, begging and begging to go. The woman finally gave in. "You've been itching for so long to see what's happening, I guess it'll be all right. But I don't believe you'll ever come home. I think you ought to take that little dog there with you, though."

"I'll kill that lion," promised the boy.

"He's killed many a better one than you," the old woman answered. "Once you leave, it'll likely be the death of you."

As the sun rose the next morning, the boy left, and before night fell, he reached Lion's den. Lion was home, sitting on his haunches out in front of a rock house. It had a rock foundation and rock steps leading up to the door. A rock fence surrounded the place.

"Little fellow, what are you here for?" asked Lion. "Why don't you come in and we'll talk."

"That's just why I came," said the boy. He went up the steps, and his little dog stretched out by the door.

The lion and the boy went inside. As they did, Lion offered, "Let me show you through the place."

The two passed through a couple of rooms with a lot of different furnishings. When they got to the third room, though, it had many firearms. The fourth room had many swords.

The boy asked, "What are these for?"

"To tickle somebody's neck."

"How about I tickle your neck first. Then you tickle mine," responded the boy. Lion said nothing.

"In that case," said the boy, "I'm going to lie on my back and whistle

47

four times. After the fourth one, if you still want to tickle my neck, you may."

The boy stretched out on his back and gave a long whistle. He gave another one even longer. About halfway through the third, the little dog trotted in the room, only now he was as big as the lion. Lion had just seized a sword and was about to start tickling. The big dog snatched hold of Lion's left thigh and tore his leg off. Lion lost his balance and crashed to the floor.

The boy urged his dog on so that he ripped off Lion's right hind-quarter. "SERVES YOU RIGHT!" the boy shouted.

Lion moaned, "If you keep that dog away and spare me, I'll make it worth your while." The boy nodded yes.

"Under me," continued Lion, "is a twenty-dollar gold piece. Keep it and you will always have good fortune."

The boy found the gold coin, but he then sicced his dog on Lion once more. The dog took him by the throat, tore his head off, and thew it to the floor. It rolled around some. Then it scooted back on Lion's body. *Zip! Zip! Zip!* This occurred several times before the boy grabbed a sword, split open Lion's jaw, and sliced off his tongue.

The boy next set the house ablaze. It got so hot that Lion's cooks, who were his pet cats, ran out from everywhere they had been hiding and took off toward the nearby settlements. While the house burned down, the dog resumed his original size. He and his master now headed home, the boy taking with him the twenty-dollar gold piece and Lion's tongue.

As the pair went along, they met a man cutting logs. He said, "I saw you and your dog pass by here on your way to visit the lion. Did you meet him? I doubt you did, or you wouldn't be here now."

"Not only did I see the lion," said the boy, "but I killed him also."

"Do you have any proof? Many greater than you have tried and failed. I believe you're just full of talk."

"Maybe other people talked big, but I killed him. Here's the proof." The boy then removed Lion's tongue from a small bag. "Here's his tongue."

"Why, Lord, have mercy!" exclaimed the fellow. "I never figured a little thing like you could have killed that lion, but you did. Can I have his tongue?"

"You really want it?"

"Of course."

"Well, you can have it," said the boy "if you let me chop off your little finger."

The man agreed, and the boy whacked off the end of the man's little finger. He then returned to the old lady's house, and the man took Lion's tongue into the nearest village.

When the woman saw her foster son come home, she asked, "Did you meet the lion?"

"I sure did," the boy said, "and I killed him and have returned home."

"Now, son, many better than you have tried to kill that lion and have been killed instead. Do you have any proof to back up your claim?"

The boy removed the tip of the man's finger from the bag. "A fellow traded me this for the lion's tongue that I cut out."

"Any other proof?" she asked, not satisfied.

"Here's this twenty-dollar gold piece the lion gave me before I killed him."

Pleased, his mother said, "Good luck is yours. Head east and get yourself a good home."

Rumor claims that living in the east is a fellow with a twenty-dollar gold piece that can talk.

Hitchiti Tales

The Wolves Try to Trick the Dogs

Wolves and dogs used to spend time together. But men started to force dogs to track the wolves' children and kill them. So, the wolves held a council. "The dogs often kill our young," some said. "We should go to the dogs' house and destroy them."

The whole council agreed. The wolves then went to where the dogs lived and howled around their house. The dogs howled back. The wolves howled in return. The dogs assembled to talk things over. While they talked, the wolves announced, "At noon, we will have chicken to eat—a big chicken dinner. Come and join us."

The dogs agreed to go. The wolves went home where they dug a pit and waited for their guests to arrive.

As the dogs prepared to set out, one of the very old ones in the house asked to go with them, but they replied, "You are too old to travel and must stay here."

"But I want to eat, too," the old dog answered.

The others, though, started off without him. He decided to follow them anyway. They looked back and saw him behind them. They whispered among themselves, "That old fellow should stay home, but here he comes."

The pack soon came to where the wolves lived. A large number had gathered there, waiting for the dogs. When everybody had arrived, the wolves said, "We'll eat once you get into that big hole and sit down." The dogs did as they requested.

The wolves asked, "Is everybody here?"

"There's still one old man on the way," the dogs said. The wolves waited.

When the old fellow finally got there, the wolves told him, "You go into the hole, too. Then we'll eat." So, the old one went down into the pit.

Four old wolves guarded the entranceway. When the old dog got settled, one of the guards raised up and declared, "Now is our chance. You have killed our children, and we are going to kill you." He continued to threaten in this manner before he sat down again. A second wolf arose and made the same promise. The third and fourth wolves did the same.

The dogs whined and howled. The old dog, though, the one the others thought ought to stay home because he was feeble and fit for nothing, now stood and said, "I am the dog who killed your young. I am old, but here is a wolf's tail. It belongs to one of your children. Kill me first." He waved the tail at the wolves, and when the old ones saw it, they jumped up and scattered.

The other dogs saw their chance. They ran out of the pit's entrance and escaped. After they had gone, the old dog left also and headed home. When he got there, the others had already arrived and were waiting.

The old dog addressed the assembly. "You told me to stay here because I could not travel. You left without me, but you could do nothing for yourselves. I followed you and rescued you. From this day forward, remember to rely upon the old. If one who is old gives you council, heed it. I will die before too long, but do not forget what I have told you. Remember that an old dog saved you."

Rabbit Does the Old Man's Bidding

Rabbit was hungry and asked an old man for food. The old man said, "Bring me an alligator you have killed. Then I will tell you the foods you can eat."

Rabbit headed toward the river and began to consider how he might kill Alligator. "What should I say to him?" Rabbit pondered. "Well, I could tell him this, or I could tell him that." He was not sure what to say.

Rabbit waded into the water and spoke out loud, hoping any nearby alligator would hear him. "Where are you, old one?"

"Here I am," Alligator said. "Why are you here?"

Rabbit answered, "They told me to bring you back to make a wooden spoon."

"Yes, I will make one," Alligator agreed and crawled onto the riverbank.

Rabbit began to walk in front of Alligator so that he put some distance between them. Rabbit grabbed a heavy stick and began to beat Alligator over and over until he dashed back to the water, with Rabbit hitting him the whole time. When Alligator splashed into the water, he swam off.

Rabbit sat down. "I do not know how to get him to come back."

Then an idea suddenly came to Rabbit. He saw a tree leaning over the river that bent down close to it, and he changed himself into a gray squirrel. He scooted up the trunk, sat in the treetop, and started complaining as loud as he could. "SQUARK! SQUARK! SQUARK!" Alligator couldn't help but hear him.

As he rested in the water, Alligator looked up and said at last, "I sure am getting sick of all your noise."

"Well," said Rabbit in disguise, "the old man sent Rabbit down here to fetch you to fashion a wooden spoon for him. I saw Rabbit on his way, but he never came back. The old man sent me to find out what happened."

"There was somebody around here who mentioned a wooden spoon," Alligator said, "but he whacked me good. I'm afraid you might be up to act the same way."

"People say that Rabbit always acts the fool. He was just being foolish. He shouldn't treat you like that. He really came to get you because the old man wants to hire you to carve him a wooden spoon. If you come on out and make the spoon, I'll take it back to the old man."

Alligator crawled out of the water and followed the squirrel. When they got to where the beating started, Alligator cried, "STOP! Right here is where he began to wallop me."

The two then went a little farther. Alligator said, "If Rabbit knew where to hit me to kill me, he could have. But he didn't. So, I'm still alive."

"Where would he have to hit you to kill you?" asked the gray squirrel.

Alligator replied, "He kept whacking my hip joint, but if he had knocked me on the back of my head, I wouldn't be here talking to you. I'd be dead for sure. He hit me in the wrong place."

While both went a little farther yet, Rabbit saw another thick stick. He picked it up, wheeled around, and whacked Alligator on his hip joint. Alligator raised his head up, and Rabbit knocked him on the back of it. Alligator dropped dead. Rabbit cut off his tail, stuck it on the stick, and returned to the old man.

The old man said, "Bring me a sackful of ants." So, Rabbit picked up a sack and left. When he got to the ants' house, he announced, "People say that ants can't fill this sack, but I say you can fill it. So, I came here to prove you can."

The ants bragged, "We are many. We can fill the sack." Rabbit then opened it, and in went all the ants. He closed it and returned to the old man.

The old man said, "Now kill me a rattlesnake and bring it here."

Rabbit left once more and headed toward Rattlesnake's house. Along the way, he found a short sick and sharpened one end. When he got there, Rabbit kept his distance and yelled, "PEOPLE SAY YOU AREN'T ANY LONGER THAN THIS STICK, BUT I TOLD THEM YOU'RE A LONG FELLOW. BUT THEY WOULDN'T LISTEN. SO, I TOLD THEM I'D GO MEASURE YOU!"

Rattlesnake was coiled up and hissed, "I'm not short." He then uncoiled and stretched out his full length. As he lay still, Rabbit began to measure him from his tail to his head. But when Rabbit got close to Rattlesnake's head, he stuck the point of the stick all the way through until it hit the ground. He picked up the dead snake and left.

When Rabbit brought Rattlesnake's body back, the old man said, "I have nothing further for you to do. Come forward."

So, Rabbit went to the old man. He pulled Rabbit's ears up, and he pulled them down. He slapped the left check with one hand and the right check with the other hand until both were flat.

And that's how the story goes.

Rabbit, Wolf, and Buzzard

One day, some people caught Rabbit while he was disturbing their garden. To punish him, they tethered him to a tree and planned to douse him with scalding water. They went to boil the water and left Rabbit waiting.

Just then, Wolf passed by the garden and saw Rabbit tied to the tree. Rabbit called out to him in a low voice. "Wolf, my old friend, the people here want me to swallow a huge hog, but I refused, So, they tethered me here, and here I sit."

Wolf thought a minute, then said, "Well, why don't I eat the hog for you?"

"All right," Rabbit replied. "Now untie me and take my place. They'll soon be back with the hog, and you can eat the whole thing."

So, Wolf freed Rabbit, and Rabbit tied him to the tree. Rabbit took off, and pretty soon the people returned. They began dipping out the boiling water from a big iron pot to pour over Wolf. He'd zig this way and zag that way, but they scalded him anyway. Figuring he'd been punished enough, they set him free.

Wolf took off after Rabbit and finally found him resting on a log. Rabbit saw Wolf and started to laugh and laugh. Wolf got so mad he wanted to kill Rabbit and went for him, but Rabbit jumped up and ran. Wolf chased as fast as he could go until he almost got him, but Rabbit slipped into a hollow tree. Perched on one of its branches, Owl saw the whole show.

Panting hard, Wolf looked up and said, "I ... want ... you ... to ... watch ... him ... while ... I ... go ... get ... an ... ax."

As Owl sat watching, Buzzard glided down and landed beside Owl. Owl said, "Rabbit's in that hole down there. I've been watching it for some time, but I'm tired. Would you watch for a spell?" Buzzard agreed, and Owl flew off.

Buzzard sat there and watched and watched. Rabbit finally called out, "Buzzard, Jump Down Here and Look at Me."

Buzzard flopped to the ground and peeped into the hole. Rabbit had a dip of snuff in his mouth and spit it right into the big bird's eyes. Buzzard couldn't see a thing. He reeled about every whichaway around the tree. Try as he might, he could not get the tobacco spit out of his eyes. Rabbit saw his chance and escaped.

In the meantime, Wolf returned with an ax and asked Buzzard, "Is he still in there?"

Still stumbling around, Buzzard answered, "I'm not sure. He spit snuff in my eyes to blind me. I still can't half see."

Wolf said, "Well, I'm going to chop this tree down, and if Rabbit's there, I'll get him."

So, Wolf chopped and chopped, but when he got to the hole, no Rabbit. "All that work for nothing," he muttered and stalked off.

Rabbit, Wildcat, the Big Tree, and the Nuts

On his travels, Rabbit once told Wildcat about a big unsteady tree near the path. Unknown to Wildcat, Rabbit happened to see him padding down the trail. Rabbit took hold of the tree and warned, "If this tree falls, it will interfere with our goings and comings. The people want it braced. So, I've been here a mighty long time holding it up. If you'll take my place, I'll search for something strong to brace it."

Wildcat looked Rabbit up and down before he agreed. "All right. I'll brace the tree."

Rabbit left and was gone for hours. Wildcat became more and more angry. "That Rabbit's not coming back. He's up to his old tricks and played me for a fool. I'm leaving."

As he went along, Wildcat would stop at different places and asked where Rabbit might be. By now, Wildcat was so mad he thought he would kill Rabbit. So, Wildcat began to hunt in earnest.

He looked everywhere he could think of, and while he looked, Rabbit spotted him and pretended to make a raft.

Wildcat came up and demanded, "What's that you're making?"

"Oh, I'm building a raft to get ready for the big flood. They say it's on the way and will be here soon. If you help me with this raft, when the flood comes, we can both survive."

Wildcat agreed to help build the raft, and when he and Rabbit finished, they carried it down to the creek. As they wobbled along, Rabbit said, "We'll try the raft out first. If it floats, you can sit on it and then I will"

At the creek, both moved the raft into the water, and it floated just fine. "Now you go ahead and sit on it, and I'll push off and then get on," Rabbit instructed.

So, Wildcat sat on the raft, and Rabbit pushed off. It quickly moved into the deep current, and Rabbit watched it fade out of sight. Rabbit headed off, while the raft floated down the creek with Wildcat until it caught in a bend in the creek. Angrily, Wildcat leapt off and went to search for Rabbit, but he had vanished again. "If I find Rabbit, I'm going to kill him for sure."

While Wildcat looked, Rabbit found a pecan and cracked the hull. As he sat eating the meat, Wildcat saw him and coming up said, "What's that you're doing?"

Rabbit replied, "I'm eating nuts" and gave a pecan half to Wildcat who liked it.

"Where did you get the nut?" Wildcat wanted to know.

Rabbit said, "If you pound your nuts, you can have a pecan, too."

Wildcat began pounding furiously until his nuts turned to pulp and he passed out. With Wildcat lying on the ground exhausted, Rabbit laughed and left.

Rabbit, Wildcat, and the Buffalo

Wildcat had not had anything to eat for a long time and was lying down nearly dead from starvation when Rabbit found him. "Old friend, what's wrong? You look almost starved to death."

"I'm so weak I can't stand up," said Wildcat. "It's been ages since I've had anything to eat."

"If I had only known," Rabbit replied, "I'd have been here sooner to tell you some buffaloes are drinking water from a creek close by. If you can get up and go down there, you might be able to catch one of the yearlings as he's drinking and get you some food."

Rabbit paused and rubbed his chin as if thinking things over. He then added, "There's a big tree by the creek that leans over it. You could climb the tree and wait until the buffaloes go down to drink. Then you can jump down on a yearling, kill it, and have a meal right there."

Wildcat staggered up and gathered his strength. He went to the creek, climbed the tree, and settled down. Soon, the buffaloes headed to the creek to drink some water. Rabbit hid in some bushes and watched while Wildcat waited in the tree. Many buffaloes came to the creek.

Wildcat suddenly jumped toward a yearling, but he misjudged and landed on an old bull. The buffalo tossed his head up high and flung Wildcat into the deepest water in the middle of the creek. There it foamed and swirled around fast. Try as hard as he might to swim free, the current held Wildcat for the longest. Finally, he swam out, struggled up the bank, and collapsed.

Rabbit saw everything and fell over, nearly dying from laughing. He then got up and went about his business.

Bear, Rabbit, and Buzzard
(or, The Bungling Host)

Bear and Rabbit had become friends and one day in the fall rambled through the countryside together. Toward the end of their travels, Bear said, "Why don't you come for a visit? I live over yonder. That tree with red leaves is my house." Both agreed to meet at an appointed time, and Bear headed home.

When the day came for Rabbit to visit, he set out and got to the tree where Bear lived. At the bottom was a hole. Bear said, "Come in and have a seat."

The two talked for a while. Then Bear got up and went out the hole and walked around to the back of the tree so that Rabbit was unable to see him. When Bear returned, he had a clump of fine lard. "I'll put this in the beans I've got cooking," he told Rabbit.

Both talked a while longer until the beans were done. Bear then put them out, and Rabbit ate as much as he could hold. They talked further about this and that, and Rabbit stood up to leave. He said, "Why don't you come to visit me at my place? Look way over yonder. You see that house low to the ground where the dry grass has turned white. I live there." Bear agreed to visit, and they set an appointed time.

When the day came, Bear started out and got to Rabbit's house made of dry grass. The two sat outside and talked for a while. Then Rabbit got up and went to the back of his house. Bear could see everything Rabbit was doing and realized he was going to hurt himself. Then he suddenly heard Rabbit squeal, "WAAH! WAAH! WAAH!"

Bear jumped up and, by the time he got to Rabbit, saw he had cut his belly and had some blue fat oozing out. "Didn't you know I'm the only one who can get lard that way?" Bear asked. "You've done gone and hurt yourself." He picked Rabbit up and put him on the bed in his house. Bear then went to get Doctor Buzzard.

When Bear got to the doctor's, he said, "Rabbit has cut himself. It looks bad. Can you treat him?"

"Why, yes," Buzzard replied. "You know I make strong medicine." So, Bear led Buzzard back to Rabbit's house where he was resting.

Doctor Buzzard took one look and said, "Boil me some hominy and bring it here."

Bear did as the doctor directed. "Now close up the house, poke a hole in the roof, and leave me to my work." Bear did as he was told and went outside.

Buzzard sat beside Rabbit and gave him the hominy. Before long, Rabbit squealed, "WAAH! WAAH! WAAH!"

By now a crowd had gathered. "What's going on in there?" they wanted to know.

Buzzard stuck his head out and answered, "He doesn't like the medicine." He then knocked Rabbit on the head, killed him, and ate him. After Buzzard had eaten all the meat from head to tail, he flapped his wings and went through the hole in the roof. But before he left, he called out, "Rabbit's in there waiting for you." He then flew off.

Bear ran inside, but no Rabbit, only his bones on the floor. Bear could not see straight he was so mad. He went back outside. A wandering orphan had arrived just then and was curious about all the people assembled. Bear explained, "I asked Doctor Buzzard to heal a bad wound Rabbit had, but the doctor ate him except for his bones and then flew off. He's circling above us, though, right now. If you can, try to shoot him."

The boy aimed one of his arrows and shot. Buzzard came crashing to the ground. Bear grabbed him and beat him until he died. Bear then hung Buzzard on a nearby branch and smoked him for many days. He started to turn yellow, and that's why Buzzard's skin is yellow even to this day.

Rabbit and the Medicine

Long ago a man lived with his wife out from a settlement. The man got sick, and his wife tried to take care of him by herself. But he took a turn for the worse, and the wife thought he needed medicine, So, she decided to go to a doctor for a cure. To carry the medicine back home, she took a tin can to put it in.

Along the way, the woman met Rabbit coming down the path. He asked her where she was headed, and she said, "My husband is sick, and I'm going to get medicine from a doctor."

Rabbit told her, "I'll save you the trouble. If you give me the can and go back home, I'll get the medicine prepared and bring it back to you."

The woman agreed and gave Rabbit the can. He went to the doctor, got the medicine, and started back with it. But about halfway to the woman's house, he got so sleepy he thought he would die. He dragged himself along, staggering over sticks and tree roots until he finally gave up and hung the can on what he believed was a branch of a fallen tree. "I've got to get some sleep," he said to himself.

But unbeknown to Rabbit, what he thought was a low tree limb were the horns of a bull elk resting along the path with his eyes almost shut. As soon as Rabbit hung the can there, the elk came to, jumped up, and crashed through the woods.

Half asleep, Rabbit shouted, "ALL RIGHT! I'LL LET YOU TAKE THE MEDICINE!" He then lay down, rested his head on a what he thought was a fallen limb, and fell asleep. However, Rabbit's pillow was no limb but a white man's arm who was taking a nap. As Rabbit dozed, the man stood up and left.

At last, Rabbit woke up. But instead of going straight to the sick man's house, he met the fellow's wife coming down the path. He stopped and asked, "You got the medicine, didn't you? I had an old man take it to you."

"You never did such a thing," said the woman. "You're nothing but a big liar."

Rabbit and the Vegetable Garden

A man planted a garden, but unknown to him, Rabbit sneaked in and ate some of the vegetables. So, the owner decided to watch carefully and catch the thief. That night, he concealed himself in the field and sat watching. Pretty soon, he spied Rabbit creeping along one of the rows and eating peas as if he owned them.

The man became so angry with Rabbit, he said to himself, "I'm going to get him one way or another."

Rabbit continued to eat. When the sun rose, he decided to leave. However, before he could get completely away, the man circled around to cut him off and started toward him. Rabbit noticed the man coming toward him and crouched down beside a tree and braced himself against the thick trunk.

The man walked up and spoke. "I've got you now, Rabbit, and I'm going to kill you for eating in my garden."

Rabbit calmly said, "If you kill me, you will die, too. This big tree growing here holds up the sky and is just about to fall. When it does, the earth and sky and everything in between will be destroyed. I'm standing here to brace the tree so that it won't fall, but I need some help. I'm tired. If you go and get some other people, together we can keep the tree steady. If you kill me, though, the earth, the sky, and all things will end."

The man stared at the tree and then looked up. The sky did appear awfully low as if it might fall at any moment. His eyes grew ever wider as he fixed his gaze on the top of the tree. It seemed to touch the sky which looked lower still.

"That tree IS about to fall," the man mumbled to himself, and he took off as fast as he could. Rabbit stood up and thought, "I guess I'd best leave as well."

Rabbit's False Talk

A fellow one time was sweet on a certain woman who lived by herself across the river from him. He'd gazed over at her place day in and day out, but he lacked the courage to talk to her. While Rabbit was making his rounds, he happened to meet the man.

They spoke for a while, and by and by, the fellow told Rabbit, "There's a woman living by herself over there across the river, and I'd like to make time with her, but I don't have the courage to approach her."

Rabbit laughed and said, "Well, if that's all that's holding you back, I'll go make your case for you."

The man looked down at the ground, then answered, "All right, but I'll go with you and keep my distance, and you can come back and tell me how things went."

The two crossed the river, and when they neared the woman's house, Rabbit said, "You wait here while I go and talk to the woman for you. If everything works out, I'll come back to let you know whether she will do it with you."

Rabbit left the man and got to the house. When he entered, the woman was there and invited him to sit down. He took a seat, and she sat across from him. Both began to talk, and they talked a long time.

The fellow who was waiting started to wonder what was happening. So, he ran over to the house and stood listening near one end. He heard Rabbit and the woman talking and figured out Rabbit was speaking for Rabbit.

"I don't want to," the woman said.

Rabbit, though, would not stop pleading. "I sure would like for you to accept my offer," he kept repeating.

Finally, since it was getting pretty late, the woman said, "I'm not really that kind of person, but I guess you talked me into it." So, Rabbit did it with her.

Now, the man had been peeping through a hole in the wall and saw everything. He became so angry that he returned to where Rabbit had left him earlier.

After a little bit, Rabbit came back. "I spoke for you as best I could, but that woman never could be persuaded. So, I decided to leave and bring you the bad news."

"You're nothing but talk, and you're full of it," the man replied. "You spoke only for yourself and never did speak for me. I heard and saw it all. You came back here after you finished with her."

The man looked so mad and red in the face Rabbit thought the fellow might kill him. So, Rabbit hightailed it out of there before the fellow could do anything.

Rabbit and the Old Man's Daughters

Rabbit knew about an old man who had two daughters, and Rabbit wanted them both. The old fellow owned a lot of hogs, but some of them started disappearing, and he could not figure out why.

Rabbit was aware of this situation and went to a place close to the old man's house and yelled, "I KNOW ALL ABOUT YOUR HOGS!"

The old man heard Rabbit shouting and went to him. There sat Rabbit holding a hog's tail stuck in the dirt. "I've heard some of your hogs have disappeared, and I came to tell you what's happened. I found they've been going underground. I grabbed one by the tail poking out and held onto it so you can see what I'm talking about."

The old man took the tail and told Rabbit, "I'll hold the tail, and you go fetch a hoe and shovel."

So, Rabbit ran to the house where the old man's daughters were outside busy with their chores. He informed them, "I ran up here because your daddy told me to get from both of you the thing that all men love."

The daughters looked up and down and snapped, "You're lying!"

At that, Rabbit shouted to their father, "YOU DID SAY BOTH, DIDN'T YOU?"

"THAT'S RIGHT. I SAID BOTH!" he hollered back.

"I know you heard that," Rabbit said.

The daughters nodded and gave Rabbit what he asked for. He then left the house while the old man, still clutching the hog's tail, waited for him to bring the hoe and shovel. The old man eventually got tired sitting there, gave the tail a hard yank, and pulled it out of the dirt. Angry, he tossed it aside and returned to the house. He asked his daughters, "Where's Rabbit?"

"Oh, he left a while back," they said. "He told both of us to give him what all men love. And we said, 'You're lying.' He then hollered out to you, 'You did say both, didn't you?' You yelled back, 'Yes.'"

When their father heard what Rabbit had done, he grew even more angry. "That's not what I intended. I told him to get both my grubbing hoe and shovel, and he ran here for them. I thought he meant THEM when he yelled to me. So, of course, I said, 'Both.' I finally got tired of waiting for him, and I pulled hard on a hog's tail he had stuck in the ground. I tossed it aside and came back to the house. I swear, if I find that Rabbit, I'm going to knock him on the head and throw him away."

Alabama Tales

Big Man-Eater's Wife Gets Fed Up

Lion had a wife, but he captured another woman and carried her off to his house where his wife lived also. The next morning, he started out to hunt, and after he had traveled a while, he returned home without killing anything to eat. So, speaking to his wife, Big Man-Eater demanded, "Slice off a piece of your flesh and roast it for me."

She cut off a small piece of herself, roasted it, and gave it to her husband. Every day, the same thing. He would go hunting, not kill anything, return home, and demand his wife give him a piece of her body to eat.

The woman captured by Big Man-Eater feared he would soon start on her. So, she decided to escape while Big Man-Eater hunted. Before she lit out, however, the first wife offered to help her and handed her four ripe huckleberries and some cut canes. "My husband will chase you. Take these huckleberries, and when he has nearly caught you, drop them on ground and keep running. Do the same with the canes."

The woman then set out for the house of her three brothers and hoped they could protect her. When Big Man-Eater came home, he called for her, but she had already run off. He followed her, and when she felt his hot breath right behind her, she tossed down the huckleberries, and Big Man-Eater stopped to eat them. He then ran after her and got close again. She threw canes on the ground. They sprouted and at once grew thick and tall, and the ground became soft and damp. Big Man-Eater could barely get through the boggy dense canebrake.

Meanwhile, the woman got to her brothers' house, and they took her in and barred the door. Big Man-Eater ran up, growling, snapping, biting, and carrying on. One of brothers shot him through a hole in the wall but only wounded him. Running out behind him, the others struck his hindquarters with thick clubs and knocked him to the ground while

63

the brother with the gun reloaded. He shot Big Man-Eater in the head and killed him.

The brothers then gathered wood, piled it on and around Big Man-Eater, and burned him up. Once the fire consumed his body, the men took shovels and threw some of his ashes high into the air. The ashes turned into bees and flew away.

The brothers threw more ashes into the air. These turned into blackbirds, and they also flew away. A third time, the brothers tossed ashes up, and crows flew away. The same happened with hornets, wasps, yellow jackets, flies, and mosquitoes, and in this manner all kinds of flying things were created.

Rabbit Kills Big Man-Eater

Lion and his wife wanted to kill the people in a certain place and eat them. The people, though, heard about this plan and in fear complained. "Big Man-Eater and his wife are going to kill and eat us."

Rabbit got wind of how the people were afraid, went to their settlement, and said, "I can help you. Bring me an old dress" They brought him an old dress.

He next said, "Bring me an old blanket." They brought him an old blanket.

Rabbit put on the old dress and wrapped the old blanket around his head. Then he set out. When he arrived at Big Man-Eater's place, he stood in front of the house and waited. Big Man-Eater's wife saw him and stepped out. "Who are you?" she asked.

Rabbit replied, "I'm your youngest aunt, and I've come to see you."

Big Man-Eater's wife said, "Well, come on in. My husband's here inside."

So, Rabbit entered, and the wife invited him to sit down. So, he sat down.

Big Man-Eater and his wife had some tough deer meat on hand and offered it to her aunt. Rabbit, though, turned it down. "I can't eat that. I don't have any teeth, but if you bring me a hatchet, I'll chop the venison into fine pieces and be able to eat it."

So, the wife handed her aunt a hatchet, and she chopped the dried deer meat into little slivers and swallowed them. The aunt said, "I always eat dried venison this way."

As it was getting late, Big Man-Eater decided to go to sleep and let the two women visit a while. They sat by the fire and talked. Rabbit asked, "When your man is asleep, what sound does he make?"

"Well, if he's not sound asleep, he wheezes sometimes ever so slightly as he breathes in and out. If he's in a deep sleep, though, you can hear the wind of his wheezes all over the place."

"If you don't mind," Rabbit told his supposed niece, "I'll stay here for the night, and in the morning I'll leave."

Big Man-Eater's wife agreed and lay down by her husband. Rabbit stayed beside the fire. As he pretended to sleep, he kept listening to how Big Man-Eater was breathing. At first, he made some shallow wheezes, but as the night wore on, Rabbit began to hear the loud breezes of his wheezes. So, he took the hatchet and slipped over to the side of Big Man-Eater.

After listening a while longer, Rabbit struck Big Man-Eater so hard on the neck his head hit the floor. Rabbit then tore off the old dress, tossed off the old blanket, and jumped up and down a few times. Just before he skedaddled out of there, he shouted loud enough to wake the dead. Big Man-Eater's wife kept on snoring.

Rabbit Frees the Sun

Long ago, before the Sun was set in the sky, an old woman caught it and put it in a clay pot where she kept it confined. Rabbit heard about what she did. He wanted to capture the Sun, so he went to the old woman's house. She told him he could stay with her. All the people gathered there, and Rabbit began to dance.

To everyone assembled, Rabbit said, "Sing for me to help me dance."

The people answered, "How shall we sing to you? We don't know how."

Rabbit called out to them, "SING THE WORDS *RABBIT, RABBIT, RABBIT!*"

"*RABBIT, RABBIT, RABBIT!*" the people sang.

Rabbit danced faster and faster, then cried, "MOVE THE JAR TOWARD ME!" And the people moved the clay pot toward him.

Again, he cried out, "MOVE THE JAR TOWARD ME! I AM DANCING LIKE A MADMAN!" And again, the people moved it toward him.

After the pot was beside him, Rabbit seized the clay pot and ran, but the people chased him. Rabbit, though, was too fast for them. As he ran through the woods, he would throw the jar against bushes, but it would not break. So, he had to pick it up over and over as he ran. Then Rabbit saw a hornbeam tree with thick ridges along its trunk. He dashed the jar against the tree, and it broke into pieces at once.

All the four-footed animals of the forest gathered, and all the creatures of the air assembled. They went to council at once, and their judgment was to place the Sun in the sky. The creatures that fly tried to move it there, but they could not.

Little Wren attempted to move it by himself, but it rose only a little, then dropped back. He said, "If any should aid me, we can put the Sun in the sky."

So, Buzzard stepped forward, and he and Wren helped each other. Buzzard held one side of the Sun, and little Wren held the other. They flew into the sky, and there they placed the Sun.

When they returned to the earth, the people ruled, "Buzzard, you will eat the creatures that have died."

To Little Wren, they said, "You will bathe in cold water each morning and thus will never know sickness."

An Orphan Outdoes Rabbit

A young fellow had no mother or father. Although he was poor, the people who took care of him dressed him in fine clothes. One day, they told him, "You are old enough to make your own way."

So, the orphan set out, taking his bow and arrows. After he had traveled a good while, he met a girl. "I want you to shoot the dove sitting in that tree over there," she said. He did as she requested and gave her the dove.

The orphan continued traveling and met a woman. Like the girl before, she said, "I want you to shoot the dove sitting in that tree over there." Again, he did as she requested.

Setting out once more, the orphan met Rabbit who had on a white deerskin over a ragged old shirt full of holes. The two agreed to travel together and soon arrived at a pond where they decided to hunt turtles. Rabbit took off his white deer hide and tied it around the orphan's fine clothes.

As the youth prepared to go into the pond, he removed the white hide along with his clothing. He then dived into the water to catch turtles. Rabbit jumped in, too, but came out while the orphan was still hunting. Rabbit grabbed the white deerskin and the fine clothes and slipped away, leaving his old shirt on the edge of the pond.

The orphan continued to hunt and caught several turtles which he strung together with a cord before he came out of the water. He immediately saw that Rabbit had taken the deer hide and his clothes and left a ragged shirt. Having nothing else to wear, he put on the old shirt.

After a while, the young man came to a ripe persimmon tree. He shook the tree hard. Down fell the fruit, and he ate as much as he could hold. From the leftover persimmons, he mashed and smeared the pulp and juice over his shirt. He then took his string of turtles and set off.

After a time, the orphan arrived at a cabin and waited outside. A young woman stepped out, then went back inside and said to her mother, "Look out there."

The mother glanced out and urged her daughter, "Go talk to him."

So, the girl went back out and said, "Why don't you come inside?"

The young man entered the house, and when he did, he saw a bed prepared for him, but he did not want to lie on it since his shirt and body had dried juice and mashed persimmons everywhere. So, he pushed the bed aside and sat on the floor.

To the daughter, he offered, "I've got a few turtles outside, and you and your mother can have them."

So, the daughter went to fetch the turtles, and she and her mother cooked them. Everybody thought they made a good meal, and once all had eaten, the daughter and the orphan got married.

After four or five days had passed, the couple decided to head down to a nearby creek. The young man said to his wife, "Be sure and comb your hair before we go." She did, and the pair left.

At the creek, the husband dived in several times and swam back and forth. When he got out of the water, he and his wife started for home. Along the way, he told her, "Go find your relatives and direct them to where I dived."

The woman made her rounds and told her kin about the creek. When they went to the bank where the orphan dived, all kinds of fish were floating on the water. So, the relatives brought baskets, filled them up, cooked all the fish, and had a fine meal.

By and by, the young man again said to his wife, "Comb your hair and part it, and we'll go back to the creek."

When the two got there, the woman thought she would wash her hair because it was full of lice. As she scrubbed her head, so many fell out that the creek filled with fish. These again floated on top of the water.

The pair returned home, and as before, the wife informed her relatives about the creek. Once again, they took baskets, filled them with fish, and had another fine meal.

Rabbit heard about what the orphan had done and thought he would imitate him. So, Rabbit went to the creek, dove in a few times, and swam back and forth. He then told his wife to go with him to gather the fish. But when they arrived, none were there, not even a minnow.

In the meantime, the orphan had gone hunting along another part of the creek where he shot a deer. He hung the body in the fork of a tree and continued to hunt. He soon killed another one and hung its body up as well. He shot several more and treated them the same way and left for home.

When he got there, he said to his wife, "Tell your people to track along the creek where I went hunting today."

The wife let her kin know about the hunt, and they set out with a horse to load the carcasses on. They carried many deer back to their cabins.

As with the fish, Rabbit heard about the hunt and wanted to copy the orphan's success. So, he tracked along the same area of the creek until he arrived at the spot where the orphan shot his first buck. Now, the young fellow had not kept the liver and had cast it aside. Rabbit found it, cut it up into small pieces, and hung them on bushes.

When Rabbit returned to his wife, he said, "Have your people go where I hunted today." They followed his trail, but they did not find any deer to take back, only small pieces of liver.

Meanwhile, the orphan instructed his wife. "Comb your hair and part it down the center, then come and sit beside me." She did as he directed, and when she sat beside him, he took a hatchet and split her in two so smartly that he had two wives now.

Rabbit heard what the fellow had done and took a notion to do the same. "After my wife combs and parts her hair, I will split her with a hatchet just as the orphan did his wife." Rabbit's wife did as he instructed, but when he hit her in her part, she dropped dead.

Rabbit became so frightened he took off, but when the people discovered his dead wife, they pursued him with dogs. After being hunted for a long time, he hid in a hollow tree. The dogs trailed him there, and the hunters set Blue Crane to guard the hole while they went to get an ax.

Before they left, however, they gave a rope to Blue Crane and said, "If Rabbit tries to escape, tie him up with this rope."

Rabbit watched, and as soon as the men were out of sight, he whispered, "Come close and look in here."

As soon as Blue Crane stuck his head inside the hole, Rabbit snatched the rope, looped it over Blue Crane's head, and tied him to the tree. Rabbit then cut a thick switch and beat Blue Crane black and blue. A man finally heard Blue Crane's cries for help and headed toward the tree, but Rabbit heard him coming and took off through the bushes. *ZIP! ZIP! ZIP!*

Later, Rabbit met the orphan and asked, "Have you repaired your house yet?"

The orphan replied, "I've about finished cutting through the old house posts."

Rabbit went home and almost cut through his old posts. That night, he went to bed. Near midnight, his house collapsed on him.

Skunk Deceives the Wolves

On one of his travels, Possum met a wolf and killed him. "I'll skin and roast him," Possum decided. When the meat was ready, he put it in a basket to carry it.

As Possum waddled along, he met some other wolves who asked, "What do you have in that basket?"

"Nothing much. Just some clay for my grandmother. She promised to make an earthen pot for me, and I'm taking her the clay."

All the wolves believed Possum's story except for one. He had one eye and followed Possum, all the while repeating "I will not stop until I see what's in your basket."

Old One Eye then ran in front of Possum, faced him, and asked, "What's in there?"

"As I said before, nothing. My grandmother told me to get some clay. She wants to make me an earthen pot."

One Eye raised his voice. "WELL! I WANT TO LOOK INSIDE!" He jumped toward Possum and pulled the basket down to see what he had. "That looks like something roasted." He then shouted to the others who had gone ahead. "COME BACK! COME BACK! POSSUM HAS SOMETHING ROASTED!" The other wolves ran back and ate the meat.

When they finished, Possum said, "You have eaten yourselves."

The wolves stared at one another and wondered, "What does he mean, 'You have eaten yourselves?'" They growled, "Let's eat him." When they tried to kill him, however, Possum scooted into a nearby hole in the ground.

As the wolves dug at the hole, along came Skunk. "Why are you digging?" he wanted to know.

"Possum is in this hole," they answered.

"I can run him out, and you can kill him," Skunk offered. "I'll go in. When I holler EEEH! EEEH! EEEH! I'm coming out with him. Get close to the hole so you can hear." Skunk then disappeared.

The wolves gathered around with their snouts almost in the hole, Old One Eye closer than everyone else. All at once, Skunk threw a stink up their noses so bad it knocked them over. Possum ran out and so escaped.

Koasati/Coushatta Tales

Rabbit Provides Fire

Long ago, this land did not have fire, for those who possessed it lived far across the ocean. Although the people wanted fire, its owners refused to let them have it.

Then Rabbit announced to the people who had assembled, "I can bring some fire to you."

A man with many daughters replied, "The one who crosses the ocean and returns with fire will have one of my daughters."

Rabbit answered, "I must have more than one."

Big Man-Eater, who wanted all the daughters, was present and declared, "I can bring back fire."

"All right," said the man, "you bring it back."

So, Big Man-Eater set out. When he arrived at the ocean, he jumped in and vanished. The peopled waited a long time, but he never returned.

Rabbit then said, "Big Man-Eater could not bring back fire. Only I can bring it back and have all the young women." The man with many daughters told Rabbit to go.

Rabbit quickly ran to the ocean, threw off his shirt, and filled it with wood spunk before he tied it up. He then placed this in the water and sat down upon it like a raft. In that way, he traveled across the ocean.

"I have come for fire," Rabbit announced to its keepers, but they refused him. So, he seized some burning sticks and fled through the woods toward the sea as the Keepers of Fire pursued him. When he came to the ocean, he paused and saw pitch oozing from a tree. He rubbed the resin on the back of his head. As one of his pursuers approached, he dived into the ocean and swam, holding the blazing wood above the water. After a while, he became tired so that the flame touched the back of his head. Still, he swam and at last reached the other side.

Rabbit met the man who sent him. "My daughters are yours," he told Rabbit.

That night, as they prepared to lie down, Rabbit said, "I must sleep in the middle."

The women spoke for moment, and together they made Rabbit's bed. "Everything is ready," they announced.

Before Rabbit lay down, the women whispered to one another, "When Rabbit gets into bed, we'll talk sweetly, smile, and laugh to make him happy, and when he gets comfortable, we'll pick him up by holding his arms on each side. Then we will carry him out, pull off his shirt, and switch him."

So, when everyone got into bed, the women comforted Rabbit and made him so happy that he suspected nothing. They then seized him by the arms, took him outside, and tried to throw him to the ground. Rabbit became scared during the struggle, and as the women held him tight, they ripped the skin off his back. Away he ran.

After Rabbit sped off, he met Big Man-Eater, who had not died at sea but had finally returned. He asked, "What happened? Where is your shirt?"

"I help many women," Rabbit returned. "I keep them very happy." Big Man-Eater did not believe a word he said.

Rabbit and Big Man-Eater Trade Shoes

While traveling, Rabbit and Lion happened to meet and became friends. Big Man-Eater saw the fine shoes Rabbit wore and said, "I'll trade you mine for yours."

Now Rabbit liked his shoes very much and refused. "No, my shoes keep out the cold, and when I run through the briars, they don't stick in my feet." Still, Big Man-Eater wanted the shoes and continued to beg his new friend to swap.

Rabbit then teased him. "When I wear these shoes, the girls can't keep their eyes off them."

Big Man-Eater now coveted the shoes even more. "Let's trade. I'll give you a woman for your shoes."

Rabbit paused before he answered. "I'd like to see her first."

"Well," said Big Man-Eater, "I'll fetch her for you tomorrow."

Rabbit was not keen on the notion. "No, I want to go see her myself."

"I'm having a dance tomorrow night. You can stop by and take a look for yourself," replied the other.

Rabbit remained where he was, and Big Man-Eater left. Pleased about meeting the young woman, Rabbit cleaned his shoes and the next day set out for the dance. When he got there, he discovered that his friend had invited everyone. Rabbit sat on the edge of the dancing ground. He planned to trick Big Man-Eater who saw him and came over to talk.

"Remember, I want to make a trade..."

"Where's the woman?" Rabbit asked.

"I'll give you that one in the middle of the dancing circle but only if you swap your shoes for her. She is my pretty daughter."

Rabbit was eager for a woman, so he said, "Bring her to me where I'll be in the dark. Then we'll swap, and you can head off. But wait until tomorrow before you wear your new shoes. Bring a big handkerchief tonight to wrap them up. Tomorrow, before the ballgame, you can put them on and invite everybody to look at your fine new shoes."

Little known to Big Man-Eater, Rabbit had brought some rotten moccasins full of holes and made for big wide feet. He concealed these from Big Man-Eater who saw only Rabbit's good shoes. So, Big Man-Eater left and brought his daughter to his friend in the dark.

"Now we'll swap," declared Rabbit.

Big Man-Eater handed over his daughter and said, "She is your wife. Take her with you when you leave." After trading the old moccasins, Rabbit and his wife left the dance.

Rabbit loved his new bride so much he could not take his eyes off her. Blinking over and over, he stared and stared and stared at her. After a while, his eyes began to bulge out of his head as they became big and hard. His ears also started growing until they became long like the those of a jack ass. His eyes and ears have stayed that way to this day.

As for Big Man-Eater, right after Rabbit left the dance, he announced, "I beat Rabbit out of his fine shoes, but I will put them on tomorrow before the ball play. All the women cannot resist looking at them."

The next day, Big Man-Eater unwrapped his new shoes in front of the people. When he saw the rotten moccasins, he quietly left in shame as the women laughed. He and everyone gathered knew Rabbit had played a trick on him.

Rabbit, Big Man-Eater, and the River

A man once said to people that rivers should run straight, without any bends and with the current in the middle. Rabbit told him, "It is not good for rivers to be straight."

The man then said, "Who would like to carry water and spill it in different places?"

Rabbit volunteered, "Let me spill the water." He waited, but the man would not let him. He went to someone else, but he refused also. Rabbit asked everyone to let him spill the water, but no one would let him. Finally, when no one was looking, he took the water and ran off.

Men hunted Rabbit for four days with dogs until, exhausted, he hid in a hollow tree. The hunters set Big Man-Eater to guard the tree while they went to get an ax. When they returned, one of them chopped into the tree and pulled Rabbit out. They then took him beside the river and made a box to hold him. They intended to leave him inside and throw it into the water.

As the men were about to fasten the lid, Rabbit said, "Nail it tight. You can't kill me. I'll just float down to the ocean, and in four days I'll return."

The hunters nailed down the lid. "This time we are rid of him." As it was noon, they went home to eat and directed Big Man-Eater to guard the box. "When we return, we will toss the box into the river."

Rabbit waited and listened until he heard the men leave, then said to Big Man-Eater, "Open the box. I have a secret to tell you. You'll like it."

With his long claws, Big Man-Eater pried open the lid and let Rabbit out. Rabbit confessed, "My friend, those men really plan to send me to a place where there are many pretty girls."

"Oh, let me go in your place," Big Man-Eater responded excitedly. "I want to see all the pretty women!"

"Of course," Rabbit agreed. So, Big Man-Eater climbed into the box and curled up while Rabbit fastened the lid tightly.

When the hunters finished eating, they came back, carried the box down to the river, and threw it in. "This box seems mighty heavy," one said. The box, however, soon floated into the ocean.

"We are now rid of that lying fool," the men said among themselves. Then they laughed for a long time and left.

In four days, though, just as he had said, Rabbit returned. "I promised you I would be back."

Rabbit Plays Pranks on Elephant

Elephant was working in his field early one morning when Rabbit came up. He inquired, "What are you doing?"

Elephant looked up and said, "I've got some seed beans at the house, and I'm clearing the ground to plant them."

Elephant continued to work, and Rabbit left. He headed toward Elephant's house, went in, spoke to his wife, and pointed. "Elephant said for you to cook those beans for me."

The wife thought Rabbit was lying. "Why, he told me he intended to plant those beans," she answered.

"He told me," Rabbit said, "go up to the house and tell my wife to cook some beans for you." She still did not believe him.

"Well, I'm sure he'll say it's all right for you to cook them." So, Rabbit stuck his head out and hollered, "DIDN'T YOU SAY SO?"

"YES, I DID!" yelled Elephant.

So, Elephant's wife cooked the beans, and Rabbit ate every one of them. As he swallowed the last few, Elephant entered the house and exclaimed, "WHY, YOU RASCAL, YOU'VE EATEN ALL MY SEED BEANS!"

"If you are angry with me," Rabbit offered, "I will stretch my body across a big box, and you can cut me in half." Rabbit lay across the box, and Elephant came down with his ax. Rabbit jumped aside. *BAM!* The ax hit the box and shattered it. Wood chips and splinters flew in all directions.

Rabbit next offered, "Let me lie on a large rock, and you can hack me in two." So, he lay on a rock, but when Elephant chopped down, again Rabbit leapt aside. *BAM!* This time, the ax broke.

Rabbit boasted, "There is but one way to kill me. You must put me inside a house and burn it down. When you hear loud cracking and popping, I will be dead."

Elephant took Rabbit to an old house, locked him inside, and set it afire. But Rabbit had already dug a hole in the floor and a tunnel some distance out. He ran through the tunnel with the house cracking and popping behind him.

As he escaped, Rabbit shouted to Elephant and his missus, "TRY AS YOU MIGHT, YOU CAN'T KILL ME, BUT LET'S BE FRIENDS ANYWAY!"

Elephant agreed, and he and Rabbit went traveling together. Dusk fell, and Rabbit urged, "Let's make camp at Tree-Falling-on-Place."

When they got to where an old dead tree stood, Rabbit said, "We'll need to gather lots of firewood before we go to sleep."

So, Rabbit shook the dead tree, and lots of sticks fell for the two to pick up. They built a big fire nearby. They then lay down to sleep.

When Rabbit heard Elephant snoring, he rubbed himself with some ashes that had cooled before he took a stick and scattered hot coals over his friend. Elephant never did go back to sleep that night.

In the morning, when the two started out once again, Rabbit said, "Let's head to the river called Jumping-Back-and-Forth-Across."

They got there around noon, and Rabbit challenged Elephant to a contest. "I'll jump back and forth over the stream first. Then you do the same."

So, Rabbit jumped back and forth. Elephant jumped over to the other side and stood there a moment. Before he returned, Rabbit widened the river so that it stretched out from east to west and became the ocean. Elephant is still on the far side to this day.

Rabbit's Grandmother Punishes Buzzard

One day, Rabbit was resting. As he gazed at the sky, Buzzard glided down to him. Stirred by Buzzard's skill, Rabbit said, "I want to go up like you."

Buzzard agreed to let Rabbit ride on his back high in the air. So, Rabbit climbed on Buzzard, who flapped his wings and flew toward the sky. They mounted higher and higher until they arrived at a door.

Buzzard directed Rabbit, "Take hold of this door." When he did, though, Buzzard flew away followed by many buzzards that lived there. Rabbit gripped the door for a long time until he became tired. He suddenly let go and fell. When he hit the ground, part of him burst open.

Seeing what happened, Rabbit's grandmother ran to him. She doctored him until at last he had healed. When he was well enough, she said, "You must get even with that Buzzard."

Heeding her words, Rabbit left and came to a marsh. He stretched out there as if asleep. Buzzard saw him and circled above several times before drifting down. Thinking Rabbit dead, Buzzard walked toward Rabbit and stood next to him. Rabbit instantly seized the big bird and held him fast by his feet.

Rabbit's grandmother ran to help. Rabbit then quickly plucked out all of Buzzard's feathers. When he finished, he tied Buzzard in the marsh and conjured cold weather to come. A chilled wind blew from the north. When it became icy cold, Rabbit's grandmother switched Buzzard with a keen hickory.

Rabbit, the Turkeys, and Spunk Soup

One day, Rabbit decided to have some fun. So, he went high up on a hill and got inside a sack. He rolled down, laughing all the way. *BABOOM! BABOOM! BABOOM! BABOOM! BABOOM!*

A flock of turkeys saw him from a distance. They enjoyed watching Rabbit and came closer.

"What are you doing?" they asked.

"Enjoying myself," he responded.

"You lie!" they taunted.

"Well!" Rabbit huffed. "Why don't one of you get inside, and I'll roll you down."

So, one of the turkeys hopped in the sack, and Rabbit got him started. *BABOOM! BABOOM! BABOOM! BABOOM! BABOOM!* The turkey laughed all the way to the bottom and told the others, "That IS fun. You should try it, too."

Now all the turkeys got into the sack, and Rabbit rolled them down. When they got to the bottom, they were too dizzy to stand, so Rabbit picked them up, slung them over his arm, and took them away. He soon came to his grandmother's place and shut the turkeys up in her corncrib. He warned her, "Do not open the corncrib." He then left.

By and by, the grandmother got curious, went down to the corncrib, and opened it. Before she could say a word, the turkeys swarmed out, flapped their wings, and flew away. *LO-PO-POP! LO-PO-POP! LO-PO-POP!* She threw her hands up and tried to grab them but caught only one by the feet.

She called for her grandson. "Rabbit, come quick. I caught a turkey by the feet."

He ran back and scolded, "I told you not to open the corncrib. I had planned to give a feast for a number of guests but go ahead and kill the one you have. You can cook it, and I'll invite just a few."

While the grandmother prepared the turkey, Rabbit left, walked around at random, and returned by the time it was done. "Hurry, a big crowd is on the way," he told her, though no one was really coming. "Bring the food down here. We'll have to eat outside off this cane stand."

The grandmother set out the food and went back to the cabin for something. Rabbit yelled so she could hear him, "ALL RIGHT! LET'S EAT!" He then made a racket like a large crowd talking as he jumped on one side of the platform and then on the other to sound like a huge number of people had gathered.

Before the old woman could return, Rabbit had gobbled down all the food. When he finished, he took some slippery elm spunk, mixed it with water, and made a soup just as his grandmother got back. "Here, eat this. That's all that's left."

"This tastes like old spunk," she said.

"Soup always tastes that way this time of year," he replied, and the two of them finished what remained.

Possum and Panther Become Partners

On one of his travels, Possum saw a parcel of deer not too far off and sat down to watch them. Panther stole up to him, and by and by said, "Possum, if you can fool those deer, I will kill one, and we will have a feast."

Possum headed toward the deer and said, "The one who once ate you is lying over there. He died a while back and is full of worms. Go dance around him and celebrate. Shout the words LONG DEAD! LONG DEAD!"

The deer went where Possum pointed, danced, and loudly sang, "LONG DEAD! LONG DEAD!" Possum sat and watched them as they celebrated around a fire they had made.

A fawn tiptoed close to the flame where Panther lay and warned, "HE IS OPENING HIS EYES!"

"YOU LIE!" Possum cried out.

Before the deer were aware, Panther jumped on an old buck, wrestled him to the ground, and choked him to death. In a flash, the rest of the herd fled. That night, Panther ate until stuffed. Possum filled up on the remains.

Natchez Tales

Perch Fools Owl

Perch swam in a small puddle that was nearly dry, and Owl swooped down and caught him. Owl was just about to eat him, when Perch said, "If you will take me to a clean and airy place, I'll sing you a song, and you can dance to it. I'm a very good singer."

"All right," Owl agreed, and he flew away with Perch. "Tell me when we reach a suitable spot."

They soon arrived at a stream where water pooled in different places. "Here is a good spot for me to sing and you to dance," Perch said.

Owl lit along the stream bank beside a pool. "Brush away the sticks and leaves so that you can easily dance back and forth four rounds," Perch told him. "Be sure to put me along your path. On the fourth round, you can eat me."

Owl brushed the ground clean, and Perch began his sweet song. Owl started his dance, but when he turned to end his fourth round, Perch flipped himself into the air, jumped into the pool of water, and swam off.

Wolf and Rabbit Cannot Get Along

Rabbit and Wolf had a problem. Both wanted to marry the same woman. Unknown to Rabbit, she had agreed to marry Wolf, but Rabbit went to try and win her over.

The woman's mother thought she should have a say in the matter. "Rabbit's come to court you, but you've agreed to marry Wolf."

Rabbit spoke up. "Here's something you may not know. Wolf is really my old saddle horse."

The mother said, "Well, if you can ride him over here, I'll take your word for it."

Rabbit left and later met Wolf. "When are you next going to visit your future bride? Let me know, and we'll go together."

Wolf agreed and stopped by Rabbit's house. "Are you ready?" he asked.

"Yes, but I'm having stomach troubles and can't walk. May I ride on your back?"

"I guess that would be all right," Wolf said.

So, Rabbit hopped up on Wolf's back. He then said, "It's awful hard for me to sit up here. Do you think we could get a saddle?"

Wolf was not too keen about the idea but after a pause, he replied, "I'll get a saddle for you." Rabbit saddled Wolf and got back on him.

Still not satisfied, Rabbit hemmed and hawed a while. Wolf asked, "What's the matter with you now?"

"If you let me put spurs on, I'll feel steadier up here." So, Wolf handed Rabbit some spurs. He fastened these to his feet and got back on.

"I'd feel even better if I had a bridle on you." So, Wolf gave Rabbit a bridle. He put it on Wolf and remounted.

"I'm ready now. Let's go," and the two set out.

Rabbit rode Wolf up to the house and called out, "I SAID I'D RIDE MY SADDLE HORSE OVER HERE."

And before Wolf could say a word, Rabbit got off and shut him in the barn. A man there put out hay and corn for Wolf to eat, but Rabbit said, "This horse won't eat that. He prefers fresh meat."

"We don't have any meat," the fellow said. So, Wolf stayed all day in the stable with nothing to eat.

In the meantime, the mother and her daughter accepted Rabbit's offer of marriage, and he spent the night. However, when dark fell, Wolf started digging until he dug his way out and ran off. The next morning, Rabbit went to the barn and discovered he had escaped. Believing that Wolf would waylay him, Rabbit got so scared he went back to the house and refused to leave. That night, though, he got hungry, went out, and started to feed in the grass and weeds.

Wolf was waiting. He lunged toward Rabbit and started to chase him. Round and round and round they went until Rabbit ran through a hole in the fence. Wolf remained, guarding the house in case Rabbit came back. Once in a while, he would return, but Wolf would chase him off. Not to be outdone, Rabbit decided to hide in the garden and feed on the vegetables, but Wolf sneaked up on him and captured him.

Wolf now started for home and carried Rabbit with him. He planned to chop Rabbit's head off. So, when he arrived, he got his ax. Rabbit bragged, "I don't give a-you-know-what if you cut off my head. When you do, there'll be two of me."

So, Wolf laid down his ax, tied up Rabbit, and kindled a big fire. He threatened to throw Rabbit in it.

"Do and I'll piss all over this fire and put it out."

Wolf then got a big iron pot full of water and hung it over the flames. "I think I'll dump you in boiling water."

"Do and I'll kick up my feet and break your pot," Rabbit said.

Wolf pointed and replied, "Then I'll just throw you into this briar patch."

"Do and I'll cry and scream as loud as I can."

Wolf seized Rabbit by the ears and flung him deep into the briar patch. Rabbit hit the ground and went "WHOOP! WHOOP! WHOOP!" and took off toward the woods as fast as he could go.

Wolf turned red with rage and chased him. Round and round they went, dodging rocks and fallen branches until Rabbit jumped into a hollow tree. Wolf tried to get him out but could not.

Wolf saw Owl perched on a nearby limb and said, "I'm going to get my ax. Don't let him out. When I come back, I'll kill him."

"Do not fear," returned Owl. "If he tries to escape, I will kill him myself."

Wolf went to get his ax. When Rabbit saw that he was gone, he told Owl, "Come down and see me. This hole is very pretty. You'll like it, my friend."

"That hole is too dim, and I do not see well." Owl declared.

"Fly down, and open your eyes as wide as possible," Rabbit instructed. He had been chewing tobacco the entire time. When owl peered into the hole, Rabbit spit in his face. Owl flew back to his limb but had such a glob of tobacco juice in his eyes he fell off and staggered around trying to clear his sight by opening his eyes as wide as he could. He then dropped a big load on the ground. SPLAT! Rabbit rushed out of the hollow tree and skedaddled off.

When Wolf returned, he asked, "Is Rabbit still in there?"

"No, he escaped," Owl replied. "But first we had a fight. Look at what happened to me. Rabbit spit tobacco juice in my eyes and almost blinded me. As we fought, he dropped that big pile over there before he ran off."

Wolf said, "I'm going to set that mess on fire."

81

Owl objected. "Oh, you need not do that."

He kept on so much about the matter that Wolf finally said, "You're acting so stingy about it I believe you wrang out that heap yourself." Then, with his ax handle, Wolf whacked Owl on the head so hard he squalled, "O-O-o-o-o! O-O-o-o-o! O-O-o-o-o!"

Since that day, Owl has always made the sound and has a swollen head with wide eyes.

Rabbit Kills Alligator

The chief of the animals offered to divide different foods among them and said, "Ask for what you like to eat." Among the requests, Squirrel wanted acorns, while Possum, Raccoon, and Fox asked for persimmons. The birds preferred grapes.

Rabbit gazed up and noticed the many sycamore balls hanging from a tree. He wanted these. The animal chief agreed. So, Rabbit sat under the tree and waited for them to drop. Instead of falling straight down, however, the balls would scatter here and there.

Rabbit finally got hungry and went to the chief again. "I'd like something else to eat."

The chief told Rabbit, "Go on a hunt and return with food I like. I will then provide you something you like."

Rabbit set out and traveled to Alligator's home. He called for Alligator to come out.

"What's all the noise about?" Alligator inquired.

"The animals want you to chop down a forked post."

"Who needs it?" Alligator wanted to know.

"It's for the chief."

Alligator said, "Well, if the chief wants a forked post, I guess I'll have to get one."

So, he and Rabbit traveled together until they came close to a canebrake where there was suitable wood. Rabbit suddenly knocked Alligator on the head, but the blow failed to kill him, and he ran off unharmed.

Rabbit returned to the chief. "I couldn't find any food you might like."

"Then you will not have anything to eat until you do," answered the chief.

Rabbit set out once more, and this time he killed a fawn and skinned it. He then draped the skin over himself and, disguised as a fawn, headed back to Alligator's home. When he got there, he shouted for Alligator to come out.

"What's all the noise about this time?" Alligator asked.

"The chief still wants you to bring him a forked post."

"I tried before," Alligator said, "but got thumped hard on the head."

"Who would do such a thing?"

"That Rabbit did it," replied Alligator.

"Oh, you should realize by now he hasn't got any sense. I'll go with you. You know a fawn like me wouldn't do such a thing. You can trust me."

"Well, all right," Alligator said. "Let's go." So, he and Rabbit left.

As the pair traveled toward the canebrake, they passed near the spot where the chief of the animals happened to be. Disguised as the fawn, Rabbit asked Alligator, "Why was Rabbit not able to kill you when he thumped you on the head?"

"He didn't hit me in the right place."

"Where's that?"

"Well," Alligator admitted, "if Rabbit had struck me in the back, I wouldn't be here. I'd be dead."

By and by, as they traveled a little farther, Rabbit picked up a heavy stick and struck Alligator over his back and killed him. Rabbit then hoisted the dead body over his shoulder and hauled it to the chief.

As Rabbit stood before him, the chief said, "Those kinds of things should not be eaten. Go where the old women have their gardens and steal vegetables out of them. And when you rob them, the dogs will give chase. Now run, Rabbit, run."

At once, the chief set his dogs on Rabbit, and he hightailed through the brush. The chief then called out, "THAT IS WHERE THEY WILL CATCH YOU AND KILL YOU!"

Ever since that day, Rabbit has liked gardens. There, he often can be found eating.

The Young Hunter's Adventures

A woman went down to a creek to wash herself and laid her baby on the ground beside it. As she dipped out water, Panther watched closely, then stole up, and snatched the child in his mouth. With her back turned, she was unaware of what had happened to the boy and, after much searching, decided he was not to be found.

Panther carried the child to his den, and he and his mate raised him as their own. After a few years, when the boy had gotten bigger, the Panthers gave him a bow and arrows. The youth would go hunting and return to the den to tell his parents that he saw something which frightened him, when all he had really seen was a bird.

Panther explained, "You can kill these birds and eat them." So, the boy would go hunting, shoot the birds, and bring them back.

One day, he returned and told his father, "Some things with slick heads frightened me."

"You can kill and eat those, too," Panther said. "They are turkeys." The next time the boy went hunting, he shot a turkey.

The boy grew into a young man and continued to hunt. He came home another time and looked scared. "Today, I saw something with slender legs and a white tail."

Panther and his mate replied, "That was a deer. It also can be killed and eaten." So, the young man took his bow and killed it.

Far off was a mountain that seemed blue from a distance. The Panthers directed their son, "Do not ever go to that blue mountain."

A few days later, the Panthers left and traveled to a certain place. Alone, the hunter wondered, "Why did they tell me not go to the mountain?" But no matter what they had told him, he decided to go there.

The young man journeyed several days, and when he arrived, he climbed to the top, and there he saw a throng of people playing ball. He also recognized his human mother among the crowd.

The hunter then returned home where the Panthers waited for him. "Have you been to the distant mountain?" they asked, and he told them he had.

"That is where you were born. That is your town. We must now prepare you for your journey."

So, the Panthers instructed the young man to shoot various kinds of birds. He did as they asked. They then told him to shoot another kind, and so he did. The Panthers repeated their counsel several times until he had shot as many kinds of birds as possible. With the feathers and the birds, the Panthers adorned the young hunter. They set a green parakeet on his head and put blue jays on both shoulders and tied various smaller birds around his waist. The Panthers brought all of these birds to life again.

"After you have traveled a while," said the father, "you will arrive at a house, and when you have passed by it, you will meet someone, but do not stop to talk." Then Panther gave the young man a horn. "Blow this, and all the birds will cry out."

So, the hunter set out, and as Panther had prophesied, he came to a house and met Rabbit standing just beyond it. Rabbit spoke to him. "Where are you traveling?"

"I am traveling to my mother's home. And you? Where do you go?"

"I'm headed to the creek to catch turtles. Your mother lives nearby. Come with me, and when we've caught enough turtles, we'll travel together to her house."

At these words, the young man turned around and went with Rabbit. They reached the creek, and the hunter removed his clothes. "Tell me how to catch turtles."

"I braid a rope from the bark of a young hickory tree, hold the end in my mouth, and dive into the water. When I catch one, I tie it to the rope, and when I have enough, I pull them out."

So, the two made hickory bark cords and waded into the creek. Rabbit said, "When I say go, we'll dive into the deep water. NOW GO!"

The hunter waded a little deeper and dived in, but Rabbit jumped out, took the clothes lying on the bank, and ran off. Meanwhile, after seizing a turtle, the young man stuck his head out of the water and waded out. He looked around and saw that his clothes were missing. Figuring he had been tricked, he hung down his head and thought, "What will I do?"

When he looked up, he noticed a persimmon tree full of fruit. He shook the tree hard and crushed the sticky fallen fruit all over himself, then left to find his mother's house. Carrying the turtle with him, he reached her place and stood in the yard. His mother was inside about to cut up a raccoon to cook later. In a low voice, he called, "Mother."

His mother, though, responded, "I'm not sure I have a child."

As the hunter started to leave, he said, "May the coon bite you if you have a son."

The dead raccoon instantly bit her, and the young man left as his mother screamed from the sudden pain. He stopped at many houses along the way, but he was so unwashed, gummy, and dirty only a few people offered him food. They said, "You can eat outside and then be on your way."

He came at last to where an old woman and her granddaughter lived in a broken-down house. Out in the unswept yard was a hole dug into a clay bank, and there he set his turtle. The old woman and her grand-daughter came out, greeted him, and made him feel welcomed. They invited him inside and offered him food.

The young man said, "Though I passed many houses, you are the first people who have welcomed me into their home, and this is the first place in which I have eaten."

The grandmother said, "No one should treat a person that way."

The hunter responded, "I do not know whether you eat turtle, but I put one in the hole outside."

"Turtle is hard for us to get," the old woman said.

The three went to the clay bank, and when they peered in the hole, it teemed with turtles, their shells clacking together and making a great noise. The hunter took one out, and the grandmother prepared it, then said, "No one ever gave us food like this before. You may have my grand-daughter as your wife."

The hunter replied, "If you have any kin, invite them to come and select a turtle. So, the old woman sent her granddaughter to inform their relatives who eagerly came for the turtles."

A little while later, the young man decided to take his bride to the creek. After he stripped off his clothes, he dived into the water and swam underneath from one side to the other. Back and forth he went, causing the fish to become raddled and float to the top.

"Go and inform your relatives and let them come and collect the fish," he told his wife. When she did, they came and gathered many.

Rabbit heard about the what the young man did and vowed, "I will do the same." He went to the creek, dived in, and swam back and forth. Yet only minnows rose to the surface. When he told the people to gather them, the minnows darted off.

"Another of Rabbit's tricks," the people muttered in anger.

After the young man had dived into the creek earlier, the dried per-simmons and filth washed off his body, and he appeared as a fine hunter. By and by, as he and his wife sat in the yard, he asked her to comb her hair and part it in the middle. After she did, he left to get a broad ax and sharpened it on a grindstone.

When he returned, he said, "I am hungry. Prepare something to eat."

His wife went inside and brought out various things to eat. "Where should I put the food?" she asked.

Her husband then rose quickly and struck her head between her parted hair. She became two people who spoke and smiled to each other.

Sitting outside his house, Rabbit heard about the hunter's action and directed his wife to do the same. "Comb your hair and part it down the middle, then bring me my ax and grindstone." While he sharpened the ax, he added, "I am hungry. Bring me something to eat."

She went inside and brought out different foods. "Where should I put these?"

Rabbit jumped up and with his ax struck the part in her hair. She instantly dropped dead on the ground.

When the animals heard about what Rabbit did, they headed to the young hunter's house and arrested him. "YOU ARE THE REASON RABBIT MURDERED HIS WIFE!" they cried. So, they put him on trial, and their sentence was death.

The animals decided that the young man should die by cutting cane for arrows in a canebrake full of rattlesnakes. But first Panther secretly visited him and brought him four balls. "Take these, and when you enter the canebrake, think on your enemies and throw each ball for them to chase. Be sure you throw the last one as far as possible."

When the animals put the young man in the canebrake, he threw the first ball, and as the rattlesnakes ran after it, he cut cane. They returned. He threw the second ball. The snakes chased it, and he cut more cane The same occurred with the third. He then flung the fourth ball as far as he could, and out of the canebrake he ran safely along the path he had cut.

The animals, however, caught the hunter and thought to give him to a cannibal who lived close by. The animals decreed, "You must cut off the cannibal's beard and dress the arrows with it."

But before they took him away, his Panther father again came to him in secret. "Go to the cannibal, and there change into Granddaddy Longlegs. Scurry to his ceiling and wait."

The animals took their prisoner to where the cannibal lived, but he was away, and only his wife was at home. The hunter persuaded her to cut off the beard of her husband when he returned. Then, turning into Grandaddy Longlegs, the hunter climbed to the ceiling and waited.

By and by, the cannibal came home. "I am tired from travel and now must sleep." He soon began to snore deeply, and his wife cut off his beard. When it was safe, the young man turned back into himself, and the woman gave him the beard. He returned with it to his captors.

The animals thought, "How can we kill this prisoner? Not one of our plans has come to pass."

"Something dangerous lives at the creek," one said. "Let us send him there and sentence him to dig up clay from the bottom."

The others agreed, but before the hunter left, his Panther father secretly came to see him once more. "You will not be able to get the clay. It is too deep, and the current too swift. Call for the one with the white collar and let him dig it for you. When he begins, sit upon the bank, and urge him to hurry."

The animals took their prisoner to the creek, threw him in the water, and left. He climbed onto the bank and said, "I seek the one who wears the white collar."

The person he called came and was the Kingfisher. The young man asked him to dive to the bottom and dig out the clay, and the Kingfisher agreed. "After I dive, watch the bubbles as they rise. If they are clear, I am safe, but if they are red with blood, you must return to the people."

The Kingfisher dived, and the hunter sat watching. The bubbles were clear, and the bird came up and told him to take the clay from his claws.

"Now strike that rock with the clay," said the bird, and when the young hunter struck the rock, the clay at once became larger. He then carried it back to those who had condemned him. Not to be outdone, they decided to punish him another way and sent him across the creek where many cannibals lived. Once more, his Panther father came and advised him. The animals then ferried the hunter across the creek.

That night, the large dogs of the cannibals pursued him, but following the counsel of Panther, the young man hid inside a hollow tree. The dogs traced his scent there. The cannibals, who could not see him in the dark, poked a stick inside the hole to force him out, but he remained hidden. Thinking the hounds had deceived them, they became angry and beat the dogs. The cannibals then went home.

Early the next morning, the young man slipped out of the hollow tree and wandered about. In time, he saw two women swimming in the creek. He took their clothing and climbed into a tree. Concealed by the limbs and leaves, he watched them. When they came out of the water, they could not find their clothes but noticed him above them. They demanded their clothes.

"And what will you give me in return?" he asked.

"We will let you be our brother."

He did not move or speak.

"You will be our nephew," the women offered.

He stayed where he was and did not answer.

"We will let you be our son," they next replied.

Again, he remained still and said nothing.

The women named all types of kinships, but the hunter's response was the same. At last, they said, "We will be your wives." He straight-away climbed down and followed them.

As the three walked together, the women said, "We have ever longed for a husband, but when we find one, our father kills him and roasts him. First, though, our father makes the man have a race with him. But he tricks the man and falls behind him so that he runs ahead to a deep place the rains have washed out. There, in the washout, our father has sharp stakes stuck up. He then chases the man hard so that he suddenly falls on them and dies."

Before long, the hunter and his new wives reached their father's house. The cannibal came out and rejoiced, shouting, "MY DAUGHTERS ALWAYS Bring HOME A FINE MAN!" He then invited the hunter to race.

He and the cannibal ran toward the washout, but when they neared it, the young man dropped back, and the old man fell into the ditch but not on the spikes. The young man stopped and helped the cannibal to his feet.

That night, the hunter put on a mask with open eyes painted on it and slept between his two wives. From time to time, to see whether his son-in-law was asleep, the old man would tiptoe over and look. But the mask with wide-open eyes fooled the cannibal, and he would go back to his pallet. Although he tried for several nights, he finally gave up his attempts to catch the young man sleeping.

So, the cannibal whispered to his daughters, "Tomorrow night, I will set the house on fire, but I will warn you beforehand."

The next night, he tiptoed over to his daughters and gently tapped them on the head to wake them. Unknown to their father, however, when they started to leave, they held their husband between them so he could not be seen in the dark. They went outside, and the cannibal set fire to his house.

CRACK, CRACK, CRACK and POP, POP, POP went the house as it burned, and while it cracked and popped, the old man laughed, "Those are the bones that I like to eat now popping and cracking." He then ran and circled the house three times, all the while laughing and rejoicing.

By and by, he gazed about and saw his son-in-law. "I thought you burned to death in the fire, and for that reason I acted strangely in my grief."

The women then said to their husband, "Our father will never cease acting this way. If you wish, go back to your home."

Before the hunter parted from his wives, they found four young pups. "Take these, and when you come to the creek, you will meet the dangerous thing with white around its neck and horns on its head. Name it 'My Friend' and ride it across."

So, he took the four pups to the wide creek and sat down, and as his wives had directed, he called for something. Different kinds of snakes and turtles raised their heads from the water.

"You are not the one I call," he said.

They answered, "We thought you called to us," then vanished beneath the water.

After a while, a huge creature with a white ring around its neck and with horns like a deer broke the surface and asked, "What troubles you?"

"Will you carry me across the water?" the young hunter responded.

The horned snake returned, "And what will you do for me?"

"My Friend, I have brought you food and will give it to you as you take me over."

The giant serpent agreed to the request, and the hunter mounted its horns. As they began to cross, he tossed before it a pup. But once the snake swallowed it, they started to sink to the bottom. The hunter threw out another pup, and they rose and continued toward the far bank. Again, when the snake ate the pup, they sank. So, the young man threw the third one before it, and they rose and moved closer to the other side. The same occurred with the fourth pup.

Then the young man began to saw off a prong from one of the creature's horns, and its dust sprinkled the water. "What is falling?" the snake asked.

"Oh, that is from some ground cornmeal I am eating."

So, they kept going, and the hunter removed the prong. When nearly to the opposite side, to confuse the snake, he shot an arrow which stuck in the soil. He pretended to shoot another arrow, then jumped on the bank.

The serpent became angry, declaring, "You should have jumped earlier and not exhausted me."

"You are too proud and easily angered," the hunter returned. "I will make the stream dry so that you have nothing to hold you up."

So, the water ran dry, and the horned serpent writhed on the muddy bottom. It cried out, "I HELPED YOU, AND NOW YOU HAVE WRONGED ME!"

The hunter then caused the water to run again, and the creature swam away. The young man returned to the Panthers who had taken care of him.

Why Possum Hangs by His Tail

One time there was a girl so pretty that all the creatures sought to marry her. Possum decided to try his luck and went to visit her. Along the way, he found some pieces of paper and stuffed them inside his pouch. When he arrived at the girl's house, a crowd of suitors had already gathered. While he waited, he took out the papers. He would look carefully at each piece and then put it aside.

The people asked, "What are you looking at."

"I used to be a soldier," he said, "and these papers are my pension pay."

When the girl heard about Possum's money, she declared at once that she would marry him. The other creatures who were there grew angry and decided to do something. "Let's get rid of Possum's bushy tail," they plotted.

So, that night, while Possum and his wife were asleep, one of the suitors slipped into the house and hid a hair-eating caterpillar in Possum's tail. By morning, the caterpillar had eaten all the hair from it.

The next morning, Possum woke up, and when he discovered how he had been deceived, he went outside and climbed up the nearest tree. When his wife awoke, she wondered where her husband was and went out of doors to find him. She searched here and there, then finally looked up and saw him sitting on a high limb.

"WHAT ARE YOU DOING UP THERE?" she yelled. "COME DOWN HERE AT ONCE!"

Possum refused.

"IF YOU DO NOT COME DOWN HERE, I'LL KNOCK YOU DOWN!"

Possum's wife then started picking up rocks and sticks to pelt him. A few of these hit him until at last one struck his head so that he slipped off his limb. As he fell, though, his tail coiled around it, and he hung there upside down. Even today, Possum can hang from a limb by his tail.

Fox and Crawfish Have a Race

Fox was hungry, so he thought he would eat Crawfish. But when Fox came to catch him, Crawfish offered, "Let's race first, and if you win, then you can eat me."

Thinking the little fellow would be easy to beat, Fox accepted the offer. They agreed to run over seven hills, and at the appointed time, they hunkered down beside each other at the foot of the first hill. Crawfish was to give the signal. Fox kept swishing his tail back and forth from one side and then over toward Crawfish.

Crawfish shouted, "LET'S GO!"

But at that moment, Fox happened to flick his tail beside Crawfish who grabbed it with one of his claws. Off they went, Crawfish flopping up and down and clinging to the bushy tail with all his might. Fox carried him over one hill, then another until they crossed the seventh. At the end of the course, Fox turned so fast that he whipped Crawfish off and hurled him some distance away.

When he landed, the little fellow hollered, "I KNEW I COULD BEAT YOU!"

Turkey Tricks Wildcat

One day Wildcat was splitting rails when he spied a turkey gobbler standing by a tree. When Wildcat picked up his gun, Turkey saw him and cried out, "WAIT! DON'T KILL ME!"

Turkey then walked up to Wildcat and said, "If you pluck off my feathers, I will go to your wife, and she can kill and cook me. That way, when you get home, you'll have something to eat."

"All right," Wildcat agreed. "Sit on this log, and I'll pick out your feathers."

After Wildcat had plucked him clean, Turkey said, "By the time you get home, I should be cooked done." He then headed toward Wildcat's house.

When Turkey got there, he told Wildcat's wife, "Your husband plucked me and sent me here with a message. He wants you to pound up cold flour for me and for me to tread on you."

Wildcat's wife at once took some dried corn, sugared it, added some salt, and beat the mixture with her pestle in a mortar. She then gave the cornmeal to Turkey, and he walked on her for a while before he took the cold flour and left.

At midday, Wildcat came home. "Is That Turkey Done? I've Been Splitting Rails All Morning, and I'm Hungry!"

"No," his wife answered. "When Turkey came here, he told me you had plucked him. He said you wanted me to fix him some cold flour and for him to tread on me. Well, I did what you said. I pounded up cold flour, he stepped on me a while, and then he went off."

After his wife told Wildcat what happened, he grabbed his gun. "In what direction did he head?"

Wildcat's wife pointed him the way, and he set off. Before long, he saw a rafter of turkeys. Walking among them was the one he had plucked. Turkey would strut around and toss the others some of the cold meal, and they would give him a feather in return. He had already stuck them all over his body. By the time Wildcat got close enough to shoot, Turkey had stuck on so many he looked just like the others.

The turkeys spotted Wildcat sneaking up and took off. He never shot a single one and went home just as hungry as ever.

The Fawn, the Wolves, the Skunk, and the Terrapin

On his travels, Wolf came upon a fawn and asked, "Where did you get your white stripes and spots?"

"The people put me about three feet deep in the ground and placed over me a cane grate with small openings. They then built a fire on top of it, and the heat splotched my hide white with spots and stripes."

Wolf thought he wanted his fur to be splotched also. So, the people dug a three-foot hole for him to get in, laid over it a cane riddle, and made a fire on the top. The people left and told the fawn to watch the fire.

In a short while, Wolf said, "I'm hot. My hair is striped and speckled like yours."

The fawn put more wood on the fire.

Before long, Wolf spoke again. "I have to pee."

The fawn threw on more wood.

Soon, Wolf said, "I've got to shit."

The fawn piled on even more wood, and the flames roared higher yet. Wolf howled and howled. By and by, nothing was left of him, only his bones among the ashes and hot coals. The fawn gathered Wolf's backbones, threaded hickory-bark twine through them, and wore them as a necklace. He then left and walked along singing when he encountered some other wolves who heard him.

"What is the meaning of your song?" they asked.

"Oh, I'm singing about how I could be wearing my own bones but am not."

The wolves at first saw no harm in these words, and the fawn kept walking. After he was a short distance from them, he began to sing again. This time, they realized the bones were those of one of their people, and they chased the fawn who fled before them through the woods. As luck would have it, he soon came to the hole of Skunk. He was sitting outside his den and watched the fawn go inside.

The wolves quickly came up and asked, "Did you see a fawn come by here?"

"Yes, he is in my house resting."

"Turn him out," they demanded. "We want him. He killed our brother."

Skunk then directed them to gather around the mouth of his den. "Get close. The fawn is swift and nimble. Do not let him run past you. I will go in and pull him out."

Skunk then entered his house and made a noise as if he were dragging something. The wolves heard the sound. *Scritch scratch. Scritch scratch. Scritch scratch.* Skunk, though, was only clawing the dirt with his paws as he worked his way out backward.

The wolves guarded the hole closely, their noses right beside the opening. Skunk suddenly threw such a stink over them that they dropped where they stood. Off ran Skunk and the fawn.

In time, the wolves revived and picked up the fawn's trail. They pursued him and got closer and closer, eventually getting so close the fawn ran to Buzzard's house and jumped in his nose. However, the deer could not squeeze completely inside so that part of one leg still hung out.

Up ran the wolves. "Has a fawn come here?" they asked.

"I have not seen one," Buzzard told them.

One of the wolf people then asked, "What is that dangling from your nose? It looks like the foreleg of a deer."

Buzzard blew his nose. The fawn shot out and took off, escaping through the woods. Still the wolves pursued him so closely he could feel their breath on his backside. So, he sprang into a tall tree. Using the bristles around their mouths, the wolves attempted to shoot him down but could not.

By and by, they remembered that Terrapin lived in that part of the woods. "He has a bow and arrows. Let's persuade him to kill the fawn," they said.

So, the wolves sent a messenger to Terrapin and told him what they wanted him to do. Terrapin answered, "I am cutting cane and making arrows. I cannot come."

The messenger returned to the others and gave them Terrapin's answer. "Go back," they said. "Tell him we think you have finished your arrows."

The wolf went back and gave Terrapin the message. "I am making my arrows straight," he said.

The wolf again returned to his people, and they sent him a third time. "I am putting feathers on my arrows," returned Terrapin.

Once more, the messenger brought back Terrapin's answer. "Go back," said the other wolves.

Terrapin told him, "I am now sharpening my arrows."

The wolf returned again, and again his people sent him back. "Tell Terrapin we think his arrows are sharp."

This time, Terrapin agreed to go. "I will shoot the deer, but I am so slow your kin must carry me to the tree."

So, three wolves went to Terrapin. One carried his bow. Another, his arrows. And another, Terrapin. They brought him to the assembled wolves and set him beneath the tree where the fawn had taken shelter. Terrapin then started to shoot arrows at him, but they missed the mark and landed in the ground some distance past the tree. The wolves ran to get them and brought them back while Terrapin kept shooting until he finally hit the deer. He tumbled from his limb, and the wolves skinned him and divided the meat so that each had a piece.

They offered Terrapin his reward. "What part will you have?" they asked. However, he did not speak.

"Do you want a hindquarter?" they asked.

"My hindquarters always hurt me, and I think the deer's hindquarter would make the pain worse."

"Will you take a shank and shoulder?"

"My shoulder pains me also," Terrapin complained. "A forequarter would not agree with me."

"Would you like a rib?"

"No, my ribs hurt me, too."

"How about the backbone?" the wolves offered.

"Oh, no, my back is always bothering me. The backbone might make it worse."

"Will you take the head?"

"I have headaches all the time, and it might give me one."

"Well, what about the jaw? Won't you take it?"

"My jaw aches right now." Terrapin groaned. "I couldn't take the jaw."

"Then we'll give you the legs and feet."

"I have pains in my knees. I'm sure the legs and feet would not agree with me."

The wolves then asked, "Could you eat the liver?"

"No, that part bothers me, too."

"Well, take the guts."

Terrapin moaned, "My stomach gives me cramps. The guts would not agree with me either."

"Take the tail then."

"My tail troubles me more than my other parts."

The head wolf finally said, "I don't think he wants anything."

With that, the wolves carried off their share of meat and left Terrapin by himself. He then edged over to where the wolves had cut up the fawn. "Why, they even lapped up all the blood," he said to himself. As he began to crawl away, however, he found a leaf with a lump of clotted blood on it. He then piled other leaves on it and made a bundle to take with him.

As Terrapin neared his house, his wife spied him and thought, "He's bringing home meat." So, she hung a pot of water over the fire.

Terrapin brought in his bundle and set it close by. His wife started to remove the leaves one by one.

"The meat's got to be in here somewhere," she muttered.

At last, she came to the last leaf. She turned to Terrapin and scolded, "WHAT DO YOU MEAN BRINGING ME THIS Little CLUMP OF BLOOD?" She at once picked it up and flung it in his eyes, and ever since then Terrapin has always had red eyes.

Seminole Tales

Rabbit Brings Back Fire

One day, Rabbit swam across the salt sea and found people who had fire. They guarded it for themselves. Round and round the fire they would dance.

Rabbit got a cloth and put some pitch on it. He wanted the fine tar to catch fire. He tied the cloth around his head so the part with pitch rested along the back of his neck. He entered the dance and went around the fire. As he circled it many times, he moved closer and closer to the flames until he danced so close the pitch caught on fire.

Rabbit then ran toward the water, and the people chased him. He waded in, but the people stopped. With the fire burning on the back of his neck, he swam across, holding his head high out of the water. In this way, Rabbit brought back fire, and since that time, he has a red place behind his head where the fire burned his neck.

Rabbit Wants a Wife

Rabbit once told everyone, "I sure would like to get married." However, nobody believed him because he was such a big liar.

Everybody said, "Before you can marry, you'll have to kill Alligator."

"All right then," Rabbit replied. So, he went to Alligator's house and spoke to him. At first, Alligator would not come out, but Rabbit wheedled for so long Alligator stuck out his head.

"I'd like for us to be friends," Rabbit cooed.

Alligator was not too keen on the notion, but Rabbit kept repeating "Let's be friends" until Alligator came all the way out of his hole.

"Why don't we go for a walk in the woods?" Rabbit eventually said.

The two went along for a while and soon began to act like old pals.

Then, before Alligator was aware, Rabbit seized a thick fallen branch and beat Alligator all over his body. The problem was that Rabbit did not strike the right place. Alligator crawled back in his hole, and Rabbit left.

He soon came back, though, and turned into a squirrel. Just like one, he scooted up a tree and chattered, fluttered his tail, and jumped from branch to branch. Nobody would have known he was Rabbit.

He called down to Alligator, "Let's be friends."

"Oh, no," Alligator said, "Rabbit asked me the same thing just before he tried to kill me."

"Everybody knows that Rabbit is a bad fellow, really bad," answered the squirrel and kept up his friendly talk.

By and by, Alligator poked his head out. "Rabbit wanted to kill me, but he didn't know my secret."

"Where should he have hit you?" the squirrel inquired.

"On the back of my head," Alligator whispered.

He still had his head sticking out, so the squirrel slipped down the tree and picked up a big stick. *BAM!* He struck the back of Alligator's head and then turned back into Rabbit. He pulled Alligator out, chopped off his tail, and took it with him.

Rabbit went along, happy and singing because he now had proof he had completed his task, but when he showed the people the tail, they said, "Now you must kill Rattlesnake."

Rabbit set out with a big stick toward Rattlesnake's hole. When he got there, the snake was asleep, sunning himself beside the door. Rabbit struck him on the head and went back to the camp.

Still, the people were not satisfied. "Go into the swamp and cut down a big tree with one chop" they demanded. "Then we will give you your bride."

"Let me rest for four days, and on the fourth, I'll chop down the tree with one blow," Rabbit bragged.

While the people thought he rested, he slipped into the swamp and met Woodpecker. "I want you to peck a circle around that big tree over yonder," Rabbit said. Woodpecker did as Rabbit requested.

On day four, Rabbit took his ax and headed into the swamp. The tree was now thin and weak where the bird had pecked. With one blow from Rabbit's ax, the big tree fell. In that way, Rabbit believed he had won his bride.

Back in those days, however, husbands usually had two wives, and like the others, Rabbit wanted two. The people said, "We'll give you another bride, but here's what you must do. Part your bride's hair down the middle. Then, with your ax, chop her in two where the part is, and you will have two wives."

Rabbit did as they directed, but when he struck his wife's part, she dropped dead from the blow. The people judged he must die, but Rabbit fled from the camp and escaped into the swamp. After all his hard work, he still did not have a wife.

The Thunder Boys Deceive and Kill an Old Woman

Long ago, right after a woman gave birth to a boy, she died. Although the afterbirth was thrown in the woods, it soon came to life as another boy. The father knew nothing about this second child who remained in the woods and was wild.

As the boys grew older, the father's son would run off and talk to his wild brother. The boy later fashioned some arrows and made two bows, one for himself and one for the wild boy.

One day, the father asked his son, "Who is the boy who lives in the woods?"

"Oh, he and I talk and play together."

Because the father wanted to catch the wild boy, he told his son, "Tell him I have gone off to hunt." He then stretched out on the ground and looked just like a log.

Pretty soon the wild boy came near. The other child said, "My father is away. Let us play around this log."

Pointing to the log, the wild boy refused and remained where he stood.

The other boy said, "That is only a log," and taking an ax, he stuck it.

The wild boy still refused to come closer. After a while, he found some small soft feathers and blew on them. He became the feathers. They floated into the air, and his brother chased after them in play.

The next day, the father set off to hunt deer. His son was just inside the woods where he and the wild boy were playing. The father called to them, "I Am Going Hunting. Do Not Leave Camp and Do Not Go Near the Lake."

As soon as the man left, however, the boys said to each other, "Let's go to the lake and catch frogs and other small water animals."

The boys caught little creatures near the water when it suddenly began to rise until it spread and covered the houses at the camp. Then, just as suddenly, the water fell until the lakebed became as dry as a sun-baked bone.

About two miles away lived the father's brother. He was old and could not do much. "Let's find the old uncle and kill him," said the wild boy. So, the pair went to his camp and killed the old man.

When the father returned from hunting, he found out what the boys did and became furious, but he decided not to say anything to them just yet and went to his brother's camp. The men there declared, "There's nothing to do but kill those boys."

Hearing about what the men intended, the two got wasps and hornets. When the men arrived, the boys set the hornets and wasps loose and killed the men instead.

"Let's head south," the boys decided.

So, they set out, and after they traveled for a while, they came to a camp where an old lady lived by herself. She greeted them and said, "Boys, bring me some firewood." They gathered a large pile and walked back and forth so much into the woods they wore down a path where Old Toad Frog sat and watched them.

The old woman next demanded, "Make me a scaffold above the firewood."

Once more, they did as she directed and had nearly completed the scaffold when Old Toad Frog saw them pass by along the path. "What are you doing?" he wanted to know.

"We're helping the old lady gather firewood and build a scaffold over it."

Old Toad Frog warned, "Well, I guess you don't know she plans to burn you up. Once you finish the scaffold, she'll kindle her fire and want you to climb up there. She'll then knock you down into the flames. You two ought to get her to climb up first to show you how it's done and push her off."

The boys followed Old Toad Frog's counsel and got the old woman to climb up first. They knocked her off. *WHOOF!* She burned up at once. Without delay, four horses leapt out. A brown horse jumped out first, then a red, black, and white one.

Mounting two of them, the boys rode off. They later came to a large body of water and shot an arrow across it. The arrow reached the other side and signaled they, too, could cross over.

The boys next arrived at a range of mountains where many animals threatened to eat them. With their bows and arrows, the boys held off the creatures.

"Let us go into the sky," the two decided. "We will be safe there."

They shot an arrow straight up. It stuck in the sky and held fast. The boys figured, "We, too, can get there." So, they became arrows and shot themselves into the sky.

When they arrived, it was like a crowded pool room with many people milling about. They questioned, "Where are you from?"

"We come from far below," answered the boys. "We did not like it there and came to live here."

Great Thunder heard them and walked over to talk. "You can live in my house."

The three then left. They arrived at Great Thunder's home and became Thunder and Lightning, or the Thunder Boys. Their new father selected two girls for them to marry. Many children resulted from this union, and none of them were good. For this reason, Indian children down here are afraid of being killed during storms.

Catawba Tales

Rabbit Steals Fire from Buzzard

Long, long ago, fire belonged to Buzzard and his people. He refused to share it with others. He and the rest of the buzzards would gather around the fire and spread their wings wide to warm themselves when it was cold. No one else could get close to the fire.

Shivering, Rabbit went to Buzzard and pled, "Please let me warm my cold foot by your fire."

"No," replied Buzzard. "No, I won't."

Rabbit hopped off and waited a little bit. Then he went around behind the other buzzards.

"Help me," he begged. "I'm almost frozen." His teeth clattered, and he made himself shake even more from the cold.

One of the buzzards saw Rabbit trembling. Feeling sorry for him, the buzzard raised his wings higher so Rabbit could get next to the fire.

Rabbit saw his chance. He began to sing and put pine splinters between his toes. Then he shot under the buzzard's wing and lit the splinters. The fire got in the wood fast and blazed up warmly.

The fire became so hot that Rabbit ran off still carrying the flaming splinters between his toes. Through the woods he ran, singing and jumping, jumping and singing.

> RABBIT IS GOOD.
> THE FIRE BIG AND WARM.
> PEOPLE MAY COME NOW
> TO REST AND GET WARM.

The Woman Who Stole a Boy and Became a Comet

There was once a poor woman who stole another woman's child. Upset at her son's disappearance, the mother could not stop crying. Woodpecker heard her sobs and, taking pity, came to her.

"Why do you cry?" asked the bird.

"Another woman has taken my son. I cannot find him."

Woodpecker said, "Give me the bright copper bands in your ears, and I will tell you where the boy is." The mother agreed, handing the bird the rings in her ears.

"Your son is on the other side of the river," said Woodpecker. "Here is some cornbread for your lost child."

The mother ate a portion of the bread and put what was left in the breast of her dress. She then crossed the river and came upon a hut made of bark. The bad woman who had kidnapped her son was away.

When the boy saw his mother, he ran to her, and she offered him the cornbread. He ate it greedily, for the woman who had captured him was very old and poor and had given him nothing to eat for several days.

The boy took his mother into the old woman's hut. "She will return soon. Hide in this hollow log."

The mother did as her son told her. He then went to hunt for deer and killed one, but he left it in the woods not far from the bark dwelling. He went back there and waited, watching for the old woman to return. When she did, he came to her.

"I have killed a deer, but I am too weak to carry it out of the woods."

"I will go and get the meat," the woman volunteered, for she was very hungry.

While she busied herself with some task before she left, the boy cut part way the straps on her pack. When she got to the deer and loaded the meat in it, the straps snapped from the weight.

"OH NO! OH NO!" she screeched as the meat hit the ground.

Suddenly, she smelled something, and when she looked up, she saw smoke coming from the direction of her house.

"OH NO! OH NO! MY HOUSE IS ON FIRE!" She left the deer where it had fallen and ran as fast as she could toward the hut.

In the meantime, the boy and his mother were trying to escape to get back to their own people. Seeing them, the woman gave chase and was gaining on them, for the boy was even slower than the old woman because he had not had much food and was tired from the hunt.

As the old woman got closer, the boy and his mother rose in the air. As they did, he let down a braided grapevine rope. The old woman stretched out her hand and grabbed the end of the rope. She rose along with the boy and his mother. When she got higher in the sky, the boy let go of the rope, and the old woman dropped fast with the grapevine trailing behind her. As she fell, she turned into a comet, with the rope flying behind as its tail. Off she sped.

The mother and her son continued to rise ever higher. At last, they reached Where They Never Die. There, the boy became a cloud in the crystal blue of heaven.

The mother exclaimed, "MY SON, MY SON IS A CLOUD!"

How Possum Tricked Deer and Wolf

Late in the fall, the weather had already turned cold, and snow covered the ground. Yet the persimmon trees still hung with ripe fruit. "Oh, how good and sweet it would taste," thought Possum.

Known as One-Tail-Clear-Of-Hair, he decided to leave his thicket and look for persimmons. As he walked over the snow, he came to one of the trees and started to sing to himself.

> I am here alone.
> What's there to be done?
> I will eat persimmons.

He climbed up high into the tree to get the ripest fruit.

While Possum was eating, Deer came down the hill. "Are the persimmons good?" he asked.

"There is one on the ground," Possum said. "Try it and see for yourself."

Deer ate the sweet, juicy fruit and liked it. "How can I get more?" he wanted to know.

Possum answered, "Go back up the hill, and run down as fast as you can until you butt your head against this tree. All the persimmons will fall down, and we will both have plenty to eat."

Deer did just as Possum told him, sped down the hill, and butted the tree as hard as he could. He dropped dead from the mighty blow.

Down the tree hurried Possum, singing while he searched his pouch for a knife to cut Deer up.

> I am here alone.
> What's there to be done?
> Deer is good to eat.

Wolf was in the woods nearby and heard Possum's singing and trotted toward it. "What are you making all the noise about?"

"Oh, nothing really. It's just a little song I was singing."

Before Possum could finish, Wolf interrupted, "If you don't tell me, I'll bite your head off."

"In that case," said Possum somewhat afraid, "I found a dead animal."

"What are you waiting for? Let me see it," growled Wolf.

The two started back to where Deer lay in the snow. When they got there, Wolf tore off a piece of Deer's insides and, throwing it in Possum's face, knocked the smaller animal to the ground.

"COOK THAT AND EAT IT!" yelled Wolf. As Possum got up and started to leave, Wolf added, "If you hear a covey of quail startled by another animal, say 'Wolf is on his way and will get you.'" He meant for his words to frighten off anyone who might try to help Possum.

Possum ran off in tears. As he went along, he stepped on some sticks and broke them. The noise startled some nearby quail who rose up, their wings making a loud fluttering noise.

When the birds settled on the ground, they went to Possum. "What's wrong?" they asked.

Possum told them how Wolf had treated him, and the quail once again flew into the air, but this time they landed near Wolf. Because of a thicket, he could not see the birds but heard their flapping wings and became scared. Thinking an enemy had scared them and might be near, away he ran, leaving the meat he had taken where it lay.

The quail found the meat and got busy. Beside the river, they made a tall rack from sticks to put the meat on and let it dry. By the time they hung all of it up, Possum returned. The quail then placed him on top of the rack where he would be safe and could guard the meat.

That evening, Wolf came back to look for the deer, but he had disappeared. Wolf searched all around but could find nothing. By chance, he walked down to the river where the meat rack stood high along its edge. Looking down in the water, he happened to see Possum's shadow. He jumped in and dived beneath the surface. No Possum anywhere.

Wolf struggled out of the water. He sniffed and looked here and looked there but did not look up. Again, he saw the shadow and jumped into the river only to find nothing. When he came to the surface, he snarled and snapped, biting at bits of fallen leaves floating where he saw Possum's shadow.

Sitting high above, Possum began to laugh. He laughed so much that his slobber drifted into the water.

Crawling out of the river, Wolf looked up and, seeing the meat, begged, "Please, Possum, toss me down just a small piece. I'll eat it and play dead like you. Then we can have a good laugh at my joke."

Possum threw down a little piece, and Wolf gobbled it up. He fell down, then got to his feet.

"Oh, Possum, throw me a bigger chunk. I'll eat it and fall down and pretend I'm dead the way you do."

Possum grinned and laughed and tossed down a bigger piece. This time, after Wolf ate it, he dropped down and lay on the ground a little longer before he got up.

"Now toss me an even bigger chunk, and I'll fall down again."

Possum showed Wolf a large piece. "Will this one do?"

"Oh, yes. That's just right," Wolf said.

Several more times, Wolf begged for meat, each time asking for bigger and bigger pieces after he played dead and got up.

Finally, Wolf said, "Throw me the largest chunk you have, and I'll pretend for sure I'm dead. We'll have the best laugh yet. You won't be able to stop grinning."

Possum picked up a big boney joint of meat. "Is this the one you want?"

"YES! YES! THAT'S IT!" Wolf howled.

Possum tossed the meat down. Wolf swallowed it in one gulp and dropped dead for sure. Ever since that day, Possum cannot stop grinning.

Pig and Wolf

One day Wolf invited Pig to visit him. "Where I live, there are lots of ripe apples. When you come to see me, we'll get some." Wolf left.

On the day Pig went to Wolf's house, Wolf said, "Oh, I've already gotten the apples." But he really did not have any.

Pig replied, "Well, you come and visit me tomorrow, and we'll get more apples."

The next day, Wolf went to see Pig. Pig said, "Oh, I've already gotten the apples." He lied just as Wolf had.

Wolf said, "Well, tomorrow, you come see me, and we can get even more apples."

Tomorrow came, and Pig went to visit. Just as before, Wolf lied. "I've already gotten some apples."

And just as before, Pig asked Wolf to visit him the next day.

Wolf again went to visit, but now he was angry. He marched into Pig's house and snarled, "Instead of Eating Apples, I'm Going to Eat You!"

Pig remained calm. "Why don't you sit for a while? I'm cooking collards, and when I'm through, I'm going to eat a big mess and get even fatter. That way, there'll be even more of me to eat."

Wolf saw a large iron cooking pot nearby with a hot fire under it. He did not know how much of a fighter Pig was.

"I've got to step outside a minute," Pig said. Suddenly, he ran back into the house and shouted, "Lots of People Are Headed This Way!"

Frightened, Wolf whined, "Where can I hide?"

"Don't worry. I'll hide you," Pig grunted.

Turning his back to Wolf, Pig stood in front of the big pot. With an iron hook, he lifted the pot off the fire and then removed the heavy lid. The pot was full of hot water rolling with a hard boil.

Looking back over his shoulder, Pig yelled, "Hurry! Over Here!"

Wolf jumped up and ran toward Pig. Grabbing Wolf, Pig shoved him into the boiling water and slammed down the lid on the pot. And that was the end of Wolf.

How Fox Took Turtle's Water

Turtle once had all the world's water. He spread himself over it and guarded it so nobody else could have any.

One day, Fox happened to walk by and, being thirsty, said, "Turtle, I'm dying of thirst. Would you please give me sip of water?"

Turtle refused. So, Fox began to scratch the ground in front of Turtle and clawed out a little trench right up to where Turtle sat.

Turtle shifted himself somewhat. A trickle of water ran out from under his shell and made a small runlet. This branch soon grew bigger and bigger until it became a river. The river formed other rivers. These ran into deep basins until they turned into oceans.

In this way, the water that Turtle guarded for himself became the creeks, lakes, rivers, and oceans for everybody to share.

How Rooster Tricked Fox

One day, as Rooster fed under a tree, he saw Fox headed his way. To escape, Rooster flapped his wings and flew onto a branch.

"Oh, don't be afraid of me," Fox called out. "Come back down. I won't do anything to you. Haven't you heard? There is now peace among all the creatures, whether the birds that fly or the animals that walk and run."

"No, I haven't heard," Rooster answered.

"Well, it's true. The news has spread, and it seems everybody knows except you."

Up on his limb, Rooster heard a noise. He looked off in the distance and saw some dogs running over a hill, barking, yapping, and following Fox's trail.

Rooster replied, "If what you say is true, I'll be right down. But I just saw a pack of dogs running this way toward..."

But before Rooster could finish, Fox took off as fast as he could.

The Cherokee Hunter Outwitted

Based on an anecdote recounted by Chief Sam Blue, this retelling is from an incident that occurred within his family in the 1850s.

My grandmother once traveled into the mountains close to the Cherokee lands in western North Carolina. She had two of her children with her—Nelson George, who was a grown boy, and her younger daughter, Margaret (Wiley) Brown, who was Nelson's half-sister and my mother. They spent several days in the woods and avoided the Cherokee since at that time the Catawba and the Cherokee were not on very friendly terms. Because my family was poor and needed provisions, my grandmother and the children were busy gathering whatever they could find in the woods.

One day, a young Cherokee hunter met them. He had been hunting in the mountains and had a long blowgun. He said he was heading home. Tied to his belt was a string of quail he had taken with his blowgun. They looked good to my grandmother.

The Cherokee boy could not speak English, and my grandmother could not speak Cherokee. So, he signaled he wanted to wrestle her son.

The Cherokee untied his string of quail, put them on the ground, and leaned his blowgun on a tree.

Nelson said he was willing to have a wrestling match. My grandmother told him to go ahead.

The two began wrestling. While they were at it, my mother and grandmother eased over to where the quail were. Pretty soon, Nelson pinned the Cherokee on the ground and kept him there on his back. Meanwhile, the women had taken the quail and slipped away safely.

Nelson let the Cherokee boy up and quietly followed the women. The boy looked for his birds, but they were nowhere to be had. He got his blowgun and left.

My mother told me the cooked quail made a good meal thanks to the Cherokee hunter.

Cherokee Tales

How Turkey Took Terrapin's Scalp

One day, Turkey and Terrapin, the land turtle, were out walking and met each other. Terrapin was on his way back from war and had taken a scalp. He had tied it around his neck with a string.

Turkey asked, "What's that hanging around your neck and dragging on the ground?"

"It's a fresh scalp I took in war?" Terrapin said.

"Well, it doesn't look right on you," laughed Turkey. "Your neck's too low to the ground and too short to wear it like that. Here, let me fix it."

"All right," Terrapin agreed.

Turkey, however, took the scalp and hung it around his own neck. "I'll walk over here so you can see how it looks," he said.

Turkey walked a short distance in front of Terrapin. "Now how do you like it?"

"Oh, it looks good on you, very becoming," Terrapin answered.

"Let me fix it a little this way, and you can tell me if you like it better." So, Turkey gave the string on the scalp a slight tug to adjust it and walked farther ahead of Terrapin.

"How about now?"

"Oh, that looks very nice," Terrapin replied.

Turkey kept on walking ahead and asking how the scalp looked.

Annoyed, Terrapin finally called, "COME BACK HERE WITH MY SCALP!"

But Turkey just walked faster and faster until he broke into a run. Terrapin had had enough. He took his bow and fired some cane splints into Turkey's legs to slow him down.

Despite the wounds, Turkey still got away. The splints, however, turned into the tiny bones in Turkey's legs. When he ran off, he became

110

so excited he accidentally swallowed the scalp. Its black hair later grew out on his neck as the dark feathers still seen today. For that reason, Turkey is the bird of war.

Terrapin Outwits the Wolves

Terrapin and Possum decided one day to hunt for persimmons. They soon came across a tree full of ripe fruit, but all of it hung high off the ground.

Possum said to his friend, "I'll climb up and toss some down." But before Terrapin could reach any, a wolf appeared and ate the persimmons as soon as they touched the ground. Sometimes he would even grab one and gulp it as it fell.

Possum watched and waited, and before long he threw down a big bone he always carried in his pouch. Before it hit the ground, Wolf lunged for it, and the bone wedged in his throat. He coughed and hacked and wheezed and gasped and soon breathed his last as he choked to death.

Terrapin called out to Possum, "JUST WHAT I NEEDED. I CAN USE HIS DRIED EARS FOR SPOONS TO EAT MY GROUND CORN!" So, Terrapin cut off Wolf's ears and headed for home, with Possum still sitting in the tree and stuffing himself with ripe persimmons.

In a little while, Terrapin arrived at a house. "Why don't you rest a spell," said the owner, "and have some sour corn mush? There's some in a jar right outside the door."

"I don't mind if I do," said Terrapin, and he sat down and scooped up some sour mush with one of Wolf's dried ears. The owner eyed his unusual spoon.

After Terrapin ate his fill, he left. Soon he came to another house. The people there invited him to stop and have some of their corn mush.

"I don't mind if I do," Terrapin repeated, and he dipped up a scoopful with Wolf's ear. After a while, he left. The people there also noticed his spoons. Pretty soon word spread that Terrapin had killed Wolf and made spoons out of his ears.

When the wolves heard the news, they sniffed out Terrapin's trail until they caught up and took him prisoner. They immediately went into council to decide his punishment. Finally, they decided, "Let's boil him alive in a clay pot."

But when Terrapin saw the pot, he laughed. "Don't you know if you put me in that thing, I'll kick it to pieces."

Again, the wolves went to council. "Let's burn him in the fire," they finally agreed.

When Terrapin heard their plan, he broke out laughing. "Go ahead. Put me in the fire. I'll just put it out."

Once more the wolves went to council. This time they decided, "Let's throw him in the deepest hole in the river. He'll drown for sure."

When Terrapin heard this punishment, he began to beg, "Oh, please don't do that. Please don't throw me in the river. I'll drown for sure."

The wolves ignored his pleas. At once, they dragged him down to the river where they tossed him in. He dived under the water where he hit a rock. His shell cracked apart in a dozen places. But Terrapin sang a medicine song.

> I sewed myself together.
> I sewed myself together.

When Terrapin came up to the opposite bank, he poked his head out of the water and laughed, "HEE-HEE! I GOT AWAY FROM YOU THAT TIME!" His shell had become whole again, though the scars from the cracks remained and are there to this day.

How Partridge Got His Whistle

In the distant long ago, Terrapin owned a whistle he liked to blow. *FWEET! Fweet fweet fweet!* was his constant sound. Partridge became jealous of Terrapin's fine *FWEET! Fweet fweet fweet!*

The two met one day. Partridge asked, "May I try your whistle?"

At first, thinking some trick was afoot, Terrapin was afraid to give it to Partridge. But Partridge promised, "You can stay and watch me practice, and when I'm through, you can have your whistle back right away." So, Terrapin handed over his whistle.

Partridge strutted around constantly blowing. *FWEET! Fweet fweet fweet! FWEET! Fweet fweet fweet! FWEET! Fweet fweet fweet!*

"How do I sound?" he wanted to know.

"Oh, you sound good," Terrapin said, walking beside him.

Partridge ran a little in front of Terrapin. *FWEET! Fweet fweet fweet! FWEET! Fweet fweet fweet!* "How do I sound now?"

Terrapin breathed hard and replied, struggling to keep pace, "Sss-sounds good." "Don't go so fast!"

FWEET! Fweet fweet fweet! FWEET! Fweet fweet fweet! FWEET! Fweet fweet fweet! "Tell me how this sounds," Partridge called a little farther away. Then spreading his wings, he flew up in a tree before Terrapin could answer.

Terrapin never did get his whistle back. This loss and the loss of his scalp to Turkey left him so ashamed he now hides in his shell when anyone comes near.

Rabbit Steals Otter's Coat

The animals all wore fur of different lengths, colors, and styles. Some had long coats, and others had short coats. Some wore coats of black, and others wore coats that were brown or yellow. Some animals had coats with tails. Some even had rings around their tails, and others had coats without tails.

With all the different coats, the animals were always arguing about whose fur looked the best. They decided to meet in council to settle the matter.

Most had heard that Otter had the best coat. But no one knew for sure because he lived by himself way back up in the woods near a creek, though he did not live in the creek itself. None of the other animals had seen him in a long time. In fact, they were not sure exactly where he lived. They just knew he lived way back up near a creek. But the animals did know that Otter would come to the council if they invited him.

Of course, Rabbit thought the animals should vote that he had the finest fur. But he feared they would say Otter's was better. So, Rabbit planned to get the council to decide in his favor. He asked around to find out what path Otter would travel to get to the meeting. Then without telling anybody, he went to find Otter.

After four days, Rabbit met another animal wearing a beautiful fur coat. It was shiny and soft and dark brown. The animal had to be Otter.

Otter politely introduced himself and asked, "Where are you going?"

"Oh," said Rabbit, "I was coming to see you. The animals are holding a council. Because you live so far away, they thought you might not know how to get there. So, they sent me to guide you."

"Thank you," said Otter, and off they went.

All day, they headed toward the council meeting but had to stop when night fell. Rabbit picked the spot to camp because Otter did not know the country there. Rabbit chopped bushes to make beds for them to sleep on. They headed out early the next day.

That afternoon, Rabbit gathered some wood and carried it on his back. "What's that for?" Otter asked.

"Tonight, I'll build a fire so we'll be warm and cozy," Rabbit said.

At sunset, they made camp and ate supper. When they finished, Rabbit took a stick and carved a paddle. Otter again asked, "What's that for?"

"If I sleep with a paddle under my head, I'll have good dreams."

Rabbit next cleared out the bushes and made a path down to the creek. Again, Otter wondered aloud, "What's that for?"

"The name of this place is Where-It-Rains-Fire," Rabbit replied. "The sky looks a little strange this evening, and we'd best be ready. I'll stay awake, but you go on to sleep. If anything happens, I'll shout a warning, and you run down the path and dive in the creek. You'll have time to hang your pretty coat on a tree. That way, it won't catch on fire."

Otter went to sleep while Rabbit pretended to keep watch. Soon the fire Rabbit made was nothing but red-hot coals. Rabbit yelled. Otter was so sound asleep he never moved. Rabbit waited, then yelled again. Otter lay as still as could be.

Rabbit shoveled some hot coals on to the paddle, tossed them high into the air, and shouted, "It's Raining Fire! It's Raining Fire!" Otter sprang up as hot coals poured down all around him.

"Run to the Creek! Run to the Creek!" shouted Rabbit. Otter hurriedly hung his coat on a limb, ran toward the water, and dived in as fast as he could. He still lives in the water to this day.

Rabbit took off his coat, put on Otter's, and headed to the council. The animals had already arrived and were waiting for Otter. Finally, they saw him walking down the trail.

"Here he comes," they said and sent a little fellow to give him the best seat. Everyone was happy Otter was there. But when they walked up to greet him, he kept his head hung low and covered half his face with a paw.

All the animals wondered "Why is he so shy?"

Then Bear went up and knocked down the paw. There sat Rabbit. Everybody knew him from his split lip. He jumped up to escape, but before he could get away, Bear grabbed his tail and pulled it off. Ever since that day, Rabbit has only a stubby tail.

Why Possum's Tail Has No Hair

At one time, Possum had a long bushy tail. He was proud of it and would comb out the briars and brambles each morning. When the animals did their dance, he even sang about his tail. He repeated his song so much that Rabbit got tired of hearing it. Of course, Rabbit really was jealous because he had no tail at all ever since Bear had pulled it off.

A big meeting of all the animals was soon to take place. There would also be a dance. Rabbit's job was to give everyone the news. As he passed near Possum's place, he thought, "Here's my chance to teach Possum a lesson." So, Rabbit stopped to find out whether Possum planned to attend.

Possum said, "I'll be there if I can sit where everybody can see my beautiful tail."

"I'll be sure you have a special seat," Rabbit promised. "I'll send someone to comb out your tail before the dance starts so you can show off even better." Delighted by Rabbit's words, Possum agreed to come.

Rabbit then went to see Cricket. The people called him barber because he could cut hair so well. Rabbit greeted Cricket and said, "Tomorrow, there's going to be a meeting. A dance will follow. In the morning, go to Possum, and dress his tail for the dance that night. Be sure to do everything I tell you."

The next morning, Cricket headed for Possum's house. "I'm here to prepare you for the dance tonight." Possum stretched himself out on the ground, got comfortable, and closed his eyes.

Cricket began to brush Possum's tail. "I'm going to wind a red string around your tail to keep it smooth until tonight." But unknown to Possum, who was almost asleep, Cricket was cutting the hair off close to the skin as he wound the string around Possum's tail.

Night came, and Possum went to where the dance was being held. He got the best seat just as Rabbit promised. Each animal had a turn dancing. When Possum's time came, he held his head high. Never looking down, he untied the string, and walked out to dance. The drummers beat their drums, and Possum started to sing:

115

See my tail,
My lovely tail.

The animals shouted, and Possum danced round and round still singing with delight:

My tail is bushy.
My tail is beautiful.
Watch it sweep the ground.

The animals yelled louder, delighting Possum even more. Again, he danced in a circle, and again he sang:

See my lovely tail.
How fine its fur.
How beautiful its color.

By now, the string had become so loose it fell off. Suddenly, the animals began to laugh, and they laughed so hard and long Possum thought, "What are they laughing at?" He peered at the animals and discovered they were pointing at him. Then looking at his tail, he found there was not a single hair on it. It was as naked as a rat's tail.

Possum was so surprised he could not say a word. All he could do was roll over and smile. Today he does the same thing. When taken by surprise, he falls on the ground and grins.

Rabbit Hunts Ducks

Rabbit loved to brag. He always boasted he could do what anyone else could do, and to tell the truth, he usually could trick the other animals into believing what he claimed.

One time, he said, "I can swim in the river and eat fish just like Otter."

"Prove it," said the others. So, Rabbit made up a clever plan so that even Otter would fall for the trick.

Not long after, Rabbit met Otter near the river. As they talked, Otter said, "Sometimes I eat ducks."

"Well, I eat ducks, too," Rabbit replied.

Otter looked as if Rabbit was telling a story. "I'd like to see you try," Otter challenged.

The two then walked beside the river until they saw some ducks paddling in the water. Quietly, they edged toward the riverbank.

"You go in first," Rabbit told Otter.

Otter slid from the bank and swam beneath the water. When he got to the ducks, he pulled one under so fast the rest never saw what happened.

By the time Otter swam back to the bank, Rabbit had made a lasso from some green bark he peeled off a sapling. "Now watch me," he said. He slipped into the water, swam under it a short way, and came up coughing. He had almost choked to death and needed to breathe.

Rabbit again dived under. When he came up for air, he was a little closer to the ducks. He went under once more. This time, when he surfaced, he was in the middle of the ducks and caught one with his lasso.

The duck fought back, flapping its wings hard until it rose from the river with Rabbit still holding on to his lasso. The duck flew and flew. Finally, Rabbit could hold on no longer and let go.

When he fell, he dropped into the bottom of a tall, hollow stump. He could not find a hole anywhere down there, and so he remained stuck without a way to escape.

Rabbit stayed so long he thought he would starve to death. Several days passed. He got hungry and began to eat his fur. Then he heard children playing around the stump, so he started singing:

> Cut a hole and peep inside.
> I'm the prettiest thing you'll eye.

Unsure what to do, children raced home to tell their father what they heard. He came back with his ax and began to chop at the stump. Rabbit kept on singing:

> I'm so pretty
> I'm a treasure.
> Cut it bigger
> To see me better.

The father took another whack at the stump. Rabbit yelled, "NOW STAND BACK SO YOU CAN GET A GOOD LOOK WHEN I COME OUT!"

The father and the children got back from the hole. Rabbit waited for his chance. *Zip! Whizz! Scoot!* He shot out of that stump and jumped clean away. And that's just one of Rabbit's tricks.

Rabbit and Possum Try to Get a Wife

Rabbit and Possum each tried to find a wife, but nobody would marry either one. As they talked things over, Rabbit said, "We'll have to go somewhere else. No one around here wants to marry us. Let's go to the next village. I'll say I have news from the big council that's ordered everyone to get married, and we'll get a wife for sure."

Possum agreed, and he and Rabbit started off for the next village. Rabbit was faster, so he got there ahead of Possum, and the villagers took him to see the chief in the council house.

"What's your business?" asked the chief.

"The head council sent me to tell you that everyone here has to get married right away," Rabbit answered.

With that, the chief summoned everybody and repeated Rabbit's message. All the animals got married at once, and Rabbit found a wife.

By the time, Possum got to the village, everyone was married, and no wife was left. Rabbit acted sorry and said, "I'll carry the message to the next village. You get there as fast as you can, and I'm sure you'll find a wife." So, Rabbit went on ahead, and Possum followed.

Rabbit got to the next village and announced, "The big council has found out that everybody's gotten lazy because we haven't had a war in a long time. It needs to start now, right here in this council house."

The animals instantly started to fight among themselves. But Rabbit took four big jumps and got out just as Possum walked in. All the animals leapt on Possum who was unarmed. He thought everyone was at peace and had not brought any weapons to defend himself.

Well, he nearly got the life beaten out of him before he dropped over and played dead. The other animals left him alone for a minute. Possum saw his chance, jumped up, and waddled out.

Possum never did get a wife. But anytime he is in danger, especially from a hunter, he just closes his eyes and plays dead.

Rabbit Escapes from Wolves

Rabbit loved to sing and always knew the latest dance. One time some wolves captured him near a field. "WE'RE GOING TO EAT YOU UP!" they snarled.

"Will you first let me show you the new dance I've been practicing?" Rabbit asked.

The wolves knew Rabbit was famous for his singing, and they were eager to learn his dance. So, they made a circle around him to watch. He tapped his paws and started to dance, all the while chanting the words:

> On the edge of the field,
> I dance, and I dance.
> Hania lil lil! Hania lil lil!

Rabbit stopped. "When I say 'on the edge of the field,' I'll go this way." He then danced in that direction. "But when I say *lil lil*, stamp your feet as hard as you can." The wolves agreed to do as asked.

Rabbit started singing and dancing again and moved a little closer toward the nearby field. When he sang *lil lil*, the wolves stamped their feet as hard as they could. Rabbit now sang even more loudly and got closer and closer to the field.

By the fourth time he sang, the wolves had all their attention on the song and on stamping their feet when their turn came. "Here's my chance," thought Rabbit. He took a long leap over the ring of wolves and made for a hollow stump where he scurried inside. The wolves chased after him.

When one wolf got there, he stuck his head through a hole in the bottom of the stump and twisted his neck to look up. But Rabbit was ready and spit in his eye. The wolf jerked his head out of the hole. None of the others would stick their head in because they were afraid of what might happen. Off they went and left Rabbit alone.

Rabbit and Tar Wolf

The weather was once so dry that all the rivers, lakes, and streams disappeared. Because there was no water, the animals met in council to see what they could do.

"Let's dig a well," one suggested.

Everyone agreed except Rabbit. He was too lazy to help. "I don't need to dig a well to get water. I can lick the dew off the grass each morning."

The other animals were not happy about Rabbit's words but dug the well without his help. The water in the well lasted for a while but started getting lower and lower and would soon run out.

Rabbit found out lapping the dew was not enough to satisfy his thirst, so he began to steal from the well. While the others suffered, he remained healthy and lively.

Wolf and Fox suspected Rabbit was up to one of his tricks. "That sneaky Rabbit must be taking our water at night," they told the animals.

"But we've got a plan to catch him." So, Wolf and Fox made a wolf out of pine gum and tar and put it by the well.

The next night, Rabbit headed to the well to take a drink just as he had been doing. As he got nearer, he saw a strange black thing.

"Who's there?" he whispered.

No answer.

Rabbit eased closer, but the tar wolf just sat there.

Louder, Rabbit asked, "WHO'S THERE?"

Still no answer.

Rabbit came closer. The tar wolf never stirred.

Braver now, Rabbit demanded, "MOVE OUT OF MY WAY, AND LET ME GET A DRINK OF WATER, OR I'LL KICK YOU!"

The thing never moved.

Rabbit was mad. He charged the tar wolf and hit it as hard as he could with his front paws which stuck to the tar.

Angrier that ever, Rabbit yelled, "LET GO, OR I'LL HIT YOU AGAIN!"

Still the tar wolf said nothing.

So, Rabbit kicked with his back feet so hard they got stuck. Now all his paws were stuck. He squirmed this way, and he squirmed that way. But the tar wolf held him fast.

In the morning, Fox and Wolf came to the well to see whether they had caught anything. And right there, stuck to the tar wolf, was the water thief. Fox and Wolf talked over what to do with him.

"Let's cut his head off," said Fox.

"Oh, that's been tried before, and it didn't hurt me at all," Rabbit argued.

Fox and Wolf then discussed other ways to kill him, but every time Rabbit told them how each method would be useless. At last, Fox and Wolf decided to let him loose in a nearby thicket to die.

When Rabbit heard this plan, he looked scared and begged, "Please don't do that! Let me live! Let me live! I'll die in that thicket!"

But the two animals refused to listen and let Rabbit loose. He instantly hopped out of reach, turned around, and whooped, "THIS THICKET IS WHERE I LIVE!"

Rabbit Escapes from Wildcat

Wolf and Fox were not the only ones who captured Rabbit. Wildcat once caught him and had him pinned to the ground. Wildcat was just about to kill him when Rabbit said, "I'm too little to eat and would be only a mouthful. But I can show you where you can find a whole flock of turkeys."

The thought of a bigger meal convinced Wildcat to let Rabbit up. "Show me where those turkeys are."

So, Rabbit took Wildcat to where the turkeys often gathered and said, "Do just as I say. Lie down and play dead. Whatever you do, don't move, even if I kick you. But when I yell JUMP, you jump up and grab the biggest one you can."

Wildcat agreed and lay down to play dead. Rabbit picked up some rotten sticks and scattered fragments and put them over Wildcat's face to make it appear covered with fly specks. That way, the turkeys would think he had been dead for a while.

Rabbit next went and found the turkeys not far off. He told them, "I was coming down the trail and saw our old enemy Wildcat lying dead alongside it. He looks like he's been dead for some time. We ought to celebrate and have a dance over him."

At first, the turkeys refused to believe Rabbit, but finally they decided to go and have a look for themselves. When they got there, Rabbit said, "Why don't you let me sing, and you can dance around him?"

The turkeys knew Rabbit had a strong voice and agreed, saying "You lead the song, and we'll dance."

So, Rabbit got a stick to keep time and sang, "Pick out the gobbler! Pick out the gobbler!"

Fearing something was afoul, an old turkey asked, "Why are you singing that?"

"Oh, it's okay," returned Rabbit. "That's what Wildcat sings when he hunts turkey. I'm just singing the way he does." So, he began his song again, and the turkeys started to dance around Wildcat.

The drove circled Wildcat several times. At last, Rabbit said, "Walk up, and hit him the way it's done in the war dance."

Believing Wildcat dead for sure, the turkeys moved in closer, and the old gobbler struck at him with his foot. Rabbit beat harder and sang as loud as he could. "PICK OUT THE GOBBLER! PICK OUT THE GOBBLER! PICK OUT THE GOBBLER!"

Suddenly, Rabbit yelled, "JUMP!" With that, Wildcat leapt up and grabbed the old turkey.

As for Rabbit, he had already taken off down the road.

How Rabbit Got a Split Lip

A long time ago, Flint Rock lived way back in the mountains. Because he had killed so many animals, all of them hated Flint. They wanted to get rid of him, but no one was brave enough to go near his house. Rabbit finally offered to do the deed and rid the animals of Flint. The animals gave Rabbit directions, and he set out for where Flint lived.

When Rabbit got there, Flint was standing outside his door. Rabbit walked up and snickered, "Are you the one called Flint?"

"Yep. That's my name," answered Flint.

"And is this your house?"

"Yep," Flint said. "I live right here."

All the while, they were talking, Rabbit looked around trying to find a way to get Flint off his guard. For a minute, he thought Flint might ask him to come in, so Rabbit waited a little.

When Flint never invited him into the house, Rabbit said, "I'm Rabbit, and I've heard a good bit about you. I thought I'd invite you to come for a visit."

"Well, sure," Flint replied. "Where do you live?"

"Why, my house is down in the broom-straw field next to the river," Rabbit said.

"I should be by in a few days," promised Flint.

Rabbit asked, "Why not come with me now and have supper?"

At first, Flint refused, but after a bit of persuading, he agreed to go. He and Rabbit went down Flint's mountain together and started across the broom-sedge field.

Rabbit stopped beside his hole. "Here's my house, but when it's hot like this, I usually stay outside where it's cooler. Let me make a fire, and we'll have supper out here."

When they finished eating, Flint stretched out on the ground. While he was resting, Rabbit took a heavy stick and with his knife carved a mallet with a vee-shape on one end. He sharpened the ends of some other sticks.

Flint looked up. "What's that for?"

"Oh, I always like to keep busy," Rabbit answered, "and this may come in handy."

Satisfied, Flint lay his head down again and fell asleep. Rabbit said a few words to him, but Flint made no reply.

Certain Flint was sound asleep, Rabbit walked over, took a sharpened stick in one paw and the mallet in the other, and hammered the stake into Flint's body. Rabbit jumped for his hole and his life as fast as he could, but before he got there—*KABOOM!* A loud explosion sounded, and pieces of Flint flew everywhere.

One piece knocked Rabbit in his hole. He stayed down there listening. When everything got quiet, he poked out his head to get a good look. *BAM!* Another piece fell and cut his lip.

Since that day, Rabbit has always had a split lip, and pieces of old Flint are scattered over many places.

Deer Gets Horns

At first, the male deer did not have horns, and his head and a doe's looked just the same. Only later did he get them.

Of all the animals, Deer was the best runner, and Rabbit the best jumper. Everyone wanted to know which one was the fastest. So, the animals decided to have a contest between the two. The prize would be a big set of horns for the winner.

The race would start on one end of a thicket. Deer and Rabbit would go through it, turn around at the other end, and race back through. The first one out would get the antlers.

When the day of the race came, all the animals had gathered. They put the horns on the ground in front of the thicket to mark the starting place. The horns made such a fine sight all the animals stood around admiring them.

Rabbit said to everyone, "Deer knows the country around here, but I don't know these parts. I'd like to take a look through the place where I'm supposed to go."

Rabbit's request seemed fair enough, so the animals agreed to let him have a look. He then went into the thicket but was gone for a long time. They waited, and they waited, and they waited.

At last, one of the animals said, "Rabbit must be up to his tricks again." So, they sent in somebody to find him.

About halfway through the thicket, the messenger caught Rabbit gnawing down brush and piling it up to clear a path all the way to the other side. The messenger backtracked quietly, returned to the other animals, and told them what Rabbit was doing.

When Rabbit finally came out of the thicket to the starting point, the animals cried, "YOU'VE BEEN CHEATING!"

"No, I haven't," Rabbit denied.

So, the animals marched into the thicket and saw the cleared path. They decided that such a trickster had no right to participate in the race. Naming Deer the fastest, they awarded the horns to him. He wears them even now.

As for Rabbit, the animals told him he should gnaw down bushes for a living. He still does to this very day.

Why Deer Has Blunt Teeth

Ever since Deer had won the horns, Rabbit was mad. "How can I get even?" he wondered.

So, Rabbit took a thick grapevine and almost gnawed it in half. He stretched the vine across the path Deer often came down. Then stepping back up the trail, Rabbit ran toward the vine and leaped high into the air when he got to it. He kept running and leaping until Deer wandered down the path.

"What are you doing?" Deer asked curiously.

"Can't you tell?" said Rabbit. "I'm so strong and such a good jumper I can bite through that grapevine in one bounce."

Deer thought Rabbit was bragging as usual and said, "I'd like to see you try."

So, Rabbit hopped back up the trail, took a good run, leapt hard, and bit through the vine where he had cut it with his teeth.

Not to be outdone, Deer said, "I think I can do just as well as you."

Rabbit immediately stretched another grapevine across the path, only this vine was thicker and not cut in half. Deer went back a piece, ran toward the vine, and jumped. He hit the grapevine right in the middle. It gave a little, sprang back hard, and flung Deer on his head.

Deer got up and tried again. Same thing. Back on his head he flew. Over and over, he tried until he was cut and bleeding.

"Let me take a look at your teeth," Rabbit said. Deer opened his mouth.

"Just as I thought," said Rabbit. "You've got long teeth like Wolf, but they're not very sharp. No wonder you can't bite that vine in two. If you want, I'll make them sharp like mine. My teeth are like a knife and can cut through anything." And with that, Rabbit sliced off a shoot from a locust tree to prove his point.

"That's just what I need," Deer thought, "teeth like Rabbit's." So, he told Rabbit to make his teeth sharp.

Rabbit took a hard stone to file Deer's teeth. And he filed, and he filed, and he filed. By the time he was through, Deer's teeth were so blunt they were nearly worn down to his gums.

"Oh, they hurt," groaned Deer.

"Well, that's to be expected," Rabbit said. "Sharp teeth always hurt a little at first. Now try them out."

Deer backed up, ran down the path, and jumped toward the grapevine. But this time, he could not even scratch it one little bit and was flung back as before. He got up, shook himself, and looked where Rabbit had been. But he had already gone, jumping through the bushes, laughing all the while.

Deer heard Rabbit holler, "I Guess You Paid for Your Horns Now!"

Since that day, Deer's teeth are so stubby he can only chew grass and leaves.

What Happened to Rabbit

Deer was angry about his blunt teeth and wanted revenge on Rabbit for filing them down.

"But I don't want to do anything too soon," Deer thought. "I'll act friendly for a while and wait until the right time to punish Rabbit when he's off guard." So, Deer pretended to be Rabbit's friend as if nothing was wrong.

Then one day, as the two were walking along and talking, Deer noticed a small stream beside their path. "Let's see who can jump the best," he said.

Rabbit, of course, thought he was the greatest jumper of all the animals and accepted the challenge right away.

"Why don't we jump over this stream beside us?" Deer asked. "Let's walk back a little way. When I say NOW, we'll both run and jump."

Rabbit agreed. So, he and Deer walked back a piece to get a good running start once Deer gave the signal.

"Now!" shouted Deer, and he and Rabbit raced for the stream. In one leap, Rabbit cleared it and landed on the far side by himself. He looked back across, and there stood Deer. He had never jumped and remained on the opposite bank, though not of a small stream but of a wide river.

Deer had used his magic to conjure the water and widen it so much that Rabbit could never return to the other side. He is there even now, and like all the animals of long ago, he is larger, stronger, and cleverer than the little rabbit seen today.

Appendix A

Story Adaptations and Authentication of Sources

From a folklorist's perspective, a folktale is not like a dried flower pressed and preserved forever between the pages of a book. Although a folktale might appear cast in final form when rendered into print by a collector, every time it is told it is created anew so that there is "no final and definitive version."[1]

Even the same storyteller will not likely tell a story the same way twice. In her analysis of Brer Rabbit tales of African American origin and parallels that derive from the Cherokee, Sandra Baringer points out oral renditions are "interactive and evolving" and these aspects are "effaced ... in the anthropologically oriented ventures" transcribing the narratives.[2] As storyteller Ruth Sawyer has noted about a story transferred to the printed page, the challenge for the person who retells it is to render "it again into living substance."[3]

In *Twenty Tellable Tales,* librarian, storyteller, and folklore authority Margaret Read MacDonald has said of collections made by anthropologists, before the days of recording devices, such texts were seldom written down from a cultural group's "teller in actual performance"[4] and thus "may be less than perfect to begin with."[5] Each subsequent telling is, therefore, a unique adaptation and becomes correct.

To refine the foregoing point further, parallel to the individual voice of the person who tells a story aloud is the distinctive voice of the person who presents a version in writing. Both may tailor a tale to a particular audience. As MacDonald indicates in her other book on storytelling, *The Storyteller's Start-Up Book*, print renditions represent "only one telling of one teller at one moment in time."[6] And yet, as Barbara Kiefer has suggested, anyone who adapts an original print version of a traditional story is obligated to inform readers of modifications.[7] However, before this information is presented, further detail on the original sources that I consulted is in order.

◈ Creek, Hitchiti, Alabama, Koasati/Coushatta, and Natchez ◈

For just over forty years, John R. Swanton was associated with the Bureau of American Ethnology of the Smithsonian Institution. As an anthropologist and linguist, Swanton (1873–1958) began his early field work among Native Americans of the Pacific Northwest. In 1905, however, he concentrated his research on tribal populations of the Southeast. One result of his new focus was the publication in 1929 of *Myths and Tales of the Southeastern Indians*. Based on material collected between 1908 and 1914, it contains a variety of stories from not only the Creek but also other members of the Creek Confederacy such as the Hitchiti, Alabama, Koasati (Coushatta) tribal groups as well as the separate Natchez Indians who were originally located along the lower Mississippi River. (**Appendix D** gives further information about these and other indigenous nations from whom I have retold their trickster tales.)

As to the Creek Confederacy, one scholar has described it as "a coalition of groups loosely committed to political agreement" and "an alliance of formerly independent tribes speaking many different languages and tracing their several pasts through quite separate and distinct histories."[8] Some groups entered as willing allies while others were remnants of Creek conquests. Within the Confederacy, its members retained many of their own distinctive traits.[9]

Besides trickster narratives, Swanton's collection includes tales about native heroes, visits to the underworld, encounters between humans and animals or supernatural figures in animal form, and native stories assimilated from European and African origins. Although Swanton used a number of informants in gathering the stories, for many of the narratives he relied heavily, as he notes in his introduction, on the previous work of William Orrie Tuggle (1841–1885) who was a pioneering folklorist from Georgia. In the 1880s, Tuggle journeyed to Oklahoma, then Indian Territory, and recorded the folktales and customs of the Creek and Yuchi who had once inhabited the Chattahoochee Valley in what is now Georgia and Alabama. In **Chart 3**, Tuggle's name is noted along with Swanton's to indicate Tuggle's contribution as a source for the Creek stories.

Swanton, however, did not realize that he had relied on an incomplete copy of Tuggle's work. In an overview of the history of Tuggle's original manuscript, Dorothy Hatfield and Eugene Current-Garcia indicate that the complete collection was found in 1960, seventy-five years after Tuggle's death and that it was dispersed among three of his family descendants.[10]

In the assessment of Hatfield and Current-Garcia, the importance of Tuggle's work cannot be overemphasized, for he gathered folktales from indigenous headmen who recounted stories and lore as passed down from one generation to another. Not only did Swanton acknowledge reliance on Tuggle, but so did James Mooney and Joel Chandler Harris.[11] Out of 91 Creek stories collected by Swanton, he attributes 46 to Tuggle.

In the original papers of Tuggle, published in 1973 under the title *Shem, Ham & Japheth,* editors Current-Garcia and Hatfield note that Swanton's use of a Smithsonian copy was "a stroke of fortune in itself" because only a few of Tuggle's stories from his original manuscript "have survived intact." To be precise, there are 16 of these.[12] Of the forty some tales presented by Swanton, he revised them for "greater accuracy and polish." In the assessment of Current-Garcia and Hatfield, Swanton may have lost some of the distinctive regionalisms found in the remaining 16 Creek narratives in Tuggle's original papers. Current-Garcia and Hatfield surmise that "...in capturing expressive native idioms, Tuggle's ear was more acute than Swanson's."[13]

Besides Tuggle, another figure of note in Swanton's work was the native informant and full-blood Creek storyteller Earnest Gouge (ca. 1865–1955). In 1915, Swanton contracted with him to write 29 tales in the Muskogee, or Creek, alphabet. These may be accessed at *www.muskogee.blogs.wm.edu/gouge-texts*, which contains photocopies of Gouge's handwritten tales. The original Gouge documents remained unpublished during Swanton's lifetime. However, 2004 saw the publication of *Totkv Mocvse/New Fire: Creek Folktales by Earnest Gouge.* Edited and translated by Jack B. Martin, Margaret McKane, and Juanita McGirt, this bilingual book has Gouge's Creek originals on the left side of the page with the English versions on the right. The collection contains several tales about Rabbit, Lion, Wolf, and Turtle (Terrapin) who, of course, are among the characters in stories I have adapted from Swanton's *Myths and Tales of the Southeastern Indians.*

❖ Seminole ❖

Clay MacCauley's *The Seminole Indians of Florida,* a monograph published in 1887 by the Smithsonian's Bureau of Ethnology, provides a detailed account of many facets of Seminole culture after their wars with the United States ended in 1858. And yet his study does not include any of the Florida natives' folktales. In 1945, nearly sixty years later, scholar Robert F. Greenlee recounted and analyzed several of their stories in *The Journal of American Folklore*. Greenlee's source for the narratives was Josie Billie, the son of Ko-nip-ha-tco. The latter had been a key informant for MacCauley's earlier report.

The Greenlee selections demonstrate the infusion of outside influences such as Christianity on Seminole culture. For instance, Josie Billie equated Jesus Christ with the indigenous figure of the Breathmaker who had created the Milky Way as the road by which spirits enter the realm of the dead. The stories also contain original native concepts such as the souls of dead animals traversing the same Spirit Road.[14] Three of the narratives are trickster tales and are listed in **Chart 3** beginning with item 50.

❖ Catawba ❖

In 1934 appeared *Catawba Texts,* a study by anthropologist and linguist Frank G. Speck (1881–1950). Four of its narratives serve as sources for my adaptations of Catawba trickster tales. In his introduction, Speck referred to his monograph as "a last feeble voice from the grave of a defunct native culture."[15] This comment reflects the highly fragmented quality of Catawba accounts of their traditions and stories.

Although Speck was a professor at the University of Pennsylvania, he spent the greatest part of his professional life engaged in field work among the indigenous peoples of North America. However, instead of concentrating on western Native Americans, in his day a more popular subject for research, Speck focused his attention on the languages and cultures of Eastern tribes. His aim was to preserve and restore where possible the remnants of their once vibrant but rapidly vanishing world.

Speck's approach as an ethnographer was to immerse himself in the day-to-day activities of the groups he studied, living closely among them and learning their customs and languages. His Catawba informants for the trickster stories were Mrs. Samson Owl, Mrs. Margaret Wiley, and Mrs. Sally Gordon. Besides the Catawba, Speck also devoted his research to other indigenous groups, including the Cherokee and Creek.

In 1947, a cache of additional Catawba stories appeared under Speck's name as the senior author in the *Journal of American Folklore*. The source for the selections was Chief Sam Blue. Speck and his co-author L.G. Carr referred to the tales as "the last combings from the chief's memory" and characterized them as a blending of "native and European motifs" that reflect "the effect of acculturation begun in the early eighteen hundreds."[16]

Of the nine folktales from Chief Blue, four are about tricksters. One of these, "Opossum Tricks the Deer and Wolves and Loses the Hair of His Tale," is a longer parallel of "Opossum Tricks the Deer and the Wolves," which Speck published earlier in 1934 in *Catawba Texts.* I have retold this older version as "How Possum Tricked Deer and Wolf." (See **Chart 3** below, item 55.)

❖ Cherokee ❖

Like Swanton, James Mooney (1861–1921) worked for the Smithsonian's Bureau of American Ethnology. But unlike Swanton and Speck, who both received exemplary university educations, Mooney was largely self-taught as an anthropologist and linguist, his highest formal education being the public schools of Richmond, Indiana. His significant early publications concerned the Plains Indians: *The Ghost-Dance Religion and the Sioux Outbreak of 1890* (1892–1893) and *Calendar History of the Kiowa Indians* (1898). Based on intermittent research over approximately thirteen years, Mooney completed *Myths of the Cherokee,* a study that focused on the Eastern Band of North Carolina. Even though the title page gives the publication date as 1900, the Bureau of American Ethnology issued the work in 1901.

Mooney's thorough text begins with a history of the Cherokee and proceeds to relate 126 sacred myths, animal stories, legends, and historical traditions. These are supplemented by a glossary of Cherokee words and extensive explanatory notes which provide frequent references to variants of some of the tales. Among Mooney's informants, two stand out. From Ayunini, or Swimmer, a Cherokee adept, steeped in his people's sacred traditions, Mooney obtained approximately three-fourths of the stories.[17] Itagunahi, or John Ax, also figured prominently as a rich repository of knowledge concerning the "humorous animal stories" and wonder tales of magic and the supernatural.[18]

❖ Original Sources and Retellings ❖

For individuals who would like to compare my retellings to the originals as rendered by Swanton, Greenlee, Speck, and Mooney, **Chart 3** lists titles, story numbers, and page numbers of their respective print recordings of Southeastern trickster narratives. Tuggle's name follows Swanton when the latter drew from the Tuggle collection as a source for some of the Creek narratives in *Myths and Tales of the Southeastern Indians*. In addition, variants contained in the larger collection of Swanton, Speck, and Mooney are also noted by both variant number and page numbers.

Chart 3: Original Written Sources for Story Adaptations

Adaptation	Source
Creek Stories	***Myths and Tales of the Southeastern Indians***
1. "The Way of Rabbit"	Swanton/Tuggle, "The Tasks of Rabbit," #66, pp. 60–61. Variants: #64, pp. 58–59; #65, pp. 59–60.
2. "Why Rabbit Steals"	Swanton/Tuggle, "Why the Rabbit Steals," #67, p. 61.
3. "The People Discover Rabbit's Ways"	Swanton/Tuggle, "Rabbit's Imposition Is Detected," #78, pp. 71–72.
4. "Rabbit Gets Lion Across the Ocean"	Swanton/Tuggle, "Rabbit Gets Man-Eater Over to the Other Side of the Ocean," #42, pp. 43–44. Variants: #40, p. 42; #41, pp. 42–43; #43, pp. 44–45.
5. "Rabbit Plays Scratch with Wildcat"	Swanton/Tuggle, "Rabbit Tries a Game of Scratch with Wildcat," #45, p. 4.
6. "Rabbit Challenges Two Tie-Snakes"	Swanton, "Rabbit Engineers a Tug of War Between Two Tie-Snakes," #49, pp. 48–49. Variants: #50, p. 49; #51, pp. 49–50.
7. "Rabbit and the Buffaloes' Tug-o-War"	Swanton, "Rabbit Engineers a Tug of War Between Two Bison," #53, pp. 50–51. Variants: #49, pp. 48–49; #50, p. 49; #51, pp. 49–50; #52, p. 50.
8. "Rabbit Fools Alligator"	Swanton/Tuggle, "Rabbit Fools Alligator," #55, pp. 52–53. Variant: #54, pp. 51–52.

Appendix A. Story Adaptations and Authentication of Sources

Adaptation	Source
9. "Terrapin Fools Rabbit"	Swanton/Tuggle, "Terrapin Races," #56 and #60, pp. 53–55. Variants: #57, p. 53; #58, p. 54; #59, p. 54.
10. "Raccoon, Panther, and the Deer"	Swanton/Tuggle, "Raccoon Gets a Deer for Panther," #48, pp. 48–49.
11. "Rabbit and the Woman's Only Son"	Swanton/Tuggle, "The Only Son and Rabbit," #9, pp. 17–18.
12. "Rabbit and Wolf"	Swanton, "Rabbit Rides Wolf," #72, pp. 64–66. Variants: #73, pp. 66–67; #74, p. 67.
13. "How Rabbit Married the Widow's Daughter"	Swanton/Tuggle, "How Rabbit Daughter Got the Widow's Daughter," #70, pp. 62–63. Variant: #69, p. 62.
14. "Rabbit Tricks Coyote"	Swanton, "Rabbit Fools Coyote," #71, pp. 63–63.
15. "Rabbit Deceives the Other Animals"	Swanton/Tuggle, "Rabbit Deceives the Other Animals," #76, pp. 69–70.
16. "Rabbit Escapes from the Box"	Swanton/Tuggle, "Rabbit Escapes from the Box," #77, pp. 70–71.
17. "How Rabbit Won a Second Wife"	Swanton, "How Rabbit Won His Wife's Sister for His Second Wife," #62, p. 57.
18. "The Boy Who Outwitted the Buffaloes"	Swanton/Tuggle, "The Flight to the Trees," #79, pp. 72–73.
19. "The Boy and the Lion"	Swanton, "The Boy and the Lion," #86, pp. 79–81.
Hitchiti Stories	**Myths and Tales of the Southeastern Indians**
20. "The Wolves Try to Trick the Dogs"	Swanton, "The Wolves and the Dogs," #20, pp. 100–101.
21. "Rabbit Does the Old Man's Bidding"	Swanton, "The Tasks of Rabbit," #26, pp. 104–105.
22. "Rabbit, Wolf, and Buzzard"	Swanton, "Rabbit and Wolf," #29, pp. 107–108.
23. "Rabbit, Wildcat, the Big Tree, and the Nuts"	Swanton, "Rabbit and Wildcat," #30, p. 108.
24. "Rabbit, Wildcat, and the Buffalo"	Swanton, "Rabbit and Wildcat," #31, p. 109.
25. "Bear, Rabbit, and Buzzard"	Swanton. "The Bungling Host," #35, pp. 111–112.
26. "Rabbit and the Medicine"	Swanton, "Rabbit Is Sent with Medicine," #36, pp. 112–113.

Appendix A. Story Adaptations and Authentication of Sources

Adaptation	Source
27. "Rabbit and the Vegetable Garden"	Swanton, "Man and Rabbit," #37, p. 113.
28. "Rabbit's False Talk"	Swanton, "Man and Rabbit," #38, pp. 113–114.
29. "Rabbit and the Old Man's Daughters"	Swanton, "Rabbit and the Old Man," #39, pp. 114–115.
Alabama Stories	**Myths and Tales of the Southeastern Indians**
30. "Big Man-Eater's Wife Gets Fed Up"	Swanton, "The Obstacle Flight," #15, p. 133. Variant: #14, pp. 131–132.
31. "Rabbit Kills Big-Man-Eater"	Swanton, "Rabbit Kills Big Man-Eater," #56, p. 161.
32. "Rabbit Frees the Sun"	Swanton, "The Rescue of the Sun," #7, p. 123.
33. "An Orphan Outdoes Rabbit"	Swanton, "The Orphan," #18, pp. 136–138.
34. "Skunk Deceives the Wolves"	Swanton, "Opossum," #52, p. 158.
Koasati/Coushatta Stories	**Myths and Tales of the Southeastern Indians**
35. "Rabbit Provides Fire"	Swanton, "Rabbit Obtains Fire," #55, pp. 203–204.
36. "Rabbit and Big Man-Eater Trade Shoes"	Swanton, "Rabbit and Big Man-Eater Swap," #56, pp. 206–207.
37. "Rabbit, Big Man-Eater, and the River"	Swanton, "Rabbit and the River," #54, pp. 204–205.
38. "Rabbit Plays Pranks on Elephant"	Swanton, "Rabbit Plays Pranks on Big Man-Eater," #57, pp. 207–208.
39. "Rabbit's Grandmother Punishes Buzzard"	Swanton, "Rabbit and Buzzard," #62, p. 211.
40. "Rabbit, the Turkeys, and Spunk Soup"	Swanton, "Rabbit and the Turkeys," #60, p. 210.
41. "Possum and Panther Become Partners"	"Opossum and Panther in Partnership," #44, p. 200.
Natchez Stories	**Myths and Tales of the Southeastern Indians**
42. "Perch Fools Owl"	Swanton, "The Perch and the Owl," #27, p. 253.
43. "Wolf and Rabbit Cannot Get Along"	Swanton, "The Wolf and the Rabbit," #32, pp. 256–258.
44. "Rabbit Kills Alligator"	Swanton, "Rabbit and Alligator," #31, pp. 255–256.

Appendix A. Story Adaptations and Authentication of Sources

Adaptation	Source
45. "The Young Hunter's Adventures"	Swanton, "The Panther Child," #9, pp. 234–239.
46. "Why Possum Hangs by His Tail"	Swanton, "The Opossum," #22, p. 249.
47. "Fox and Crawfish Have a Race"	Swanton, "The Fox and the Crawfish," #25, p. 252.
48. Turkey Tricks Wildcat"	Swanton, "Turkey and Wildcat," #29, p. 254.
49. "The Fawn, the Wolves, the Skunk, and the Terrapin"	Swanton, "The Wolves and the Fawn," and the "Terrapin" #23, pp. 249–252.
Seminole Stories	**"Folktales of the Florida Seminole," The Journal of American Folklore**
50. "Rabbit Brings Back Fire"	Greenlee, "Rabbit Lies and Runs Away with Fire," p. 143.
51. "Rabbit Wants a Wife"	Greenlee, "Rabbit Wants to Marry," p. 144.
52. "The Thunder Boys Deceive and Kill an Old Woman"	Greenlee, untitled, pp. 141–143.
Catawba Stories	**Catawba Texts**
53. "Rabbit Steals Fire from Buzzard"	Speck, "The Rabbit Steals the Fire from the Buzzard," #9a, pp. 8–9. Variant: #9b, pp. 8–9.
54. "The Woman Who Stole a Boy and Became a Comet"	Speck, "The Bad Woman Who Stole a Boy and Became a Comet," #1, pp. 1–3.
55. "How Possum Tricked Deer and Wolf"	Speck, "Opossum Tricks the Deer and the Wolves," #16, pp. 15–17. Variant: #115, pp. 84–88.
56. "Pig and Wolf"	Speck, "The Pig Outwits the Wolf," #116, pp. 88–91.
"Catawba Folk Tales from Chief Sam Blue"	**The Journal of American Folklore**
57. "How Fox Took Turtle's Water"	Speck and Carr, "How Water Was Taken from the Turtle and Spread Over the World," p. 81.
58. "How Rooster Tricked Fox"	Speck and Carr, "Rooster and Fox," p. 81.
59. "The Cherokee Hunter Outwitted"	Speck and Carr, "A Catawba Family Outwits a Cherokee Hunter," pp. 83–84.

Appendix A. Story Adaptations and Authentication of Sources

Adaptation	Source
Cherokee Stories	**Myths of the Cherokee**
60. "How Turkey Took Terrapin's Scalp"	Mooney, "How the Turkey Got His Beard," #37, pp. 287–288, 455 n37.
61. "Terrapin Outwits the Wolves"	Mooney, "The Terrapin's Escape from the Wolves," #31, pp. 278–279.
62. "How Partridge Got His Whistle"	Mooney, "How the Partridge Got His Whistle," #40, p, 289.
63. "Rabbit Steals Otter's Coat"	Mooney, "How the Rabbit Stole the Otter's Coat," #17, pp. 267–268.
64. "Why Possum's Tail Has No Hair"	Mooney, "Why the Possum's Tail Is Bare," #18, p. 269.
65. "Rabbit Hunts Ducks"	Mooney, "The Rabbit Goes Duck Hunting," #16, pp. 266–267.
66. "Rabbit and Possum Try to Get a Wife"	Mooney, "The Rabbit and the Possum After a Wife," #22, p. 273.
67. "Rabbit Escapes from the Wolves"	Mooney, "The Rabbit Escapes from the Wolves," #24, p. 274.
68. "Rabbit and Tar Wolf"	Mooney, "The Rabbit and the Tar Wolf," #21, pp. 271–272. Variant: #21, Second Version, pp. 272–273.
69. "Rabbit Escapes from Wildcat"	Mooney, "How the Wildcat Caught the Gobbler," #19, pp. 269–270.
70. "How Rabbit Got a Split Lip"	Mooney, "Flint Visits the Rabbit," #25, pp. 274–275.
71. "Deer Gets Horns"	Mooney, "How the Deer Got His Horns," #26, pp. 275–276.
72. "Why Deer Has Blunt Teeth"	Mooney, "Why the Deer's Teeth Are Blunt," #27, pp. 276–277.
73. "What Happened to Rabbit"	Mooney, "What Became of the Rabbit," #28, p. 277.

❖ Procedures Used in Adaptation ❖

In retelling indigenous selections from Swanson/Tuggle, Greenlee, Speck, and Mooney, I have adhered to the events presented in each story so that neither the plots nor the attributes of characters are altered. However, I have made adjustments as any storyteller would.

On average, the source tales have readability levels of approximately grade nine. Based on Raygor and SMOG methods, my retellings have an average readability level of fifth grade. This level provides greater accessibility to a wide variety of audiences from young adult to adult readers and approximates the less complicated nature of oral language. Compared to written text, oral language has shorter sentences and less complex vocabulary with fewer syllables.

Of course, readability measures are generally considered broad and imprecise estimates of text difficulty and do not account for the background of experience and prior knowledge individuals bring to passages they read.[19] Higher readability levels also have nothing to do with the quality of a piece of writing and may indicate a text is not reader friendly and lacks clarity because of excessively long sentences and bloated vocabulary.

Besides lowering readability levels, I have also considered procedures recommended for oral storytelling. Along with enhancing tales told aloud, these recommendations can imbue written narratives with added vigor, particularly with stories that spring from the oral tradition.

Consequently, I have often changed indirect conversation to direct dialogue. Storytelling experts Norma Livo and Sandra Rietz have commented that such modifications "strengthen the overall effect and credibility" of a tale.[20] Another benefit of direct dialogue is that it gives an adaptation a heightened pace and briskness that indirect dialogue lacks. Jayanta Kar Sharma points out that the effect is to help "control the pacing and raise tension" for the listener.[21] Thus, as an alteration grounded in oral storytelling, direct dialogue moves a story along and renders it more dramatic.

I have also, on occasion, embellished the content of some stories, not to dilute the text's authenticity but to fortify it. For instance, a selection may allude to a cultural circumstance or artifact not within the reader's experiential background. Rather than offering a clarification through footnotes or endnotes, I have embedded an explanation within the context of the passage itself. This approach results in a text being what experts in reading comprehension refer to as "considerate" text.[22]

Translators often have engaged in the same procedure to make an allusive text more reader friendly. Although early British translators did not have as complete a conception of considerate text as have their more recent counterparts, there is nothing new about amplifying a passage to enhance its sense. In his 1680 "Preface to the Translation of Ovid's Epistles," the first great critic of English literature, John Dryden, remarks that his aim as a translator is to "paraphrase, or translate with latitude."[23] In his view, strict deference to the words of a work is less important than maintaining its sense, even to the point of amplifying but not altering it to enhance its aesthetic appeal.

Modern translators have defined the idea of amplification to entail embedding clarification of meaning within the work itself as opposed to having separate explanatory notes. For example, in discussing his translation of the second-century CE Latin work *The Golden Ass* of Apuleius, famed English poet, novelist, and classicist Robert Graves says that "to avoid the nuisance" of explanatory notes, he "brought their substance up into the story itself" whenever a passage read "obscurely."[24]

Classical studies professor at Indiana University, Betty Rose Nagle, indicates much the same idea in comments concerning her acclaimed translation of *Ovid's Fasti: Roman Holidays*. Describing how explanations external to a narrative can break and dilute its impact, she terms her in-text embellishments "internal glosses." Their purpose is to render references in the original work "immediately accessible" to readers.[25]

An allusion in the Cherokee story "Terrapin Outwits the Wolves" illustrates how amplifying the source text from Mooney adds authenticity to the adaptation and makes it more considerate for readers who might have limited knowledge about a topic. Titled "The Terrapin's Escape from the Wolves" in Mooney's account, the story relates how Terrapin is invited to eat "some *kanahe'na* gruel from a jar that is always set outside the door."[26] Besides changing the scene in which this phrase is included into a direct dialogue between Terrapin and the character who invites him to eat the *kanahe'na*, I have incorporated into my adaptation an explicit explanation of this dish as sour corn mush. Mooney, of course, defines what *kanahe'na* is, but he presents his definition in supplementary notes[27] to the story and in his Glossary of Cherokee Words.[28] To embed this kind of allusive information within adapted selections renders them more reader-friendly for an audience than are the original sources from which they are retold.

Another modification worth noting that deviates from the original transcriptions is my variations in print styles to suggest the use of voice in an oral presentation. The research of Anne Pellowski, who has investigated the history of storytelling and its many manifestations throughout world cultures, points out that capturing oral components of style such as voice changes is a difficult, often "insurmountable," endeavor.[29] Of course, had a scribe of the ancient world been fortunate enough to hear and record a Native American tale, the transcription on a scroll would have had no spacing between words, no difference between lower case and capital letters, and no punctuation such as periods and commas. This out-loud culture would have relied on the reader's ear to "disentangle what to the eye seemed a continuous string of signs."[30]

Today, besides conventional punctuation, added forms of print can suggest to readers effects that might be achieved if the indigenous tale were rendered aloud as in storytelling. For instance, to suggest a character's speaking in a loud voice, I have written the dialogue in all capital letters. I have also inserted sound effects when insinuated by a tale. These are in *italics*.

My adaptation of Mooney's version of the Cherokee story "How Partridge Got His Whistle" serves as a case in point for imitations of sound. Mooney's rendition indicates that Terrapin once possessed a whistle on which he blew all the time. Jealous, Partridge requested to hold the whistle, strutted around constantly blowing it, and eventually flew off, tricking Terrapin out of his instrument. Mooney merely states that Terrapin and later Partridge blew on the whistle and does not provide a print analogue. After listening to various recordings of a partridge's "whistle," I thought the onomatopoetic phrase *FWEET! Fweet fweet fweet!* suggested a similar sound and rhythm, with the first "fweet" in all capital letters to capture the stress of the bird's first note and the succeeding lower-case "fweets," without any punctuation between them, imitating the rapid fire of the bird's last three staccato tones.

Some critics might object to such print alterations and additions. However, this objection is based on mistaken assumptions about transcriptions made by folklorists, ethnologists, and anthropologists, as if their recordings constitute the final, frozen forms of a traditional narrative.

Comments by folklore expert David Elton Gay on Swanton's *Myths and Tales of the Southeastern Indians* illustrate the types of problems that can result from assuming such compilations to be pristine expressions of indigenous material. Among the limitations in Swanton's collection is that there are no texts in the native languages of the Southeast, thus creating challenges in comparing the stories to original versions. Another issue is that Swanton recast his Creek borrowings in the first section of his book from Tuggle so that Swanton's texts are further removed from those Tuggle heard and recorded during his sojourn in the Territory of Oklahoma. As reported by Gay, Swanton himself was aware of these kinds of issues in his work.[31]

One facet of Swanton's collection that I have not seen addressed by critics and that impacts its authenticity is his reliance on Latin to present certain parts of different stories. Although instances of Latin renderings are rare in Swanton, they surface whenever a tale becomes indelicate, off-color, or sexually suggestive.

An example of what might be considered an uncouth episode occurs in the Hitchiti story "Rabbit and Wildcat." At the end of the tale, as a victim of one of Rabbit's pranks, Wildcat has vowed to kill the trickster. Upon their next encounter, Wildcat finds Rabbit sitting with a cracked pecan and inquires what he is doing. To save himself, Rabbit gives Wildcat the nut to eat. Wildcat likes it so much he asks Rabbit where he can find some pecans also.

In Swanton's version, Rabbit then makes his earthy reply in Latin which begins *Si testiculos tuos percutias, pecana habebis.*[32] Following Rabbit's answer, the narrator then continues with another sentence in Latin to conclude the tale. In my adaptation, I have translated the passage into English. However, had I rendered it into a literal translation of Swanton's Latin, the text would sound absurdly out of place. Rabbit's response to Wildcat would read "If you pound your testicles, you will have a pecan." The word "testicles" for *testiculos* would give Rabbit's advice to Wildcat a clinical air.

I doubt Swanton's informant used such incongruous English diction. In my adaptation, "Rabbit, Wildcat, the Big Tree, and the Nuts," I have translated the Latin so that it is in keeping with the style of the rest of the story. Therefore, my freer rendering of the complete conclusion is as follows:

> Rabbit said, "If you pound your nuts, you can have a pecan, too."
> Wildcat began pounding furiously until his nuts turned to pulp and he passed out. With Wildcat lying on the ground exhausted, Rabbit laughed and left.

Another instance among several of Swanton's defaulting to Latin, this time for a suggestive sexual encounter, occurs in his version of the Hitchiti tale titled "Rabbit and the Old Man." Here, the trickster desires (Swanton writes "wanted") a man's two daughters. Rabbit uses a ruse to get the man away from his daughters who are at his house. Sent there to fetch the man's hoe and shovel, Rabbit meets the two daughters and explicitly asks for sex.

Swanton phrases the request in Latin as Rabbit tells the daughters he has come to them because their father told him *rem habere cum ambabus.*[33] This phrase could be politely translated as "to have an affair with both [of you]." In my version, "Rabbit and the Old Man's Daughters," because such a delicate rendering seems out of character for the trickster's libidinous nature, I have framed Rabbit's solicitation of the women as "I ran up here because your daddy told me to get from you *the thing all men love.*" Although my version of Rabbit's request, as indicated in the foregoing italics, is not an exact translation, it is more pointed in its sexual implications and better matches the overall style of my adaptation. For readers who want to explore potential reasons for Swanton's use of Latin for portions of his stories, **Appendix C** details the social climate of Swanton's day regarding publications that might have then been legally considered obscene and offers possible causes for his choice of Latin.

In addition to problems with authenticity, another limitation with anthropological print recordings is that they sometimes read as dry and lifeless, although this issue was not necessarily present in the sources I consulted. One reason for this wooden effect is researchers were often outsiders from the group they investigated and recorded their written versions from native informants as cultural artifacts, not as tales told by the group's storytelling adepts before a live audience.

In contradistinction to certain transcriptions, Anne Pellowski's review of some Native American styles of storytelling indicates that their oral presentations were not colorless affairs as sometimes implied in print recordings but dramatic events resulting from the use of voice and delivery techniques like gesture and pantomime.[34] Among several anecdotes related by Pellowski, one recounts how a storyteller among the Coeur d'Alene—originally located in Montana, Idaho, and Washington State—presented a story in such a dramatic fashion that, when he pantomimed sneaking up on a tent in the dark, he lay down and crawled upon his stomach, all the while continuing to tell the tale.[35]

Details concerning a Cherokee story collected by Charles Lanman underscore Pellowski's findings. Fellow nineteenth-century American Washington Irving referred to him as "the picturesque explorer of the United States."[36] Besides exploration, among Lanman's many vocations and pursuits, he was famous as a biographer, essayist, and librarian for the United States War Department and later for the House of Representatives, as well as a painter associated with the Hudson River School.

Lanman was also a travelogue writer. In the fifteenth letter from his 1849 book, *Letters from the Allegheny Mountains*, he describes his journey through Hickory Nut Gorge in North Carolina and gives a vivid account of the gorge's river, granite precipices, and other topography such as Chimney Rock. At the end of the letter, he relates a story told to him by a Cherokee headman named both All Bones and Flying Squirrel.

This untitled narrative is a *pourquoi* tale that explains how the Cherokee lost the tobacco weed and suffered great afflictions from being deprived of its healing powers. However, a mighty wizard, often called a conjuror in other Cherokee stories, helped the people recover the precious plant. Whereas Lanman's print version runs to approximately 450 words, he informs his readers that, when the Cherokee chief told the story, it lasted "no less than two hours."[37] Surely this extended rendition must have contained dramatic features like noticeable voice changes, sound effects, expressive gestures, and conspicuous facial expressions. In adapting the trickster tales of Southeastern Native Americans, I have attempted to capture in print something of these first two components of storytelling.

Appendix B

Sovereignty and Appropriation

A current matter of debate that touches on retelling the traditional literature of non-white minorities in the United States such as Native Americans concerns the twofold issue of *sovereignty* and *appropriation.* In *Multicultural Children's Literature*, Donna E. Norton summarizes the competing viewpoints.

One perspective holds that only indigenous people should have complete ownership of their past traditions and customs.[1] This position obviously extends to their folklore and overlaps with concerns about authenticity. Matt Dembicki, a comic book creator and the editor of *Tricksters: Native American Tales, A Graphic Collection,* voices this belief in an addendum to his book. In "From the Editor," he states that he "wanted the stories to be authentic, meaning they would have to be written by Native American storytellers."[2] An alternative argument advocates that non-natives who know and respect the history and culture of Native Americans can write authoritatively about them.[3]

In her guide to selecting books for children and young adults about indigenous groups, Mary Jo Lass-Woodfin finds merit in both points of view. She states, "...while it true that no one knows an experience as deeply as one who has lived it, it is equally true that an observer can sometimes see processes that the person involved in the events cannot see until later, if ever."[4]

As an instance of overgeneralization, the first part of Lass-Woodfin's statement requires qualification. While it may be true that lived experience might assist a writer create a work with authenticity, this assertion has greater application to literary genres like lyric poetry, which is written to convey deep personal feelings; modern realism; and obviously autobiography. In these, firsthand knowledge of lives lived may be significant in accurately portraying events, situations, and emotions from cultural perspectives or personal experiences.

In other genres, being a member of a cultural group counts for little

Appendix B. Sovereignty and Appropriation

when compared, not to experience lived, which may be irrelevant to the genre, but to knowledge gained through study and inquiry. In historical fiction, background accuracy and verisimilitude are crucial so as not to distort the historical record. In biography, research is essential to depict an individual's life fairly and truthfully. In other informational texts in areas like science, getting factual details correct is critical. In folktales, mythology, and legends, a knowledge of components like fanciful plots, talking animals, supernatural phenomena, magic makers, and other unreal characters may be helpful since these may not be aspects and preoccupations in the daily lives of members of a culture from whom the lore derived in the distant past has been erased from memory or only spottily recalled.

In fact, over generations of recounting their traditional narratives, indigenous storytellers sometimes have added out-of-place details. In discussing selections of the Oklahoma Cherokee collected by John and Anna Kilpatrick in *Friends of Thunder*, Robert J. Conley notes that, even though many of the narratives "are ancient," native storytellers "incorporated modern elements" as they adapted the tales over the years.[5] A conspicuous example of such an addition occurs in an untitled Seminole story collected by Robert F. Greenlee in the 1940s. In describing the Upper World where Thunder lives, Greenlee's informant, Josie Billie, compared it to a pool hall with a crowd of people roaming around.[6] I have retold the story as "The Thunder Boys Deceive and Kill an Old Woman," and I included the strained simile because it shows how folktales are not static.

But back to Lass-Woodfin. She further notes that much of the folklore of Native Americans would not exist today if anthropologists and other non-native academics and writers not collected and preserved them.[7] In *A Critical Handbook of Children's Literature*, Rebecca Lukens goes so far as to say today's readers are "fortunate" that scholars preserved stories from past oral cultures so that their folktales "have become the property of all people."[8]

In *The Storyteller's Start-Up Book*, Margaret Read MacDonald clinches the foregoing perspective. She finds the notion of "cultural exclusiveness" a threat to the continued viability of folktales which changed and developed over time as they passed from one storyteller to another. In MacDonald's view, the "world is as rich as it is because we have shared our stories across cultures, and with them our hopes, our beliefs, our ways of seeing. Now is not the time to freeze all story into pockets of ethnicity. Now more than ever we need each other's stories."[9]

Appendix C

Social Climate and Swanton's Use of Latin

Appendix A discusses the inauthenticity of Swanton's rendering into Latin earthy portions of his *Myths and Tales of the Southeastern Indians.* Some readers today might berate Swanton for his squeamishness in not putting into English parts of indigenous stories expressing what today seem mildly naughty matters. Some readers might even go so far as to describe him as Scarlett O'Hara characterized her future husband Tom Kennedy: "an old maid in britches." Yet such a depiction does not account for the context of Swanton's contemporary social climate. As Frank Fureli has stated, anything during the nineteenth century through much of the twentieth that smacked of the indecent or salacious was "available only on the margins of society."[1] Now, however, far more explicit material no longer lurks in the shadows but lives in the light of common day, particularly via the Internet, so that in the West there has been a "normalisation of a culture of pornography in *adult* society."[2]

Even before the widespread availability of internet smut, communications scholars such as Neil Postman in *The Disappearance of Childhood* (1982) and Joshua Meyrowitz in *No Sense of Place* (1985) detailed how electronic media like television tended to destroy information barriers that separated different social groups such as children and adults. When knowledge results primarily through print, it separates individuals into distinct groups because its form and content impose different degrees of reading ability, interests, and background experiences that serve as keys to unlocking meaning. Postman concluded that both television and film share a perception of children who are "in social orientation, language, and interests no different from adults."[3] Meyrowitz arrived at a similar verdict. As opposed to a culture in which access to information is dominated by books, in which the secret underside of

145

adult life was less readily available to developing children and adolescents, television provided them access to the inaccessible.[4]

Both applause and scorn have greeted these cultural changes. In discussing the relatively recent pornification of Western society, Susanne Paasonen has observed a positive outcome is that what was once taboo has become more publicly visible and acceptable, thereby promoting sexual freedom and diversity. On the other hand, she notes that to some critics the pervasiveness of offensive material has further promoted male "sexualized hierarchies of privilege" and intensified the oppression of women.[5]

Howsoever one might regard the revelation of adult secrets through the mainstreaming of pornography, restrictions and sanctions against indecency were rife in Swanton's time. In the United State during the Gilded Age, approximately the last three decades of the nineteenth century, there was a common understanding of what comprised offensive publications. Paul S. Boyer refers to this "sweet accord" as the "genteel literary code" that was informally enforced among the era's organizations for the prevention of vice, mainstream publishers and authors, and prominent members of society's privileged ranks. The result of this tacit agreement was "to purge books of any erotic aspect" and to permit "only hints" of sexual attraction between men and women.[6] Although Boyer concentrates on literary works offered for reading in the home market, then considered a refuge of safety and tranquility which must be safeguarded without fail,[7] his analysis suggests the repressive atmosphere of the period into which Swanton was born.

More vigorous than the literary world in efforts to suppress vulgar, degrading, and consequently perilous material were actions by the vice societies. These organizations "became dangerously addicted to sweeping generalizations about the horrid effects of improper books."[8] At the time Swanton collected his tales, primarily between 1908 and 1914, the repressive reign of Anthony Comstock still flourished, and although Comstock died in 1915 as a "laughingstock" to many supporters of free speech, his legacy of censorship continued long after his death, with some postal inspectors unable to differentiate "between a D.H. Lawrence and a Larry Flynt"[9]

In the 1870s, Comstock received public acclaim for his privately initiated crusade in New York City against a vendor of "smut." For his efforts and with the aid of philanthropist Morris Jesup, he became secretary of the city's newly founded Committee for the Suppression of

Vice. Within a year, Comstock had confiscated 200,000 offensive items such as "photographs, rings, knives, song-lyric sheets, playing cards, and what he referred to as 'obscene and immoral rubber articles.'"[10] With the aid of congressional republicans and Grant's corrupt Vice President, Schuyler Colfax, Comstock worked to have a national anti-obscenity bill passed. On March 3, 1873, Grant signed the first of what would later be called "the Comstock Laws." Comstock also received an appointment as special agent to the postal service to enforce the legislation.[11]

Comstock was not without his detractors. Taken from a much longer work, a 25¢ pamphlet, published by D.M. Bennett in New York in 1878 and titled *Anthony Comstock and His Career of Cruelty and Crime,* castigated the half a dozen Comstock acts "as subversive of the very principals of American liberty and destructive to individual rights guaranteed by the Constitution of our country."[12] Bennett further assailed Comstock as laboring under the guise of eliminating "obscene literature" while causing "the arraignment of numerous persons who had not the slightest intention of violating the rules of propriety and morality."[13]

To give the flavor of the legislation, Bennett quoted the entirety of Section 3893 of one of the acts. It forbade people from sending by the United States Postal Service any "obscene, lewd, or lascivious book, pamphlet, picture, paper, print, or other publication of an indecent character." Among other enumerated items such as "scurrilous epithets" upon postcards, the section prohibited mailing or delivering "any article or thing designed or intended for the prevention of conception or procuring of abortion." Considered guilty of a misdemeanor if convicted, individuals could be fined between $100 and $5000 for each offense or "imprisoned at hard labor not less than one year, nor more than ten years, or both."[14]

By 1914, which overlaps the time Swanton collected most of his narratives, Comstock brought about the conviction of 2,740 individuals out of 3,697 indicted, a 74 percent success rate. For those convicted, the fines amounted to $237,134.30. These aided in paying for the prison sentences which totaled some 565 years.[15]

Before his death on September 15, 1915, Comstock devoted much of his energy to harassing birth control activist Margaret Sanger, who would later found the American Birth Control League, the progenitor of Planned Parenthood. In 1914, she was indicted by a federal grand jury for sending her monthly, *The Woman Rebel,* through the mail. The publication's central purpose in advocating for birth control was that women should have control of their own bodies.[16] Emily Taft Douglas' biography of Sanger details that she had only eighteen hours to decide her future. If convicted on all counts, she faced forty-five years in prison.[17] Fearing an unfriendly court, Sanger hastily made a few arrangements, then boarded a train leaving New York City for Montreal. From Canada, she sailed to exile in Britain.[18] During the train ride, Sanger adopted the name Bertha Watson to avoid extradition. She would use this name over the coming year.[19]

Sanger's husband, however, did not escape legal action. One of Comstock's toadies had asked William Sanger for a copy of *Family Limitation*, an unpublished pamphlet on birth control. Comstock himself made the arrest. The conviction carried a fine of $100 or thirty days in jail. William Sanger opted for the latter.[20]

In such a climate as his contemporaries Margaret and William Sanger endured, Swanton had every reason to be concerned about anything indecorous in his compilation of indigenous tales, particularly anything sent through the mail to the Bureau of Ethnology. As evidenced by the following additional explanation for Swanton's use of Latin, scholarship and science did not always protect research from slavering censors and legal prosecution.

This parallel explanation derives from concepts about pornography that developed after the gradual unearthing of Pompeii. According to Walter Kendrick, from the earliest excavations that began in the mid–1700s, artifacts came to light which, because of what authorities deemed their salacious nature, created consternation. For example, a "particularly outrageous artifact" discovered in 1758 was a small marble sculpture that realistically portrayed a satyr engaged in sex with a goat.[21]

King Charles, the Bourbon monarch of Naples, prohibited his royal sculptor from letting anyone see the statue. And yet the English classical scholar Richard Payne Knight in his 1786 book on ancient phallic cults, *Discourse on the Worship of Priapus*, alluded to the concealment of the piece in the Neapolitan Royal Museum of Portici. As Kendrick notes, the fact that Knight knew about the supposedly forbidden object suggests the process had already begun by which "a gentleman with appropriate demeanor (and ready cash for the custodian) would be admitted to the locked chamber where controversial items lurked." This "makeshift practice" excluded the poor, who could not afford the cost of admittance, and both women and children of all economic brackets.[22]

Selective exclusion of certain groups expanded to include denial of entry to the brothels of Pompeii as these were uncovered.[23] Difficulties, however, arose with the printing of guidebooks and catalogues describing the new discoveries which were obviously part of everyday life in Pompeii and pointed to drastically different values between ancient pagan and contemporary Christian European worldviews. Kendrick indicates that from this clash of cultures, art historians misappropriated the word "pornography" to categorize "Pompeii's priceless obscenities." The word originally had appeared in a work in the second century CE by the Greek writer Athenaeus and referred to "whore-painters."[24] Only after the Pompeian discoveries and subsequent scholarly writings about them did the term "pornography" come to denote lasciviousness and something to be hidden and safeguarded in "the Secret Museum."[25]

Scholars eventually began to apply analogous safeguards to written works, correspondingly withholding accessibility to what might be offensive. Erudition became the means of denying women, children, and the poorer classes from obtaining admission to supposed taboos in print, for there was little distinction between pornography that encompassed ancient culture and that designed to stir prurient interests. The physical Secret Museum accordingly became a "metaphoric" one.[26] Only the educated elite could be admitted.

In *A History of Pornography*, an anecdote given by H. Montgomery Hyde illustrates how esoteric language could serve as a gatekeeper of secret information. Hyde's example relates to English translations of one of Boccaccio's ribald narratives in *The Decameron*. But first a brief recapitulation of the tale based on John Payne's 1886 English translation.

Boccaccio's tenth story of the third day concerns how an innocent young pagan woman of the Barbary coast named Alibech wants to learn the tenets of Christianity. Upon the advice of a friend, she travels into the "solitudes of the deserts of Thebais"[27] and seeks to be taught by the holy hermits who live there in severe self-denial. Fearing they might succumb to carnal temptation, each older man she encounters keeps sending her for instruction to another until finally the young hermit, Rustico, agrees to be her spiritual preceptor. Entranced by Alibech's beauty, Rustico begins a lengthy disquisition on the eternal war between God and the Devil. He tells Alibech that the greatest duty of a Christian in service to God is to put the Devil back in Hell, should he escape from where he was originally consigned.

Rustico next instructs Alibech to imitate his example. He takes off his clothes, and she takes off hers. She gazes upon his nakedness, and he on hers. Rustico, now "being more than ever inflamed in his desires," then experiences an erection, or "the resurrection of the flesh" as the Victorian John Payne cautiously phrases it.[28] Alibech naively queries Rustico about what he possesses which "thrusts forth thus" and which she lacks.[29] He answers that what she beholds is the Devil, who rises up and torments him almost beyond endurance.

However, Rustico informs her that she has something which he has not, and that is Hell. He then convinces the neophyte that she will give him "the utmost solacement and will do God a very great service" if she will permit him to put the Devil back in Hell.[30] Over time, Alibech becomes so enamored of this Christian duty that Rustico grows exhausted from the activity. To his "great satisfaction," he at last finds relief from her excessive devotion to God when she is called home to inherit her father's "ample" fortune and to take a husband whom she hopes will also want to put the Devil in Hell.[31]

Hyde relates that Payne's translation was not originally available to the public but was printed in 1886 as a private edition for the Villon Society. He further states that, unlike Payne's rendition, most English versions of *The Decameron* left the part about Rustico and Alibech's proclivities in medieval Italian.[32]

Swanton's use of Latin in indigenous tales of the Southeastern United States is an analogue to translators retaining Boccaccio's vernacular Florentine wording of the fourteenth century. Generally inaccessible to most people, such languages kept the indecorous portions of their narratives in the secret museum of print for educated individuals and functioned to prevent the alleged susceptible minds of certain groups like women and children from capitulating to corrupting influences. With legal undergirding, so held the beliefs of the day.

Yet scholarly works larded with technical language in English for their limited readership and the vendors who sold these publications were not immune from censors and legal prosecution for obscenity. The scientific publications of Havelock Ellis, a contemporary of Swanton, illustrate this point.

English physician Henry Havelock Ellis (1859–1939) was a pioneering researcher in human sexual behavior. Published over the years between 1897 and 1928, his seven-volume *Studies in the Psychology of Sex* broke constraints of the time by frank and scientific discussion of human sexuality. Like groundbreaking works by Freud, Kraft-Ebbing, and other investigators at the close of the nineteenth century, Ellis pre-sented evidence that individuals were capable of eroticizing "the unlike-liest objects and actions … somewhere, at least once."[33]

The first volume, *Sexual Inversion,* however, was initially published in 1896 in German as a medical text, the English translation not avail-able until the following year. The book contained case histories that detailed intimate relations between men and presented the research in "a reasonably sympathetic manner."[34] In 1898, a London bookseller, George Bedborough, sold a copy to an undercover policeman who had developed a friendship with the bookseller "in order to entrap him."[35] Despite the attempt by Ellis to defend the work as a scientific investiga-tion and written support from noted figures like George Bernard Shaw, the court was not swayed and considered any scientific justification a pose and trick to sell an obscene book. Found guilty, the bookseller was fined 100 pounds and released.[36]

The legal basis for rulings of guilt in obscenity cases like the one involving Ellis rested upon the "Hicklin test" as expounded by Chief Justice Cockburn in the famous 1868 case of *Regina v. Hicklin.* While it was by no means the first court case concerning obscenity, Cockburn's decision contained a definition that would serve as the standard test in both British and American law well into the twentieth century.[37] As cited by Hyde, Cockburn's definition is as follows:

> I think the test of obscenity is this, whether the tendency of the matter charged as obscenity is to deprave and corrupt those whose minds are open to such immoral influences, and into whose hands a publication of this sort may fall.[38]

The case involved an appeal against an English country magistrate named Hicklin who had ordered the destruction of a militant antipapist pamphlet, *The Confessional Unmasked.* The work contained quotations from Catholic manuals which contended that, during certain confes-sions by women, a priest might without blame experience sensations of sensuality coursing through his body. The pamphlet provided "consid-erable detail" about these corporeal sensations yet also assured a priest who encountered them that he would be without guilt—but only if he never derived pleasure from the exposure.[39]

While *The Confessional Unmasked* may have had a worthy pur-pose in exposing clerical corruption, its descriptions were nevertheless judged by Cockburn to be "indecent and likely to exert a depraved and corrupting influence on its readers."[40] In cases involving novels, these readers became young people even though novels were read by all ages and levels of society.[41] The Hicklin test thus relegated the content of reading material to what would not tend to corrupt what Kendrick calls "the Young Person," an imaginary social construct.[42] In Europe, this invented individual was usually female and in the United States usually male, with these fictional characters only existing in the fretful minds of men like Comstock who saw themselves as the guardians of morality supported by law.[43]

By the beginning of the twentieth century, the public had grown less narrow minded, and courts sometimes ruled against cases Comstock pursued as obscene.[44] Yet societies for the suppression of vice still maintained public respect, and although Comstock himself had become in many quarters something of a clown, periodicals and newspapers offered encomiums to his memory when he died of pneumonia in 1915. The *New York Times* praised him as a "benefactor and a hero" in a worthy cause.[45]

As for the Hicklin test articulated in 1868 by Chief Justice Cockburn, not until 1959 was it retired from the English statute book. The new Obscene Publications Act required that, instead of a few parts, a work must be considered in its entirety as to whether it might corrupt or deprave susceptible persons likely "to read, see, or hear it."[46]

Two years earlier in 1957, the United States Supreme Court in *Roth v. United States* had rejected the Hicklin test in similar terms. The majority opinion stated that, although the Constitution did not protect obscenity, the new criterion for determining it in a work was "Whether to the average person, applying contemporary community standards, the dominant theme of the material taken as a whole appeals to prurient interest."[47] Perhaps if Swanton had published *Myths and Tales of the Southeastern Indians* at the end of the 1950s or later, instead of 1929, he would have kept all parts of the stories in English.

Historical Sketches of Southeastern Native Groups and Commentary on Selected Variants

❖ Creek ❖

This sketch of the Creek provides broad information about this Southeastern native coalition. More specific details will follow about indigenous groups who were allied with them but who retained much of their own cultural identities. These include the Hitchiti and the Alabama-Coushatta, Coushatta being another name for the Koasati which is the designation Swanton used in his *Myths and Tales of the Southeastern Indians*. The Alabama and Coushatta are discussed together because of their early proximity to each other and because of the close correspondence of their histories.

In his 1952 *Indian Tribes of North America*, Swanton says that the indigenous people who later composed the most numerous members of the Creek Confederacy at first lived in the 1500s in the Spanish province of Guale which lay along the coast of present-day Georgia. Because of conflicts with Europeans, they moved inland where they formed the Creek Confederacy.[1] The lands this population came to occupy, until their removal west of the Mississippi River in the 1830s, comprise today's southwest Georgia and northern and central Alabama. Muskogee is also another name for the group.

The origin of the name "Creek" was once thought to have been applied by the colonists of South Carolina to the Muskogee because they lived near or along their land's many streams. Research of colonial documents by Vernon W. Crane, however, reveals the etymology likely derives from a group dwelling in the vicinity of the Upper Ocmulgee River, then known as "Ocheese Creek." Gradually shortened to "Creek," the word came to designate all members of the alliance.[2] Historian Alan

Appendix D. Historical Sketches and Commentary

Gallay describes this loosely associated population in the eighteenth century as "an array of native peoples" who, for defensive purposes, had "converged to form the Creek Confederacy."[3]

Until the 1760s, the Creek population exceeded both the English settlers and enslaved blacks of Georgia, according to *New Georgia Encyclopedia*. This source further indicates that, through trade and intermarriage, white colonists developed close ties with the Creek. As fugitives from slavery, many Africans settled among the Creek and forged cultural connections as well.[4]

Before Georgia's founding as a colony by General Oglethorpe in the 1730s, however, South Carolina became involved in Creek affairs. Captain Tobias Fitch's account of his mission to the Creek Confederacy illustrates the complex international interactions, both military and commercial, among Native Americans, the English of Carolina, and Spanish and French colonial interests. Fitch was a planter who had emerged as one of the leaders in the South Carolina Common House of Assembly.[5] Sent from Charleston in 1725, Fitch had as his ostensible primary aim that the Creek give restitution to John Sharp, a white trader to the Cherokee. Several young warriors of the Creek had wounded Sharp and stolen from him a slave woman and her children along with trade goods such as Sharp's "Best Case of Pistoolls."[6]

Arriving at Oakfuskee, the principal town of the Upper Creek on the Tallapoosa River, Fitch addressed a paramount chief named "Gogell Eys" (Goggle Eyes) and sixty headmen from twenty additional settlements. Besides demanding payment for Sharp's losses, Fitch harangued the gathered assembly and astutely reminded them of their benefits from trade with Carolina:

> I must tell your young men that, if it had not been for us, you would not have known how to war nor yet have anything to war with. You have nothing but bows and arrows to kill deer; you had no hoes and axes then [but] what you made of stone. You wore nothing but skins; but now you have learned the use of firearms ... to kill deer and [the use of] other provisions to wage war against your enemies. And yet you set no greater value on us who have been good friends to you than on your greatest enemies.[7]

Besides the issue of restitution to John Sharp, Fitch met with other problems. In the Hitchiti town of Apalachicola on the Chattahoochee River, he encountered a Spanish embassy sent by the governor of St. Augustine. The leader of the commission claimed that the Creek Emperor Brims, whom he referred to as "old Brinimes," had sent for him. Overhearing the conversation, one of the Creek headmen declared to Fitch "The Spaniard lies."[8] Although England and Spain were then at peace, Fitch was not pleased with what he perceived as a covert attempt to influence the Creek to join with the Yemasee of Florida who often raided Carolina and were Spanish allies. He thereupon threatened to seize the envoy along with a black slave he had with him, Fitch claiming that the Yemasee had captured the slave from his rightful English owner.[9] Fitch did make good on his intention to confiscate the slave, although the man later escaped with the assistance of a Creek leader by the name of "Squire Mickeo."[10]

Other complications arose during Fitch's sojourn. Eager for the Creek and Cherokee to cease their depredations against each other, he hoped to establish peace between them to develop increased trade with Charleston. To thwart the attempt, Seneca emissaries arrived from the Iroquois League. They declared that, although the Creek should keep peace with the English, they should not halt their war with the Cherokee who were enemies of the Seneca. Should the Creek conclude a peace treaty, the Seneca would consider them to be enemies as well.[11]

As with the Spanish of Florida, Fitch was just as eager to suppress friendly relations between the Creek and the French of Louisiana. In a speech to the Lower Creek, he said that French traders were unable to supply the Creek with cloth and that, while he did not forbid commerce with the French, he requested that the Creek permit the English to have free access to trade.[12] Like the previous examples discussed from Fitch's journal, this one also demonstrates the tangled and elaborate involvement between Europeans and Native Americans of the Southeast, an involvement constantly shaping native culture.

From these close and ongoing interactions, there should be no surprise that indigenous peoples assimilated and adapted stories from one another and from other world folktales. Swanton's collection contains borrowings not only from other native groups like the Yuchi but also from African and European sources. For instance, although "The Monkey Girl" is not a trickster tale, it concerns a monkey troop which ruins a field of corn whenever a girl sings a song. With the girl eventually turning into a monkey, the story is clearly African in its roots as Swanton notes.[13]

Creek and Cherokee tales about Terrapin and Rabbit further illustrate the comingling of narrative traditions. Swanton includes five Creek variants under the title "Terrapin Races."[14] The first four have animals other than Rabbit as the land turtle's racing antagonist—three with Deer and one with Wolf. Only the fifth story pits Terrapin against Rabbit. It thus more nearly resembles the single Cherokee version in Mooney—"How the Terrapin Beat the Rabbit," a narrative which Mooney notes is so like "the well-known story of the race between the Hare and the Tortoise" that the comparison "seems almost superfluous."[15] Obviously, the Creek and Cherokee renditions of the fable from Aesop are appropriations and likely were heard through interaction with white traders or settlers. A key difference, though, between the European fable and the Creek and Cherokee adaptations is that the latter turn the tortoise into a Native American trickster who uses guile to out trick a figure notorious for unrivaled duplicity—namely, Rabbit. My adaptation "Terrapin Fools Rabbit," relies on merging parts of two Creek tales. Item 9 of **Chart 3** in **Appendix A** provides additional details.

❖ Hitchiti ❖

Next are trickster narratives from allies within the Creek Confederacy. I chose these selections based on whether they were different or did not significantly overlap as parallels with trickster stories from the Creek proper as classified in Swanton's *Tales of the Southeastern Indians* or other sources such as Mooney's collection of Cherokee tales. As in Swanton's arrangement, the Hitchiti adaptations follow those of the Creek.

The Hitchiti were part of the Creek Confederacy that coalesced in the mid–1700s along the Chattahoochee, Tallapoosa, and Alabama Rivers.[16] While the confederation bolstered the strength of its members against outside interests, whether Indian or European, each town kept its independence. This type of loose political organization operated among other Southeastern groups as well such as the Cherokee.[17]

The Hitchiti spoke a variant of the Muskogean language, a variant that extended beyond their immediate location and was even spoken by the Seminole of Florida until the Creek-American War of 1813–1814,[18] also called the Redstick War and the Creek Civil War. Swanton suggests that, before joining the Creek Confederacy, the Hitchiti lived in northern Florida and like many native groups participated in depredations that decimated or destroyed other tribes of the region.[19] More recent research by Ethridge confirms that, like the Yamasee and Apalachicola, between approximately 1710 to 1715, the Hitchiti made raids deeper and deeper into Spanish Florida to capture other Indians for the slave trade.[20]

The Hitchiti later relocated to the lower Ocmulgee River, a western tributary of the Altamaha, before they established themselves on the east bank of the Chattahoochee River in what is now Chattahoochee County in central Georgia.[21] This county borders today's state of Alabama. At the new settlements, the Hitchiti, Apalachicola, and others received fugitives fleeing from the effects of ongoing conflict with the Yamasee which led to "disruptions, displacements, and reconfigurations" of Southeastern Native Americans and which "ravaged" indigenous populations of the Southeast.[22]

According to the Peach State Archaeological Association, in 1799 United States Indian Agent Benjamin Hawkins reported that the Hitchiti had further expanded into two branches. The Tutalosi occupied an arm of Kinchafooni Creek twenty miles west of the "Little Hitchiti" who lived on both sides of the Flint River.[23]

Artifacts discovered by archaeologists at one Hitchiti site reveal an extensive trade in furs with the English colonists. Although closely associated with the Creek, the Hitchiti retained their own linguistic identity and customs.[24] By 1839, however, as with other allies within the Creek Confederacy, the Hitchiti were forced to leave their traditional homeland in Georgia and relocate to Indian Territory. In the words of historian Angie Debo, they and other members of the Confederacy "were cleared from the path of the white man, but the eager settlers who plowed their fertile fields and built rich cities along their streams never understood the cost of their expulsion."[25] An 1891 census by the Creek governing body in the territory of Oklahoma revealed that the Hitchiti had a population of 182 out of 13,000 of the total Creek population.[26]

Along with other remnants of the Creek Confederacy, some of the Hitchiti migrated to Florida and became associated with the Seminole. Concealed within the Everglades, they fought alongside other coalescent Indians against the United States in the Seminole Wars that occurred in the first half of the 1800s.[27] In 1962, however, the Hitchiti obtained separate status when the United States recognized them under the official name of the Miccosukee Tribe of Florida.[28]

Regarding Hitchiti myths and folktales, they often parallel those of the Creek and associated polities. For instance, the Creek, Hitchiti, Alabama, and Koasati (Coushatta) have tar-baby stories. The same holds true for the Cherokee and Natchez of the Southeast.

❖ Alabama-Coushatta ❖

Along with other native populations of the Southeast, the ancestors of the Alabama and Coushatta were part of the Mississippian civilization, or what Etheridge calls "a purely Indian world"[29] which flourished roughly from 800 CE to 1600 CE. They were also among the earliest indigenous peoples to encounter the pressures of European outsiders. Even before contact with non-natives, Indians of the Southeast suffered from the effects of diseases which "outran their European hosts" and which caused "extensive decimation" so that the Mississippian culture was drastically changed prior to Europeans entering its chiefdoms.[30]

One of the most devastating events for the forebears of the Alabama and Coushatta Indians was the "unparalleled destruction" wreaked by the conquistador Hernando de Soto and his army of some six hundred men in the early 1540s.[31] Through war, enslavement, and the continued exposure to European diseases such as measles and smallpox, wherever Soto's expedition went in search of fabled riches, it left in its wake depopulated and destroyed chiefdoms, which had prospered for centuries, and initiated a chain of events that caused them to swirl "into oblivion in less than twenty years."[32] Such was the case with the Mississippian chiefdoms of Moundville and Coosa from which the historic Alabama and Coushatta respectively descended.[33]

Vulnerable to raids by the Chickasaw from west and by the Cherokee from the north and east, the Alabama and Coushatta eventually merged and settled along the protective bluffs of the Alabama River at the confluence of its tributaries, the Coosa and Tallapoosa. Both groups were part of the Upper Creek division of the Confederacy. As with other tribes within the alliance, Alabama and Coushatta towns were autonomous and under the governance of a council of elders, a war leader, and a headman called a miko. Through extensive intermarriage, close kinship ties developed between the Alabama and Coushatta.[34]

According to Howard N. Martin, who has written extensively on the Alabama-Coushatta, the name "Alabama" at one time was thought to mean "Here we rest." Further research, however, suggests that the term is a combination of Muskogean words meaning "vegetable gatherers." Regarding the Coushatta, Martin states the name comes from the Koasati dialect and indicates "white cane," a meaning that reflects an environmental feature of the group's surroundings.[35]

During the colonial period, both the English and French courted the Alabama and Coushatta to establish trade. Like other natives within the Creek alliance, they frequently took a neutral stance with European powers to gain commercial advantages. The Alabama and Coushatta, though, had French leanings. In 1717, the former tribe invited the French to build a fort and trading center on their lands, and both the Alabama and Coushatta provided labor for the construction.[36] Situated on the Tallapoosa River and known as Fort Toulouse, or the Alabama Fort, it was the remotest outpost of the French in Louisiana and, as historian Roger L. Nichols notes, was designed to challenge trade from Carolina with the Southeastern Indians.[37] The fort would remain in French hands until 1763.

For both tribes, Fort Toulouse brought greater dependence on European goods as well as racial intermixture between indigenous women and the men of its French garrison. However, the Alabama-Coushatta maintained facets of their indigenous culture. For instance, despite the presence of several priests at the fort, there is nothing to indicate the clerics realized any success in converting the Alabama-Coushatta to Catholicism. Sustained Christian missionary efforts would have to wait for one hundred and fifty years.[38] And yet, some changes in religious beliefs resulted from contact with French missionaries in the eighteenth century. For example, the Life Giver became associated with the Christian God, the Horned Serpent grew more malign as a Satanic figure, and the dual concepts of heaven and hell entered into beliefs about the afterlife whereas, before close French contact, a person's earthly behavior bore no relationship to notions of reward or punishment in the next world.[39]

From 1756 to 1763 during the French and Indian War, Great Britain and France struggled for control of North America. Although the Alabama-Coushatta attempted to maintain neutrality, some of them sided with the French and helped to garrison Fort Toulouse.[40]

With the signing of the Treaty of Paris at the end of the war, Great Britain gained possession of most of France's vast former colonies. Rather than remain in their homeland, the Alabama-Coushatta in 1764 began to follow their French relatives to Louisiana, which fell under Spanish governance as a result of the treaty. This migration occurred because of the longstanding native connection with the French, the desire to avoid British control, and the inflow of English settlers onto Indian lands. The move did not occur all at once but transpired over several decades.[41]

Appendix D. Historical Sketches and Commentary

By 1800 through negotiations with Spain, Napoleon secretly transferred the province of Louisiana back to French control. Three years later with the Louisiana purchase, the United States bought the territory. However, the border between the new territory acquired by the United States and Spanish holdings in the northern reaches of New Spain was not firmly established. The Alabama and Coushatta, who had been migrating into this contested region of Texas since the 1780s, capitalized upon the situation by receiving presents from both the United States and Spanish authorities and affirming loyalty to each.[42]

In 1807, conflicts developed between tribal members remaining in Louisiana and white residents, both sides accusing the other of murdering individuals in their respective communities. Rather than contend with further dissension, the rest of the Alabama and Coushatta population moved into the southeastern area of Spanish Texas and settled in the remote Big Thicket area because of its natural abundance and their desire to be free of outsider influence.[43] Historian Sheri Marie Shuck-Hall describes this part of Texas as a "location with vast prairies and gently rolling hills interspersed with timber, numerous rivers, clear-running streams, and rich black soil." She also observes that herds of buffalo to the west served as a further food source.[44]

The government of New Spain considered Indian groups in East Texas as a buffer against further expansion by United States citizens into its holdings there and welcomed migration by the Alabama and Coushatta.[45] Despite fighting among the different Native Americans in Texas, the two groups thrived in this region for a time.[46] However, when Mexico achieved independence from Spain in 1821 and Texas declared independence from Mexico in 1836, the political situation changed for the Alabama and Coushatta once again. The senate of the new Republic of Texas failed to endorse a treaty that would have secured for them a significant land grant. After Sam Houston's presidency ended in 1838, the new president, Mirabeau B. Lamar, promoted a policy toward Indians characterized by the expulsion of those who were friendly and the extermination of those who were hostile. And yet this severe policy was never imposed upon the Alabama and Coushatta.[47]

Life became more precarious for the two groups when Texas entered the Union in 1845. In the past, once a territory became a state, the federal government took over the administration of Indian affairs, but in the case of Texas, it retained control, with all its territory belonging either to private individuals or to the state.[48] After much debate between federal and state authorities, in 1854 Texas eventually granted the Alabama official title to a little over eleven hundred acres in the Big Thicket area of Polk County. Minuscule in comparison to their former lands on which the tribe ranged, this land grant, which became known as the Big Sandy Reservation, resulted from the leadership of Chief Antone and Alabama subchiefs and from the support of Sam Houston and local white citizens. Unfortunately, an 1855 Texas land grant of 640 acres to the Coushatta never materialized because settlers already had legal claims to the allotment.[49]

Shuck-Hall observes that most of Coushatta at this time "wandered across the state, homeless."[50] The majority, according to Hook, returned to a former settlement in Louisiana. In 1859, the Alabama made provision for the remainder to live with them at the Big Sandy Reservation,[51] and by 1862, a sizable number of Coushatta had settled there. Despite the accomplishment of the Alabama and Coushatta as the only Indians to obtain a reservation and remain in Texas in the 1800s, their success came at a heavy cost. Sickness and deprivation, coupled with and often caused by long periods of uncertainty and bouts of a nomadic existence ravaged their numbers.[52]

The long-term result of the Alabama-Coushatta "migration and diaspora" was their forging a common identity. In her study of their trials and triumphs, Shuck-Hall says that their folktales express the significance of the "sacred space" of their former homeland along the Alabama River. For there they had first joined together and had forged a lasting connection through much hardship. As the "Our History" of their website notes, the cultures of the two tribes 'have some differences but for the most part are identical.[53] Today, their reservation in Polk County, Texas, comprises 4,593.7 acres.[54]

❖ Natchez ❖

During the historical period, when Europeans and Native Americans began to encounter one another in the Southeast, the Natchez lived along the eastern side of the lower Mississippi River. At the time of French colonization in the early 1700s, their population numbered approximately 6,000 people who occupied nine villages.[55] Like the Alabama and Coushatta, the ancestors of the Natchez were part of the Mississippian World, sometimes termed the "Southern Cult," or the "Southeastern Ceremonial Complex."[56] While living in separate chiefdoms, if judged on the basis of their common ceremonial regalia and objects having sacred symbolic significance, its people likely held common religious assumptions.[57]

According to early Spanish and French descriptions, the various chiefdoms also had a similar hierarchical social order.[58] However, following the collapse of the Mississippian World, power became more diffuse as indigenous people of the Southeast realigned and organized in the late seventeenth century and through the eighteenth into smaller political groups that comprise many of the Indian tribes known today. Some exceptions to this reconfiguration occurred along the lower Mississippi River and continued the outward signs of the former Southeastern Ceremonial Complex. Hudson describes these new polities as "far more modest chiefdoms" than those that existed earlier.[59]

As recorded by the French from 1700 to 1731, the trappings of the former Mississippian World were especially marked among the Natchez in the territory of Colonial French Louisiana.[60] Hudson gives a cogent overview of their social hierarchy. From top to bottom, its ranks included Suns, Nobles, Honored People, and "Stinkards." The first three categories composed the Natchez upper class while the Stinkards, or Commoners, formed the lower. Because kinship and descent were matrilineal, when a female Sun married a Stinkard, her children retained the status of a Sun. Similarly, the children of a female from the other two upper orders kept the same title as their mother. On the other hand, the children of a male who married a woman of a lower class sunk to her level. Thus, if a male Sun married a female Stinkard, his offspring would be Stinkards because of matrilineal descent. Unlike the practices of European blue bloods, who married within their own ranks, the Natchez class system forbade Suns, whether men or women, to marry other Suns.[61]

At the very top of the Natchez hierarchy was the Great Sun who "commanded more veneration and had more power" than other Southeastern chiefs and headmen of the historical period.[62] To express their veneration for this individual, the Natchez offered him generous gifts of food which included sacred corn grown in a special field. The Great Sun did not retain sole possession of these presents but was expected to show largesse and return portions of these offerings to the people.[63] Custom required the Natchez to pay other forms of deference to him. For instance, a French illustration from 1758 depicts his being carried in a litter by eight bearers.[64] A retinue of several wives and retainers attended him and upon his death were sacrificed along with any others desirous of joining him in the afterlife.[65]

Yet Hudson cautions that the Great Sun's power lacked the absolutism the French thought he possessed.[66] This conclusion is supported by the following details from historian Roger L. Nichols' account of conflicts between the French colonists and the Natchez that ultimately led to the Indians' eradication.

When the French settled in Mobile Bay in 1699, they gained diplomatic ties and commercial access to tribes along the lower Mississippi. These included the Natchez. Hoping to construct a fort and trading center in their territory, the French sought to challenge English traders from Carolina before they could establish connections with indigenous groups of the region as they had already done with other Southeastern natives. However, French diplomatic efforts with the Natchez were less than successful in the early decades of the seventeenth century. Traveling up the Mississippi in 1715, the new governor of Louisiana slighted their leadership by failing to stop at their settlements. On his journey downstream, he halted only to reprovision his supplies and maladroitly offended Natchez diplomatic sensibilities by not smoking the calumet, a long-stemmed ceremonial tobacco pipe. To the Great Sun, this omission signaled disrespect.[67]

Natchez and French relations continued to deteriorate. In 1716, a band of Natchez warriors attacked and killed some French boatmen going downriver. This aggression spurred the colonial government to send fifty men under the command of Jean Baptiste Bienville into the Natchez domain to build a small fort. Within his palisaded camp, Bienville met with the Great Sun, the Tattooed Serpent, and the Little Sun to resolve difficulties. Bienville demanded justice for the slain boatmen and reminded these leaders that the French had on former occasions surrendered whites guilty of transgressions against the Natchez. He made clear to the three that they should similarly reciprocate. They answered that internal tribal conflicts prevented them from responding in the same manner.[68] This incident provides evidence for Hudson's contention that the Great Sun "reigned more than he governed" and did not possess the central authority credited to him by French observers of the time.[69]

Eventually, to gratify French demands, the Natchez leaders showed Bienville two decapitated heads of the offenders along with a third head of an executed individual. Still unsatisfied, Bienville executed two

Appendix D. Historical Sketches and Commentary

Natchez chiefs whom he held as hostages and who had expressed pro–English sentiments. No further incidents resulted, and the French built Fort Rosalie on Natchez lands. Although the Natchez in their sympathies were divided into French and English factions, Nichols observes that the Great Sun and the Tattooed Serpent were pro–French but did not hold sway over all the settlements.[70]

Typical of interactions between whites and indigenous people in the Southeast, various issues persisted between the French and Natchez and often led to violence. Problems generally resulted from trade disputes between native adherents of the French and those of the English, from debt owed to whites and Indian failure or unwillingness to settle accounts, and from encroachments by colonists onto tribal lands. In the case of the Natchez, there is also the possible offense of the French establishing a settlement on a sacred mound where an old temple once stood. A deadly smallpox outbreak had further soured relations. Adding to the volatile environment was the death in 1725 of the Tattooed Serpent who may have been among the Natchez the staunchest bulwark against anti–French forces.[71]

Yet what ignited into violence the smoldering resentments of the Indians was the ineptitude of Sieur de Chepart, the commander of Fort Rosalie. "A notorious drunk," he had earlier overseen the government of the Natchez District but had been dismissed because of his highhanded treatment of both settlers and Indians. Pardoned by the French governor, he returned as the commander of Fort Rosalie.[72] During the tribe's most important sacred celebration, the Green Corn Festival, Chepart informed the Natchez that they must abandon their surrounding villages and give over their cleared fields for French use. The Indians in silent anger complied but bided their time. Then, in November of 1729, a party entered the fort on the pretext that Chepart smoke the calumet with them to confirm the transfer of the old fields. The French captain contemptuously demanded their departure, and Natchez warriors fired their muskets, killing him and ultimately slaying numerous soldiers and others within the fort as well as settlers at nearby farmsteads. By day's end, the warriors had killed 237 whites and mounted their heads atop the fort's palisade. As for survivors of the attack, the Natchez enslaved and distributed them among their villages.[73]

By the end of the conflict in 1731, the French and their Indian allies, most notably the Choctaw, had destroyed the Natchez as an independent tribe. James Adair, a white trader among the Southeastern Indians and author of the early important source on them, *The History of the Native Americans*, reports that during battles with the Natchez their Choctaw foes "captivated a great number of them and carried them to New Orleans, where several were burned and the rest sent as slaves to the West India Islands...."[74] Most of the tribe joined the pro–English Chickasaw[75] while other remnants sought refuge with the Creek, Catawba, and Cherokee.[76]

Mooney remarks "such admixture" in the case of the Cherokee, who "have strains" not only of Natchez but also of Creek, Catawba, Uchee, Iroquois, Osage, and Shawnee "blood," illustrates the insurmountable difficulty in tracing the origins of their Southeastern indigenous folktales. He states that "Indians are great wanderers," and long visits to other tribes, often lasting for several weeks or months, produced cultural exchanges through dancing, feasting, trading, and storytelling.[77]

In "Comparison of Myths," the concluding section of *Myths and Tales of the Southeastern Indians*, Swanton underscores Mooney's observation. Swanton gives a digest of variants and parallel plot details not only to stories in his collection but also to additional indigenous narratives described in research or contained in compilations by other scholars. He thus notes similarities across the folklore of members of the Creek Confederacy, of their indigenous neighbors like the Cherokee, Natchez, and Choctaw, and of more distant native groups like the Iroquois of the Northeast and the Plains Indians of the West such as the Ponca, Pawnee, Shoshoni among others.[78] Swanton's comparisons strongly imply the impossibility of knowing where borrowings occurred among different native peoples. Furthermore, as he indicates in his opening remarks to his volume, some of the stories derive from European and African sources.[79]

❖ Seminole ❖

Unlike other indigenous peoples of the Southeast, the origins of the Seminole are relatively recent as a tribe that coalesced in what is now the state of Florida. As to the different groups that eventually formed the Seminole, accounts vary somewhat in their explanations of how this development occurred.

The designation "Seminole" derives from the Spanish *cimarron*, a word that connotes a "wild one" or a "runaway." The Spanish also used the related term "maroon" to indicate a community of escaped

Appendix D. Historical Sketches and Commentary

African slaves. In *A People's History of Florida*, Adam Wasserman suggests this usage indicates an early connection between Native Americans and fugitive slaves from Britain's Carolina and later Georgia who sought freedom to their south in Spain's colony of *La Florida*.[80] Indeed, in 1693, an edict by Charles II of Spain granted freedom to runaways at St. Augustine if they became Catholics.[81] This policy served as a way for Spain to impair the economy of the Carolina plantation system and lasted until 1763 when Spain ceded its Florida holdings to England at the end of the French and Indian War.[82]

In Wasserman's view, the formation of the Seminole could be described as an alliance of "Afro-indigenous" groups.[83] The Oconee, however, formed the indigenous core of the Seminole. Originally part of the Creek Confederacy, the Oconee had relocated to the essentially uninhabited Alachua prairie of north-central Florida between 1730 and 1750. Aiding in the earlier destruction of the Yamasee in 1715, the Oconee after resettlement later joined with escaped black slaves, other migrating members of the Creek Confederacy, Yamasee fugitives, and remnants of original Florida tribes such as the Apalachee.[84] By the mid–1700s, these groups formed what Wasserman terms "the Seminole nucleus."[85] Although differing in some details, the website of the *Peach State Archaeological Society* essentially agrees that "the history of the Seminole is to a considerable extent a continuation of the history of the Oconee."[86]

Differing significantly from Wasserman is the explanation by Hudson on the formation of the Seminole. Hudson states that they originated primarily from separate groups of the Creek Confederacy who entered Spanish Florida in the eighteenth and nineteenth centuries once the aboriginal natives had been destroyed through disease, forced labor, and slave raids from English colonies like South Carolina and their indigenous allies. Most of the newcomers were Hitchiti speakers although a large minority spoke varieties of the Muskogean language and could communicate with other constituents of the Creek alliance such as the Alabama and Yuchee.[87] By the 1770s, whites in Florida began to use the name "Seminole" to refer to the Creek in the area near today's Gainesville.[88]

After the defeat of the Upper Creek by Jackson's militia and his Lower Creek auxiliaries at the Battle of Horseshoe Bend in 1814, around 2,500 of the Upper Creek relocated to Florida because of Creek territory ceded to the United States. This migration swelled the Seminole population to approximately 6,000. As had been the case for many previous decades, escaping slaves further enlarged the number of Indians in Spanish Florida.[89]

Like other Southeastern natives such as the Creek and Cherokee, the Seminole had long owned slaves. However, the Seminole practiced a milder form of slavery than the chattel slavery of the American South. The black slaves of the Seminole lived in separate communities in what Hudson characterizes as "comparative freedom," obligated but once a year to pay their owners a quota of produce, livestock, or animal hides.[90] These African slaves plus the runaways who became free blacks constituted a sizable portion of the Seminole and united with them in later resisting removal west of the Mississippi in the 1800s.[91]

Although there is some disagreement over the matter, the population of slaves and freedmen may have been the major cause of the Seminole wars. Hudson argues that the desire by whites for Seminole land was not the major reason for the conflict because much of it consisted of swamps and therefore was not valuable for agriculture. Rather than territory, whites coveted the blacks who lived among the Indians and wanted to eliminate Florida as a place of refuge for runaway slaves.[92] Josephy similarly indicates that, even before Spain ceded its colony to the United States in 1823, "marauding whites from Georgia" entered Florida and claimed they were seeking fugitive slaves living among the Seminole.[93]

On the other hand, in their book on the Seminole wars, John and Mary Lou Missall caution against overstating the pressure from slave states as a cause for pursuing conflict with the Seminole, especially the prolonged war between 1835 and 1842. For peace negotiators, the primary consideration, rather than obtaining free blacks or capturing runaways, was agreeing to a treaty for the war's end.[94] In fact, during the Second Seminole War, most black Seminole did not participate because of casualties, capture, or capitulation. While many were returned to the slave states, a large proportion had already moved to Indian Territory as free blacks. Those remaining in Florida, hoping to gain white allies and protectors for self-preservation and good pay, served as scouts and translators for the military. Some of the Seminole still resisting removal to the West saw them as traitors and attempted to kill such Black Seminole leaders as "Gopher John" Cavallo.[95]

The First Seminole War occurred roughly between 1817 and 1818 and resulted over what whites saw as threats to slavery and their encroachments onto land occupied by the Seminole in the north of Florida and southeast of Georgia. After the American Revolution, Great Britain had returned Florida to Spain. The Seminole consequently made punitive and sometimes brutal raids into Georgia. Not only was the United Sates angered by these actions and the failure of Spanish officials to control the native population, but the young nation was also alarmed by reports of British intrigue among the Indians.[96] In 1817, military forces from the United States entered the Spanish colony with instructions not to attack Spanish settlements. However, under the command of Andrew Jackson, an army of regulars, along with volunteers from Tennessee and a large contingent of Lower Creek allies, sacked two Spanish forts and captured the city of Pensacola.[97] Besides crushing the Seminole, one of Jackson's motives for invading foreign soil was to capture numerous blacks who lived there.[98]

The conclusion of Missall and Missall concerning Jackson's campaign is that it left the once thriving and relatively secure Seminole "destitute and homeless" and "dealt them a blow from which they were never able to recover."[99] The campaign also hastened Spain's desire to sell Florida to the United States.[100] Negotiations for the purchase concluded in 1819.

With passage of the Indian Removal Act by Congress in 1830, the Second Seminole War began in late 1835 as the Seminole and allied tribes like the Miccosukee resisted attempts to force them and their black compatriots and slaves to relocate west and merge with the Creek already in Indian Territory.[101] Although the Battle of Lake Okeechobee was the largest battle of the war, the Seminole for the most part engaged the United States army and navy in minor strikes and skirmishes, making the conflict "the nation's first large-scale guerrilla war"[102] and revealing "a general lack of competence" by senior military officers.[103] By 1842, campaigning had essentially ceased as small bands agreed to removal.[104] Josephy gives four thousand as the number sent west. Describing the conflict from the perspective of the United States, he characterizes it as the "longest, costliest, and least successful Indian war," with military deaths at fifteen hundred and a financial expenditure of between forty and sixty million dollars. Yet, at the end of the war, small groups of Seminole and Miccosukee still held out in "the fastnesses of the Everglades."[105]

The federal government built additional forts to pressure the few remaining Seminole and Miccosukee to leave Florida. The Indian response was to avoid conflict by shunning contact with whites. Legend indicates that the spark igniting the third war commenced when a military survey party in 1855 stumbled upon an abandoned Seminole settlement of Holata Micco, also known as Chief Billy Bowlegs. Supposedly, one or more members of the party destroyed his banana trees. Early the next morning, thirty warriors attacked the sleeping soldiers, killed four, and wounded four.[106]

Lasting until 1858, the third conflict was again primarily a guerrilla war.[107] Over the course of two and a half years, the Indians were "hunted and pursued to exhaustion."[108] Finally persuaded by a delegation of Seminole who had removed west, Billy Bowlegs and his people agreed to emigrate. Missall and Missall estimate that probably 150 refused to leave. The same held true for Sam Jones, or Abiaca, an ancient medicine man of the Miccosukee, and many of the "intractable" members of his tribe.[109]

A little over twenty years after the third war, Major John Wesley Powell, the first director of the Bureau of Ethnology at the Smithsonian Institution, commissioned Clay MacCauley "to inquire into the condition and to ascertain the number of Indians commonly known as the Seminole" who lived in Florida.[110] MacCauley found that the tribe numbered 208 individuals of seven family groups living in five settlements. The distances between these ranged from forty to seventy miles in "an otherwise almost uninhabited region."[111] He also observed that the Seminole were a polygamous society in which more males were born than females, a fact that he thought might impede an increase in their population. MacCauley's overall assessment of the tribe's situation was positive, with his noting that the people were not prone to either intemperance or licentiousness. He further maintained that there were no mixed-breed whites among them because, should an Indian woman produce a half-white child, her punishment was execution by the tribe. MacCauley, however, stated that the Seminole did have mixed-breed members from Indian fathers and black women who had been adopted by the tribe. He surmised that the group's "health, climate, food, and personal habits apparently conduce to an increase in numbers."[112]

Summarizing MacCauley's research, Robert F. Greenlee concluded that the location of the Florida Seminole in the Everglades and Big Cypress Swamp had isolated them from outside influences and brought little change to their way of life since the end of the third war.[113] However, this relative seclusion was "rudely broken" when the Tamiami Trail

Appendix D. Historical Sketches and Commentary

was built through their territory and opened in 1928. It ran from Tampa to Miami. This highway brought white influences that altered customs and folklore such as clan origins.[114]

Time has proven the veracity of MacCauley's prediction that the Seminole population of Florida would likely increase, although figures are inconsistent. Writing for the website *United States Now,* Summer Banks gives the number of Florida Seminole in 2010 as approximately fifteen thousand.[115] A 2022 article titled "Seminole Tribal Extension" from *https://tribalextension.org* indicates that the tribe has around four thousand registered members.[116] Be that as it may, the Seminole Nation of Florida controls some ninety thousand acres of land in Florida and occupies several reservations.[117] Its income derives mainly from tobacco sales, tourism, and the gaming industry, according to Banks.[118]

For the Seminole of Oklahoma, the website *Southern Plains Tribal Health Board* cites a population of around seventeen thousand.[119] This number closely matches the eighteen thousand cited by Banks from 2010 data.[120] Fourteen bands compose this group, two of which are known as Freedmen Bands. Also called the Black Seminole, a significant number of their members trace their ancestry to former slaves.[121]

Regarding the narratives of the Seminole, Greenlee states that "It is difficult to speak of a distinct Seminole mythology and folklore since their tales have recognizable elements common to the entire region of the Southeast."[122] The three Seminole stories that I have retold obviously have obvious parallels with tales of other Southeastern groups.

One selection presented by Greenlee as "Rabbit Lies and Runs Away with Fire"[123] and rendered here as "Rabbit Brings Back Fire" is a variant of the "theft of fire," myth in which the trickster exemplifies heroic qualities to benefit humanity. Readers may want to compare this story to two other variants I have retold: "Rabbit Provides Fire" (Koasati/Coushatta) and "Rabbit Steals Fire from Buzzard" (Catawba).

A second story adapted from Greenlee's collection having salient commonalities with other regional tales is "Rabbit Wants to Marry."[124] The title character must complete several tasks before he wins his bride. One task is to kill Alligator. By shapeshifting into a squirrel, Rabbit tricks Alligator into revealing his vulnerable spot where he can be struck and killed. Similarly, in Swanton's Natchez story "Rabbit and Alligator," Rabbit becomes a seemingly innocent fawn to trick Alligator into giving up his secret.[125] A second strong parallel in the Seminole story is contained in Swanton's Alabama tale "The Orphan."[126] Both selections have the motif of creating two wives through splitting one wife into two by hitting her with a hatchet where her hair is parted in the middle of her head. Readers who want to compare these similarities will find them in my retellings of "Rabbit Wants a Wife" (Seminole), "Rabbit Kills Alligator" (Natchez), and "An Orphan Outdoes Rabbit" (Alabama).

A third Seminole story from Greenlee is untitled.[127] I have retold it under the title "The Thunder Boys Deceive and Kill an Old Woman." This narrative, while not as well developed, has parallels with Mooney's Cherokee tale "Kanati and Selu: The Origin of Corn and Game."[128] In both selections, there are two brothers—one born in the usual manner to his parents and one born from discarded fleshly remains. In Mooney, these remains are from animals that Selu, or Corn, has cleaned by the river's brink. In Greenlee, they are the afterbirth of a naturally born son which his mother has the tossed into the forest. From both sets of remains in the two stories, the younger brother, or the Wild Boy, comes to life and is a rule-breaker, much more mischievous than his older brother. In the Cherokee version, the Wild Boy transforms himself into the soft down of a bird which the wind carries to his father the great hunter Kanati. In this disguise, the Wild Boy secretly learns to make arrows. He and his brother then misuse them to slaughter all the game, thus making their hunter father furious. In the more truncated Seminole myth, the shapeshifting of the Wild Boy amounts to no more than a slight allusion. The Wild Boy simply finds some feathers and blows on them. As they float away, his brother playfully chases them.

Although I have not retold the Cherokee story of "Kanati and Selu" in this collection, readers may find additional similarities to its Seminole counterpart. However, it is clear in the conclusion of the Seminole myth that, as in "Kanati and Selu," the two boys are the sons of Kanati, who is also the "Great Thunderer." According to Mooney, this figure is "the thunder of the whirlwind and the hurricane, who seems to be identical with Kanati himself."[129]

❖ Catawba ❖

Following the Seminole stories are seven retellings of trickster tales from the Catawba. This group traditionally inhabited the Piedmont area of North and South Carolina and was a powerful yet smaller political entity than some of the other native populations of the Southeast. The research of anthropologist Robbie Etheridge suggests that various tribal societies such as the Wisacky, Yssa, Ushery, Catawba, and Sugarees began to unite in the late 1600s along the lower Catawba River in the middle of what is now upstate South Carolina. Their banding together marked the formation of the Catawba and may have been spurred by self-preservation to escape slave raids by the fierce Westo Indians,[130] reputed at the time to be cannibals.[131] In his extensive book on the history of South Carolina, Walter Edgar says the "loose grouping of often unrelated villages and peoples" forced the creation of the Catawba Nation because of outside pressures from indigenous foes and European settlers. In Edgar's assessment, the Catawba "managed to survive" despite "war, disease, trade, settlement, and internal division."[132]

Smallpox was particularly hard on the Catawba. As with other native peoples of the Southeast, the disease drastically reduced their number, perhaps more so than with neighboring groups. In 1760, a virulent outbreak of the contagion decimated the Cherokee by an estimate of one-third. However, the pestilence so ravaged the Catawba that their population, not numerous to begin with, dwindled to no more than five hundred. Edgar reports that this number meant that, since the late 1600s, almost 90 percent had died.[133]

Except for the Yamasee War from 1715 to 1717, the Catawba remained faithful allies to the colony and later state of South Carolina. Yet they became more culturally splintered than their larger neighbors and sometimes enemies, the Creek to their south and the Cherokee to their west and northwest. According to data presented by historian Chapman J. Milling, by the 1830s most of the Catawba were living an impoverished, "wandering life" without fixed lodgings or the means of accumulating the kinds of livestock of hogs, cattle, and chickens they once owned.[134] Underscoring Milling's observation, Charles Hudson's anthropological study from the 1960s, *The Catawba Nation*, concludes that, by the end of the 1800s through the early twentieth century, the Catawba were "steadily losing their culture."[135]

Stated in even stronger terms is Sandra Baringer's more recent assessment that, unlike the Southeast's Five Civilized Tribes of the Cherokee, Creek, Choctaw, Chickasaw, and Seminole, smaller polities of the region like the Catawba "were diminished almost to the point of extinction."[136] In 1840, the number of tribal members in the traditional homeland of the Catawba had shrunk to 88 people, only four of whom were men, the remainder being women and children.[137] Such circumstances account for the fact that fewer of their folktales are preserved than those of surrounding native groups. The stories transcribed from Frank G. Speck's informants in *Catawba Tales* are often highly fragmented.

In 1959 the Bureau of Indian Affairs terminated its recognition of the Catawba as a tribe by the federal government. In 1993, however, both the United States and South Carolina re-established their tribal status. The Catawba have since made a resurgence, with their nation numbering around 3,300, according to the website *https://catawbanation.com/about-the-nation*. Many members of the tribe today live on their federally recognized reservation near the city of Rock Hill, South Carolina.

Only one Catawba tale included here concerns Rabbit ("Rabbit Steals Fire from Buzzard"). An instance of Catawba storytellers refashioning a narrative from non–Indians is "Pig and Wolf," an obvious adaptation of the English folktale "The Three Little Pigs," first collected in 1842 by English Shakespearean scholar and antiquarian James Halliwell-Phillipps[138] and included a few decades later in *English Fairy Tales* of 1898 by folklorist Joseph Jacobs.[139] The story would appear in later editions of each man's work and in other offerings for young children. An interesting facet of the appropriated Catawba version is that, instead of three little pigs, there is only one big pig who is not only a wily deceiver but also a formidable fighter against Wolf.

The Catawba tale "How Rooster Tricked Fox" also resonates with European folktales. *Perotti's Appendix*, a Renaissance manuscript having 32 of Aesop's fables as reputedly retold by the Latin writer Phaedrus, contains "The Ground-Swallow and the Fox" which has the same plot line of a "wicked little fox" attempting to lure a victim out of a tree.[140] The Catawba story is even closer to the Russian fable "The Fox and the Thrush." Not only does the latter have a fox and a bird as his potential prey, but like the rooster in the Catawba tale, the Russian thrush also scares off the fox by pretending to hear approaching hounds.[141]

❖ Cherokee ❖

Trickster tales of the Cherokee are next. As a native population, the Cherokee primarily occupied the mountain regions of what is now western South and North Carolina, eastern Tennessee, northwest Georgia, and the tip of western Virginia. In early colonial times, because of the isolation afforded by the southern Appalachians, particularly the slopes and valleys on the western side of the Eastern Continental Divide,

Cherokee culture was less subject to European influences.[142] However, like the Creek, the Cherokee developed extensive trade with the English colonists and became dependent upon it. Yet, unlike the Creek, the Cherokee were less subject to such colonial powers as the French.

Among much evidence for Cherokee dependence on European goods are incidents recorded by Colonel George Chicken in his 1725 journal which details his second embassy to the Cherokee. Its aim was to establish trade and buttress military alliances between the colony of South Carolina and the Cherokee. The entry for July 18 recounts a speech given by King Crow in the lower Cherokee town of Tomasee. In the council house, King Crow stressed to the assembled English and Cherokee "what a good thing it was to be friends with the English who they would always stand by and bid them to remember what good times it was now to what it hath been before the English came among them."[143]

After various stops at other Cherokee settlements, Chicken arrived at the Overhill town of Tunisee, in other colonial accounts sometimes spelled Tanasee from which Tennessee is a derivative. There, before the people of the town and the Charleston deputation, the Head Warrior extolled the benefits of commerce with the English. He exhorted the assembled Cherokee to "consider that all the old men were gone" and that all the younger people "have been brought up after another manner than their forefathers" so that now "they could not live without the English."[144] Recall that in the same year Captain Fitch expressed similar sentiments on the advantages of trade in the talk he made to Goggle Eyes and the sixty headmen of the Creek. (See page 154.)

Again, as with other Indians of the Southeast, early on there was interaction with English colonists. Indeed, John Henry Logan's history of the South Carolina backcountry prior to the American Revolution reports that a Virginia trader named Daugherty arrived among the Cherokee in 1690 before Charlestonians had learned about them.[145]

Whether through initial dealings with coastal tribes or later commerce with those of the interior like the Creek and Cherokee, the rise of trade, as historian Verner W. Crane states, "produced among the Indians an economic and social revolution." The steadily developing interaction throughout the eighteenth century "bred new habits and ways of living." These, in turn, "bred dependence on the white man."[146]

In the nineteenth century, about eight thousand Cherokee had already settled west of the Mississippi before the Indian Removal Act of 1830. Known as "Old Settlers," these Western Cherokee had gone to Indian Territory and received lands in the northeastern part of the present state of Oklahoma.[147] Like other indigenous populations of the Southeast such as the Creek two years earlier, most of the Cherokee who remained on their traditional lands were forcibly removed in 1838 in what is referred to as the Trail of Tears. One Cherokee group, however, hid in the mountains of western North Carolina to avoid removal and is known today as the Eastern Band of Cherokee Indians. Native informants from this group were the main source for anthropologist James Mooney who in the 1890s collected their folklore.

As with native groups already discussed, adaptation and integration of stories occurred from Cherokee contact with other cultures. One interesting example Mooney cites concerns a migration legend of the Western Cherokee of Oklahoma. Part of the Reverend Daniel Sabin Buttrick's *Antiquities of the Cherokee Indians*, the legend is comingled with the biblical account of Moses and the Israelites. Mooney says that separating the native story from the one in the Bible is "almost impossible."[148] In support of his contention, he gives a detailed comparison between the leadership of great Cherokee prophet Wasi and that of the Old Testament leader Moses.[149]

Notes

Preface

1. Paul Hazard, *Books, Children, and Men*, 5th ed., trans. Marguerite Mitchell (Boston: Horn Book, 1983), 3.

2. George E. Lankford, *Native American Legends of the Southeast: Tales from the Natchez, Caddo, Biloxi, Chickasaw, and Other Nations* (Tuscaloosa: U of AL Press, 1987), 222.

3. C.G. Jung, "On the Psychology of the Trickster Figure," in *The Archetypes and the Collective Unconscious*, 2nd ed., Vol. 9, Part 1, ed. Herbert Read, Michael Fordham, Gerhard Adler, trans. R.F.C. Hull (Princeton, NJ: Princeton UP, 1969), 262.

4. C.G. Jung, "The Fight with the Shadow," in *Civilization in Transition*, 2nd ed., Vol.10, ed. Herbert Read, Michael Fordham, Gerhard Adler, trans. R.F.C. Hull (Princeton, NJ: Princeton UP, 1970), 223.

5. Jung, "The Fight with the Shadow," 219.

6. William J. Hynes and William G. Doty, "Introducing the Fascinating and Perplexing Trickster Figure," in *Mythical Trickster Figures: Contours, Contexts, and Criticisms*, ed. William J. Hynes and William G. Doty (Tuscaloosa: U of AL Press, 1993), 8–9.

7. Charles Hudson, *The Southeastern Indians* (Knoxville: U of TN Press, 2007), 156.

8. James Mooney, *Myths of the Cherokee*, 1900, in *James Mooney's History, Myths and Sacred Formulas of the Cherokees* (Fairview, NC: Historical Images, 1992), 231.

Introduction

1. Daryl Grabarek, "Around the World with Tricksters," *School Library Journal* 1 Dec. 2009, par. 1, https://www.slj.com/story/around-the-world-with-tricksters. Accessed 9 June 2018.

2. Louis Henry Gates, "The Blackness of Blackness: A Critique of the Sign and the Signifying Monkey," in *Literary Theory: An Anthology*, 2nd ed., ed. Julie Rivkin and Michael Ryan (Malden, MA: Blackwell, 2004), 988.

3. Jonathan Brennan, "Introduction: Recognition of the African-Native American Literary Tradition," in *When Brer Rabbit Meets Coyote: African-Native American Literature*, ed. Jonathan Brennan (Urbana and Chicago: U of IL Press, 2003), 53–54.

4. David Elton Gay, "On the Interaction of Traditions: Southeastern Rabbit Tales as African-Native American Folklore," in *When Brer Rabbit Meets Coyote: African-Native American Literature*, ed. Jonathan Brennan (Urbana and Chicago: U of IL Press), 105.

5. Gay, 110–111.

6. Paul Mattick, Jr., "Hotfoots of the Gods," *The New York Times*, 15 Feb. 19, par. 3, https://www.archivenytimes.com. Accessed 15 Oct. 2020.

7. Hynes and Doty, 2.

8. Paul Radin, *The Trickster: A Study in American Indian Mythology* (New York: Schocken, 1972), xxiii.

9. Radin, xxiii.

10. Sheldon Cashdan, *The Witch Must Die: The Hidden Meaning of Fairy Tales* (New York: Basic Books, 1999), 13.

11. Cashdan, 13.

12. Cashdan, 13.

Notes—Introduction

13. Cashdan, 8.

14. Cashdan, 9.

15. David L. Russell, *Literature for Children: A Short Introduction*, 5th ed. (Boston: Pearson, 2005), 156.

16. William J. Hynes, "Mapping the Characteristics of Mythic Tricksters: A Heuristic Guide," in *Mythical Trickster Figures: Contours, Contexts, and Criticisms* ed. William J. Hynes and William G. Doty (Tuscaloosa: U of AL Press, 1993), 35.

17. Mooney, 262.

18. Terrell A. Young and Phyllis M. Ferguson, "From Anansi to Zomo: Trickster Tales in the Classroom," *The Reading Teacher* 48.6 (March 1995): 490.

19. Margaret P. Baker, "The Rabbit as Trickster," *Journal of Popular Culture* 28.2 (Mar. 2004): 149–150.

20. Paul Oppenheimer, *A Pleasant Vintage of Till Eulenspiegel* (Middleton CT: Wesleyan UP, 1972), xvii.

21. Sandra K. Baringer, "Brer Rabbit and His Cherokee Cousins: Moving Beyond the Appropriation Paradigm," in *When Brer Rabbit Meets Coyote: African-Native American Literature*, ed. Jonathan Brennan (Urbana: U of IL Press, 2003), 119.

22. Mac Linscott Ricketts, "The North American Trickster," *History of Religions* 5.2 (Winter 1966): 334–335.

23. Hudson, *The Southeastern Indians*, 145.

24. Hudson, *The Southeastern Indians*, 126.

25. Hynes, 39–40.

26. Hynes, 39–40.

27. Carl G. Jung, et al., *Man and His Symbols* (Garden City, NY: Doubleday, 1964), 112.

28. Jung, *Man and His Symbols*, 113.

29. Jung, *Man and His Symbols*, 113.

30. Lewis Hyde, *Trickster Makes This World: Mischief, Myth, and Art* (New York: Farrar, Straus, and Giroux, 1998), 13, 20, 22–23, 31, 39, 41, 43, 46–47, 51–52, 57, 96–97, 120, 125, 140, 188–191.

31. L. Hyde, 167.

32. Hynes, 42.

33. John R. Swanton, *Myths and Legends of the Southeastern Indians* (Wash-ington, D.C.: Smithsonian Institution, Bureau of American Ethnology, Bulletin 88, 1929), 57.

34. Baker, 153.

35. Baker, 154–155.

36. Hudson, *The Southeastern Indians*, 500.

37. Eugene Current-Garcia and Dorothy B. Hatfield, eds. *Shem, Ham, and Japheth: The Papers of W.O. Tuggle* (Athens: U of GA Press, 1973), 89.

38. Hudson, *The Southeastern Indians*, 201.

39. Hudson, *The Southeastern Indians*, 201.

40. Margaret Atwood. Rev. of Lewis Hyde's *The Gift* and *Trickster Makes This World*, *Los Angeles Times* 25 Jan. 1998, par. 1, https://www.latimes.com/archives/la-xpm-1998-jan-25-bk-11790. Accessed 3 Apr. 2022.

41. L. Hyde, 335.

42. L. Hyde, 335–336.

43. L. Hyde, 335.

44. L. Hyde, 337–338.

45. L. Hyde, 338.

46. Marilyn Jurich, *Scherherazade's Sisters: Trickster Heroines and Their Stories in World Literature* (Westport, CT: Greenwood, 1998), 29.

47. Jurich, 29.

48. Jurich, xvii.

49. Jurich, 3.

50. Jurich, 3.

51. Jurich, 198.

52. Jurich, 199 *ff.*

53. Jurich, 201.

54. Hudson, *The Southeastern Indians*, 186.

55. L. Hyde, 339.

56. Margaret A. Mills, "The Gender of the Trick: Female Tricksters and Male Narrators," *Asian Folklore Studies* 60 (2001): 238.

57. Mills, 238–239.

58. Mills, 239.

59. John Minton, "Trickster," in *Encyclopedia of Folklore and Literature*, ed. Mary Ellen Brown and Bruce A. Rosenberg (Denver, CO: ABC-CLIO, 1998), 663.

60. Julius Lester, *More Tales of Uncle Remus: Further Adventures of Brer*

178

Rabbit, His Friends, Enemies, and Others (New York: Dial, 1988), ix.

61. Jung, "On the Psychology of the Trickster Figure," 269–270.

62. Jung, "On the Psychology of the Trickster Figure," 269–270.

Appendix A

1. Rebecca Lukens, *A Critical Handbook of Children's Literature* 8th ed. (Boston: Pearson, 2007), 23.

2. Baringer, 120.

3. Ruth Sawyer, *The Way of the Storyteller*, 1942 (New York: Viking, 1962), 59.

4. Margaret Read MacDonald, *Twenty Tellable Tales: Audience Participation Folktales for the Beginning Storyteller* (New York: H.W. Wilson, 1986), 192.

5. MacDonald, *Twenty Tellable Tales*, 193.

6. Margaret Read MacDonald, *The Storyteller's Start-Up Book: Finding, Learning, Performing, and Using Folktales* (Little Rock, AR: August House, 1993), 11.

7. Barbara Kiefer, *Charlotte Huck's Children's Literature* 9th ed. (Boston: McGraw Hill, 2007), 278.

8. Michael D. Green, "Alexander McGillivray," in *American Indian Leaders: Studies in Diversity*, ed. R. David Edmunds (Lincoln: U of NE Press, 1980), 43.

9. Green, 43.

10. Dorothy Hatfield and Eugene Current-Garcia, "William Orrie Tuggle and the Creek Indian Folk Tales," *Southern Folklore Quarterly* 25.4 (Dec. 1961): 246.

11. Hatfield and Current-Garcia, "William Orrie Tuggle and the Creek Indian Folk Tales," 254.

12. Current-Garcia and Hatfield, *Shem, Ham, and Japheth*, 115–116, 161.

13. Current-Garcia and Hatfield, *Shem, Ham, and Japheth*, 163.

14. Robert F. Greenlee, "Folktales of the Florida Seminole," *The Journal of American Folklore* 52:228 (Apr.-June 1945): 138–139.

15. Frank G. Speck, *Catawba Texts* (New York: Columbia UP, 1934), xiv.

16. F.G. Speck and L.G. Carr, "Catawba Folk Tales from Chief Sam Blue," *Journal of American Folklore* 60.235 (Jan.–Mar. 1947): 79.

17. Mooney, 236.

18. Mooney, 237.

19. Richard T. Vacca, Jo Anne L. Vacca, and Maryann Mraz, *Content Area Reading: Literacy and Learning Across the Curriculum* 10th ed. (Boston: Pearson, 2011), 113.

20. Norma J. Livo and Sandra A. Rietz, *Storytelling: Process and Practice* (Littleton, CO: Libraries Unlimited, 1986), 97.

21. Jayanta Kar Sharma, "Oral Storytelling and Its Techniques," *International Journal of English Language, Literature, and Humanities* 4.2 (Feb. 2006): 273.

22. Marjorie Y. Lipson and Karen K. Wixson, *Assessment and Instruction of Reading and Writing Difficulties: An Interactive Approach* 4th ed. (Boston: Pearson, 2009), 40–41.

23. John Dryden, "Preface to the Translation of Ovid's Epistles," in *Essays of John Dryden*, ed. W.P. Ker (Oxford: Clarendon Press, 1900), 237 and 243.

24. Robert Graves, trans., *The Transformations of Lucius Otherwise Known as The Golden Ass*, 1951 (New York: Farrar, Straus, and Giroux, 1967), xi.

25. Betty Rose Nagle, trans., *Ovid's Fasti: Roman Holidays* (Bloomington: Indiana UP, 1995), 31–32.

26. Mooney, 278.

27. Mooney, 452.

28. Mooney, 524.

29. Anne Pellowski, *The World of Storytelling* (New York: Bowker, 1977), 108–109.

30. Alberto Manguel, *A History of Reading* (New York: Penguin, 1996), 48.

31. Gay, 103.

32. Swanton, *Myths and Tales of the Southeastern Indians*, 108.

33. Swanton, *Myths and Tales of the Southeastern Indians*, 114.

34. Pellowski, 110.

35. Pellowski, 110.

36. "Charles Lanman," in *Appletons' Cyclopedia of American Biography*, Vol. 3, ed. James Wilson Grant and John Fiske

(New York: Appleton and Company, 1887), 614.

37. Charles Lanman, *Letters from the Alleghany Mountains* (New York: Putnam, 1849), 120.

Appendix B

1. Donna E. Norton, *Multicultural Children's Literature: Through the Eyes of Many Children*, 3rd ed. (Boston: Pearson, 2009), 82.

2. Matt Dembicki, ed. *Trickster: Native American Tales: A Graphic Collection* (Golden, CO: Fulcrum Books, 2010), 225.

3. Norton, 82.

4. Mary J. Lass-Woodfin, ed. *Books on American Indians and Eskimos: A Selection Guide for Children and Young Adults* (Chicago: American Library Association, 1978), 4.

5. Robert J. Conley, Foreword in *Friends of Thunder: Folktales of the Oklahoma Cherokee*, 1964 (Norman: U of OK Press, 1995), xii.

6. Greenlee, 142–143.

7. Lass-Woodfin, 4.

8. Lukens, 24.

9. MacDonald, *The Storyteller's Start-Up Book*, 92.

Appendix C

1. Frank Fureli, "The Mainstreaming of Porn," *Spiked*, 6 July 2018, par. 1. https://www.spiked-online.com/2018/07/06/the-mainstreaming-of-porn. Accessed 20 June 2022.

2. Fureli, par. 14.

3. Neil Postman, *The Disappearance of Childhood* (New York: Delacorte, 1982), 124–125.

4. Joshua Meyrowitz, *No Sense of Place: The Impact of Electronic Media on Social Behavior* (New York: Oxford UP, 1985), 5–7.

5. Susanne Paasonen, "Pornification and the Mainstreaming of Sex," *Criminology and Social Justice, Oxford Research Encyclopedia*, 26 Oct. 2016, pars. 4 and 5. https://doi.org/10.1093/acrefore/9780190264079.013.159. Accessed 20 June 2022.

6. Paul S. Boyer, *Purity in Print: Book Censorship in America from the Gilded Age to the Computer Age*, 2nd ed. (Madison: U of WI Press, 2002), 16.

7. Boyer, 16.

8. Boyer, 20.

9. Devin Leonard, *Neither Rain nor Snow: A History of the United States Postal Service* (New York: Grove Press, 2016), 63–64.

10. Leonard, 53.

11. Leonard, 54–56.

12. D.M. Bennett, *Anthony Comstock and His Career of Cruelty and Crime: A Chapter from Champions of the Church* (New York: Liberal and Scientific Publishing House, 1878), 1014.

13. Bennett, 1010.

14. qtd. in Bennett, 1015.

15. Kenneth L. Donelson and Alleen Pace Nilsen, *Literature for Today's Young Adults*, 7th ed. (Boston: Pearson, 2005), 365.

16. Emily Taft Douglas, *Margaret Sanger: Pioneer of the Future* (Garrett Park, MD: Garrett Park Press, 1975), 50.

17. Douglas, 52.

18. Douglas, 55–56.

19. Douglas, 57.

20. Walter Kendrick, *The Hidden Museum: Pornography in Modern Culture* (Berkeley: U of CA Press, 1996), 155.

21. Kendrick, 6.

22. Kendrick, 6–7.

23. Kendrick, 7.

24. Kendrick, 11.

25. Kendrick, 2 and 11.

26. Kendrick, 15–17.

27. Giovanni Boccaccio, *Decameron*, rev. ed., trans. John Payne, ed. Charles S. Singleton (Berkeley: U of CA Press, 1982), 277.

28. Boccaccio, 279.

29. Boccaccio, 279.

30. Boccaccio, 279.

31. Boccaccio, 281.

32. H. Montgomery Hyde, *A History of Pornography*, 1964 (New York: Dell, 1966), 79.

33. Kendrick, 67.

34. Kendrick, 163.

35. Kendrick, 162.
36. Kendrick, 162.
37. Donelson and Nilsen, 376.
38. *qtd. in* H.M. Hyde, 182.
39. H.M. Hyde, 183.
40. H.M. Hyde, 182.
41. Kendrick, 92.
42. Kendrick, 123.
43. Kendrick, 142–143.
44. Leonard, 63.
45. *qtd. in* Boyer, 29.
46. H.M. Hyde, 183.
47. *qtd. in* Donelson and Nilsen, 379.

Appendix D

1. John R. Swanton, *Indian Tribes of North America* (Washington, D.C.: Smithsonian Institution, Bureau of American Ethnology, Bulletin 145), 107–108.

2. Verner W. Crane, "The Origin of the Name of the Creek Indians," *The Mississippi Valley Historical Review* 5.3 (Dec. 1918): 339 and 342.

3. Alan Gallay, *The Indian Slave Trade: The Rise of the English Empire in the American South, 1670–1717* (New Haven: Yale UP, 2002), 12.

4. Claudio Stuart, "Creek Indians," in *New Georgia Encyclopedia* 2 Feb. 2022, pars. 1,7, and 8. https://www.georgia encyclopedia.org. Accessed 8 Aug. 2002.

5. M. Eugene Sirmans, *Colonial South Carolina: A Political History, 1663–1763* (Chapel Hill: U of NC Press, 1966), 152, n62.

6. Tobias Fitch, *Journal of Captain Tobias Fitch's Mission from Charleston, S.C., to the Creeks, 1726* [1725] in *Travels in the American Colonies*, ed. Newton D. Mereness (New York: Macmillan, 1916), 179–180.

7. Fitch, 181.
8. Fitch, 187.
9. Fitch, 186.
10. Fitch, 210–211.
11. Fitch, 188–189.
12. Fitch, 199–200.
13. Swanton, *Myths and Tales of the Southeastern Indians*, 85.
14. Swanton, *Myths and Tales of the Southeastern Indians*, 53–55.

15. Mooney, 270–271 and 450.

16. Robbie Ethridge, *From Chicaza to Chickasaw: The European Invasion and the Transformation of the Mississippian World, 1540–1715* (Chapel Hill: U of NC Press, 2010), 74.

17. Gallay, 139–140.

18. Swanton, *Indian Tribes of North America*, 131.

19. Swanton, *Indian Tribes of North America*, 111.

20. Ethridge, 286.

21. Swanton, *Indian Tribes of North America*, 111.

22. Ethridge, 244.

23. "Hitchiti," *Peach State Archaeological Society*, 2022, par. 2. http://www.peachstatearchaeologicalsociety.org/index.php/11-culture-culture-historic/249-hitchiti-indians. Accessed 6 May 2022.

24. "Hitchiti," par. 7.

25. Angie Debo, *The Road to Disappearance: A History of the Creek Indians* (Norman: U of OK Press, 1941), 103.

26. Debo, 332–334.

27. "Miccosukee Tribe of Indians of Florida," *Office of Environmental Management, Federal Department of Transportation*, n.d., par. 1, https://www.fdot.gov/environmental/na-websitefiles/miccosukee.shtm#. Accessed 8 July 2022.

28. "Hitchiti," par. 7.

29. Ethridge, 2.

30. Jonathan B. Hook, *The Alabama-Coushatta Indians* (College Station: Texas A&M UP, 1997), 20.

31. Alvin M. Josephy, Jr., *500 Nations: An Illustrated History of North American Indians* (New York: Gramercy Books, 1995), 142.

32. Josephy, 153.

33. Sherie Marie Shuck-Hall, *Journey to the West: The Alabama-Coushatta Indians* (Norman: U of OK Press, 2008), 14–16.

34. Shuck-Hall, *Journey to the West*, 36–37.

35. Howard N. Martin, "Alabama-Coushatta Indians," *Texas State Historical Association*, 29 Sept. 2020, par. 1, https://tsha.org/handbook/entries/alabama-coushatta-indians. Accessed 5 May 2022.

36. Shuck-Hall, *Journey to the West,* 53.
37. Roger L. Nichols, *Indians in the United States and Canada: A Comparative History* (Lincoln: U of NE Press, 1998), 104.
38. Hook, 23.
39. Shuck-Hall, *Journey to the West,* 56.
40. Sherie Marie Shuck-Hall, "Alabama-Coushatta in Alabama," *Encyclopedia of Alabama,* 19 Jan. 2017, par. 9, https://encyclopediaofalabama.org/h-2352. Accessed 5 May 2022.
41. Hook, 28–29.
42. Martin, par. 7.
43. Martin, par. 8.
44. Shuck-Hall, *Journey to the West,* 142.
45. Hook, 30–31.
46. Shuck-Hall, *Journey to the West,* 142.
47. Martin, par. 13.
48. Hook, 32.
49. Shuck-Hall, *Journey to the West,* 187–188.
50. Shuck-Hall, *Journey to the West,* 188.
51. Hook, 32.
52. Shuck-Hall, *Journey to the West,* 189.
53. "Our History," *Alabama-Coushatta Tribe of Texas,* n. d., par. 2, https://www.alabama-coushatta.com/about-us-our-history. Accessed 8 July 2022.
54. Martin, par 1.
55. "Natchez," *Encyclopaedia Britannica Online,* 4 July 2019, par. 1, https://www.britannanica.com/topic/Natchez-people. Accessed 15 June 2022.
56. Hudson, *The Southeastern Indians,* 86.
57. Hudson, *The Southeastern Indians,* 86.
58. Hudson, *The Southeastern Indians,* 205.
59. Hudson, *The Southeastern Indians,* 206.
60. Hudson, *The Southeastern Indians,* 206.
61. Hudson, *The Southeastern Indians,* 207.
62. Hudson, *The Southeastern Indians,* 206–207.
63. Hudson, *The Southeastern Indians,* 209.
64. Hudson, *The Southeastern Indians,* 205.
65. "Natchez," par. 4.
66. Hudson, *The Southeastern Indians,* 210.
67. Nichols, 104.
68. Nichols, 104.
69. Hudson, *The Southeastern Indians,* 210.
70. Nichols, 104–105.
71. Nichols, 105–106.
72. Christopher Waldrep, "French-Natchez War," *Mississippi Encyclopedia,* 14 April 2018, par. 4, https://mississippiencyclopedia.org.entries/french-natchez-war/. Accessed 16 May 2022.
73. Nichols, 106.
74. James Adair, *The History of the American Indians,* 1775, ed. Kathryn E. Holland Braund (Tuscaloosa: U of AL Press, 2005), 355–356.
75. Adair, 356.
76. Hudson, *The Southeastern Indians,* 122.
77. Mooney, 234–235.
78. Swanton, *Myths and Tales of the Southeastern Indians,* 267–275.
79. Swanton, *Myths and Tales of the Southeastern Indians,* 1.
80. Adam Wasserman, *A People's History of Florida, 1513–1876: How Africans, Seminoles, and Lower Class Whites Shaped the Sunshine State,* 4th ed. (N. p.: n. p., 2010), 114.
81. Wasserman, 85.
82. Wasserman, 90 and 101.
83. Wasserman. 114.
84. Wasserman, 110 and 114.
85. Wasserman, 114.
86. "Oconee Tribe," *Peach State Archaeological Society,* 2022, par. 6, https://peachstatearchaelogicalsociety.org/index.php/11-culture-history/315-oconee-indians. Accessed 16 June 2022.
87. Hudson, *The Southeastern Indians,* 5 and 464.
88. Hudson, *The Southeastern Indians,* 464–465.
89. Hudson, *The Southeastern Indians,* 465.

90. Hudson, *The Southeastern Indians*, 465.

91. Hudson, *The Southeastern Indians*, 466.

92. Hudson, *The Southeastern Indians*, 465.

93. Josephy, 319.

94. John Missall and Mary Lou Missall, *The Seminole Wars: America's Longest Indian Conflict* (Gainesville: U of FL Press, 2004), 180.

95. Missall and Missall, 179–180.

96. Missall and Missall, 33–35.

97. Missall and Missall, 41–43.

98. Missall and Missall, 41.

99. Missall and Missall, 50.

100. Missall and Missall, 51.

101. Hudson, *The Southeastern Indians*, 466.

102. Missall and Missall, 125.

103. Nichols, 183.

104. Nichols, 183.

105. Josephy, 320.

106. Missall and Missall, 213.

107. Missall and Missall, 216.

108. Missall and Missall, 221.

109. Missall and Missall, 221.

110. Clay MacCauley, *The Seminole Indians of Florida: Fifth Annual Report* (Washington, D.C.: Smithsonian Institution, Bureau of Ethnology, 1887), 478.

111. MacCauley, 477–478.

112. MacCauley, 479–480.

113. Greenlee, 130.

114. Greenlee, 141.

115. Summer Banks, "Who Are the Seminole Indians?" *United States Now*, 22 June 2022, par. 4, https://www.united statesnow.org/who-are-the-seminole-indians.htm#. Accessed 9 July 2022.

116. "Seminole Tribal Extension," 2022, par. 1, https://tribalextension.org/project/seminole. Accessed 16 June 2022.

117. "Seminole Tribal Extension," par. 1.

118. Banks, par. 4.

119. "Seminole Nation of Oklahoma," *Southern Plains Tribal Health Board*, 10 April 2017, par. 6, https://spthb.org/about-us/who-we-serve/seminole-nation-of-oklahoma. Accessed 16 June 2022.

120. Banks, par. 4.

121. Banks, par. 5.

122. Greenlee, 140.

123. Greenlee, 143.

124. Greenlee, 144.

125. Swanton, *Myths and Tales of the Southeastern Indians*, 255–256.

126. Swanton, *Myths and Tales of the Southeastern Indians*, 136–138.

127. Greenlee, 142–143.

128. Mooney, 242–249.

129. Mooney, 435.

130. Ethridge, 106.

131. Chapman Milling, *Red Carolinians* (Columbia: U of SC Press, 1969), 39 and 83.

132. Walter Edgar, *South Carolina: A History* (Columbia: U of SC Press, 1998), 14–15.

133. Edgar, 157–158.

134. Milling, 256.

135. Charles Hudson, *The Catawba Nation* (Athens: U of GA Press, 1970), 77.

136. Baringer, 121.

137. Louise Pettus and Ron Chepesiuk, "The Nation Ford Treaty," in *The Palmetto State: Stories from the Making of South Carolina* (Orangeburg, SC: Sandlapper Publishing, 1991), 157.

138. James Orchard Halliwell [-Phillips], ed., "The Story of the Three Little Pigs, in *The Nursery Rhymes of England*, 5th ed., illus. W.B. Scott (Frederick Warne, 1886), 36–41.

139. Joseph Jacobs, ed. "The Story of the Three Little Pigs," in *English Fairy Tales*, 3rd rev. ed., illus. David D. Batten (London: David Nutt, 1898), 68–72.

140. Ben Edwin Perry, ed. and trans., "The Ground-Swallow and the Fox," in *Babrius and Phaedrus* (Cambridge, MA: Harvard UP, 1965), 415–417.

141. Mirra Ginsburg, ed. and trans., "The Thrush and the Fox," in *Three Rolls and One Doughnut: Fables from Russia*, illus. Anita Lobel (New York: Dial, 1970), 48.

142. Gallay, 15.

143. George Chicken, *Journal of Colonel George Chicken's Mission from Charleston, S.C., to the Cherokees, 1726* [1725] in *Travels in the American Colonies*, ed. Newton D. Mereness (New York: Macmillan, 1916), 108.

144. Chicken, 112–113.

145. John Henry Logan, *A History of*

the Upper Country of South Carolina from the Earliest Periods to the Close of the War of Independence (Charleston, SC: S.G.G. Courtenay; Columbia, SC: P.B. Glass, 1859), 168.

146. Verner W. Crane, *The Southern Frontier, 1670–1732* (Durham, NC: Duke UP, 1928), 116.

147. Gerard Reed, "Post Removal Factionalism in the Cherokee Nation," in *The Cherokee Nation: A Troubled History*, ed. Duane H. King (Knoxville: U of TN Press, 1979), 150.

148. Mooney, 231.

149. Mooney 428–429.

Bibliography

Adair, James. *The History of the American Indians*. 1775. Ed. Kathryn E. Holland Braund. Tuscaloosa: U of AL Press, 2005.

Atwood, Margaret. Review of Lewis Hyde's *The Gift* and *Trickster Makes This World*. *Los Angeles Times*, 25 Jan. 1998, https://www.latimes.com/archives/la-xpm-1998-jan.-25-bk-11790-story.html. Accessed 3 Apr. 2022.

Baker, Margaret P. "The Rabbit as Trickster." *The Journal of Popular Culture* 28.2 (Mar. 2004): 149–158.

Banks, Summer. "Who Are the Seminole Indians?" *United States Now*, 22 June 2022, https://www.unitedstatesnow.org/who-are-the-seminole-indians.htm#. Accessed 9 July 2022.

Baringer, Sandra. "Brer Rabbit and His Cherokee Cousin: Moving Beyond the Appropriation Paradigm." In *When Brer Rabbit Meets Coyote: African-Native American Literature*. Ed. Jonathan Brennan. Urbana: U of IL Press, 2003. 114–138.

Bennett, D.M. *Anthony Comstock and His Career of Cruelty and Crime: A Chapter from The Champions of the Church*. New York: Liberal and Scientific Publishing House, 1878.

Boccaccio, Giovanni. *Decameron*. Rev. ed. Trans. John Payne. Ed. Charles S. Singleton. Berkeley: U of CA Press, 1982.

Boyer, Paul S. *Purity in Print: Book Censorship in America from the Gilded Age to the Computer Age*. 2nd ed. Madison: U of WI Press, 2002.

Brennan, Jonathan. "Introduction: Recognition of the African-Native American Literary Tradition." In *When Brer Rabbit Meets Coyote: African-Native American Literature*. Ed. Jonathan Brennan. Urbana: U of IL Press, 2003. 1–97.

Cashdan, Sheldon. *The Witch Must Die: The Hidden Meaning of Fairy Tales*. New York: Basic Books, 1999.

"Charles Lanman." In *Appletons' Cyclopaedia of American Biography*. Vol. 3. Ed. James Wilson Grant and John Fiske. New York: Appleton and Company, 1887. 614.

Chicken, George. *Journal of Colonel George Chicken's Mission from Charleston, S.C., to the Cherokees, 1726* [1725]. In *Travels in the American Colonies*. Ed. Newton D. Mereness. New York: Macmillan, 1916. 93–172.

Conley, Robert J. Foreword. In *Friends of Thunder: Folktales of the Oklahoma Cherokees*. 1964. By Jack F. Kilpatrick and Anna G. Kilpatrick. Norman: U of OK Press, 1995.

Crane, Verner W. "The Origin of the Name of the Creek Indians." *The Mississippi Valley Historical Review* 5.3 (Dec. 1918): 339–342.

_____. *The Southern Frontier, 1670–1732*. Durham, NC: Duke UP, 1928.

Current-Garcia, Eugene, and Dorothy B. Hatfield, eds. *Shem, Ham, Japheth: The Papers of W.O. Tuggle*. Athens: U of GA Press, 1973.

Debo, Angie. *The Road to Disappearance: A History of the Creek Indians*. Norman: U of OK Press, 1941.

Dembicki, Matt, ed. *Trickster: Native American Tales, A Graphic Collection*. Golden, CO: Fulcrum Books, 2010.

Donelson, Kenneth L., and Alleen Pace

Bibliography

Nilsen. *Literature for Today's Young Adults.* 7th ed. Boston: Pearson, 2005.

Douglas, Emily Taft. *Margaret Sanger: Pioneer of the Future.* Garrett Park, MD: Garrett Park Press, 1975.

Dryden, John. "Preface to the Translation of Ovid's Epistles." In *Essays of John Dryden.* Ed. W.P. Ker. Vol. 1. Oxford: Clarendon Press, 1900. 230–243.

Edgar, Walter. *South Carolina: A History.* Columbia: U of SC Press, 1998.

Ethridge, Robbie. *From Chicaza to Chickasaw: The European Invasion and the Transformation of the Mississippian World, 1540–1715.* Chapel Hill: U of NC Press, 2010.

Fitch, Tobias. *Journal of Captain Tobias Fitch's Mission from Charleston to the Creeks, 1726* [1725]. In *Travels in the American Colonies.* Ed. Newton D. Mereness. New York: Macmillan, 1916. 173–212.

Fureli, Frank. "The Mainstreaming of Porn." *Spiked,* 6 July 2018, https://www.spiked-online.com/2018/07/06/the-mainstreaming-of-porn. Accessed 20 June 2022.

Gallay, Alan. *The Indian Slave Trade: The Rise of the English Empire in the American South, 1670–1717.* New Haven: Yale UP, 2002.

Gates, Louis Henry. "The Blackness of Blackness: A Critique of the Sign and the Signifying Monkey." In *Literary Theory: An Anthology.* 2nd ed. Ed. Julie Rivkin and Michael Ryan. Malden, MA: Blackwell, 2004. 987–1004.

Gay, David Elton. "On the Interaction of Traditions: Southeastern Rabbit Tales as African-Native American Folklore" In *When Brer Rabbit Meets Coyote: African-Native American Literature.* Ed. Jonathan Brennan. Urbana: U of IL Press, 2003. 101–113.

Ginsburg, Mirra. "The Fox and the Thrush." In *Three Rolls and One Doughnut: Fables from Russia.* Illus. Anita Lobel. New York: Dial, 1970. 48.

Gouge, Earnest. *Totkv Mocvse/New Fire: Creek Folktales of Earnest Gouge.* Trans. and ed. Jack B. Martin, Margaret McKane Mauldin, and Juanita McGirt. Norman: U of OK Press, 2004.

Grabarek, Daryl. "Around the World with Tricksters." *School Library Journal,* 1 Dec. 2009, https://slj.com/story/around-the-world-with-tricksters. Accessed 9 June 2018.

Graves, Robert, trans. *The Transformations of Lucius Otherwise Known as The Golden Ass.* 1951; rpt. New York: Farrar, Straus, and Giroux, 1967.

Green, Michael D. "Alexander McGillivray." In *American Indian Leaders: Studies in Diversity.* Ed. R. David Edmunds. Lincoln: U of NE Press, 1980.

Greenlee, Robert F. "Folktales of the Florida Seminole." *The Journal of American Folklore* 58.228 (Apr.-Jun. 1945): 138–145.

Hatfield, Dorothy, and Eugene Current-Garcia. "William Orrie Tuggle and the Creek Indian Folk Tales." *Southern Folklore Quarterly* 25.4 (Dec. 1961): 238–255.

"Havelock Ellis." *Encyclopaedia Britannica Online,* 29 Jan. 2022, https://www.britannica.com/biography/Havelock-Ellis. Web. 30 June 2022.

Hazard, Paul. *Books, Children, and Men.* 5th ed. Trans. Marguerite Mitchell. Boston: Horn Book, 1983.

"Hitchiti." *Peach State Archaeological Society.* 2022, http://www.peachstate archaeologicalsociety.org/index.php/11-culture-culture-historic/249-hitchiti-indians. Accessed 6 May 2022.

Hook, Jonathan B. *The Alabama-Coushatta Indians.* College Station: Texas A&M UP, 1997.

Hudson, Charles. *The Catawba Nation.* Athens: U of GA Press, 1970.

_____. *The Southeastern Indians.* Knoxville: U of TN Press, 2007.

Hyde, H. Montgomery. *A History of Pornography.* 1964. New York: Dell, 1966.

Hyde, Lewis. *Trickster Makes This World: Mischief, Myth, and Art.* New York: Farrar, Straus, and Giroux, 1998.

Hynes, William J. "Mapping the Characteristics of Mythic Tricksters: A Heuristic Approach." In *Mythical Trickster Figures: Contours, Contexts, and Criticisms.* Tuscaloosa: U of AL Press, 1993. 34–45.

_____, and William G. Doty. "Introducing

Bibliography

the Fascinating and Perplexing Trickster Figure." In *Mythical Trickster Figures: Contours, Contexts, and Criticisms.* Tuscaloosa: U of AL Press, 1993. 1–12.

Josephy, Alvin M., Jr. *500 Nations: An Illustrated History of North American Indians.* New York: Gramercy Books, 1995.

Jung, Carl G., "The Fight with the Shadow." In *Civilization in Transition.* 2nd ed. Vol. 10. Ed. Herbert Read, Michael Fordham, Gerhard Adler. Trans. R.F.C. Hull. Princeton, NJ: Princeton UP, 1970. 218–226.

_____. et al. *Man and His Symbols.* Garden City, NY: Doubleday, 1964.

_____. "On the Psychology of the Trickster Figure." In *The Archetypes and the Collective Unconscious.* 2nd ed. Vol. 9. Part 1. Ed. Herbert Read, Michael Fordham, and Gerhard Adler. Trans. R.F.C. Hull. Princeton. NJ: Princeton UP, 1969. 255–272.

Jurich, Marilyn. *Scheherazade's Sisters: Trickster Heroines and Their Stories in World Literature.* Westport, CT: Greenwood Press, 1998.

Kendrick, Walter. *The Secret Museum: Pornography in Modern Culture.* Berkeley: U of CA Press, 1996.

Kiefer, Barbara. *Charlotte Huck's Children's Literature.* 9th ed. Boston: McGraw-Hill, 2007.

Lankford, George E. *Native American Legends of the Southeast: Tales from the Natchez, Caddo, Biloxi, Chickasaw, and Other Nations.* Tuscaloosa: U of AL Press, 1987.

Lanman, Charles. *Letters from the Alleghany Mountains.* New York: Putnam, 1849.

Lanz, C.K. "What Is the Miccosukee Tribe?" *United States Now,* 7 May 2022, https://unitedstatesnow.org/what-is-the-miccosukee-tribe.htm. Accessed 27 May 2022.

Lass-Woodfin, Mary J., ed. *Books on American Indians and Eskimos: A Selection Guide for Children and Young Adults.* Chicago: American Library Association, 1978.

Leonard, Devin. *Neither Snow nor Rain:* *A History of the United States Postal Service.* New York: Grove Press, 2016.

Lester, Julius. *More Tales of Uncle Remus: Further Adventures of Brer Rabbit, His Friends, Enemies, and Others.* New York: Dial, 1988.

Lipson, Marjorie Y., and Karen K. Wixson. *Assessment and Instruction of Reading and Writing Difficulties: An Interactive Approach.* 4th ed. Boston: Pearson, 2009.

Livo, Norma J., and Sandra A Rietz. *Storytelling: Process and Practice.* Littleton, CO: Libraries Unlimited, 1986.

Logan, John Henry. *A History of the Upper Country of South Carolina from the Earliest Periods to the Close of the War of Independence.* Charleston, SC: S.G. Courtenay; Columbia, SC: P.B. Glass, 1859.

Lukens, Rebecca. *A Critical Handbook of Children's Literature.* 8th ed. Boston: Pearson, 2007.

MacCauley, Clay. *The Seminole Indians of Florida: Fifth Annual Report.* Washington, D.C.: Smithsonian Institution, Bureau of Ethnology, 1887.

MacDonald, Margaret Read. *The Storyteller's Start-Up Book: Finding, Learning, Performing, and Using Folktales.* Little Rock, AR: August House, 1993.

_____. *Twenty Tellable Tales: Audience Participation Folktales for the Beginning Storyteller.* New York: H.W. Wilson, 1986.

Manguel, Alberto. *A History of Reading.* New York: Penguin, 1996.

Martin, Howard N. "Alabama-Coushatta Indians." *Texas State Historical Association,* 29 Sept. 2020, http://tsha.org/handbook/entries/alabama-coushatta-indians. Accessed 27 May 2022.

Mattick, Paul, Jr. "Hotfoots of the Gods." *The New York Times,* 15 Feb. 1998, https://www.nytimes.com1998.02.15/books.hotfoots-of-the-gods. Accessed 15 Oct. 2021.

Meyrowitz, Joshua. *No Sense of Place: The Impact of Electronic Media on Social Behavior.* New York: Oxford UP, 1985.

"Miccosukee Tribe of Indians of Florida," *Office of Environmental Management, Federal Department of Trans-*

Bibliography

portation, n.d., https://www.fdot. gov/environmental/ne-websitefiles/ miccosukee.shtm#. Accessed 8 July 2022.

Milling, Chapman J. *Red Carolinians*. Columbia: U of SC Press, 1969.

Mills, Margaret A. "The Gender of the Trick: Female Tricksters and Male Narrators." *Asian Folklore Studies* 60 (2001): 237–258.

Minton, John. "Trickster." In *Encyclopedia of Folklore and Literature*. Ed. Mary Ellen Brown and Bruce A. Rosenberg. Denver, CO: ABC-CLIO, 1998. 662–666.

Missall, John, and Mary Lou Missall. *The Seminole Wars: America's Longest Indian Conflict*. Gainesville: U of FL Press, 2004.

Mooney, James. *Myths of the Cherokee*. 1900. In *James Mooney's History, Myths, and Sacred Formulas of the Cherokees*, 2–576. Fairview, NC: Historical Images, 1992.

Nagle, Betty Rose, trans. *Ovid's Fasti: Roman Holidays*. Bloomington: Indiana UP, 1995.

"Natchez." *Encyclopedia Britannica Online*, 4 July 2019, https://www. britannica.com/topic/Natchez-people. Accessed 11 May 2022.

Nichols, Roger L. *Indians in the United States and Canada: A Comparative History*. Lincoln: U of NE Press, 1998.

Norton, Donna E. *Multicultural Children's Literature: Through the Eyes of Many Children*. 3rd ed. Boston: Pearson, 2009.

"Oconee Tribe." *Peach State Archaeological Society*, 2022, https://peachstate archaeologicalsociety.org/index. php/11-culture-history/315-oconeeindians. Accessed 16 June 2022.

Oppenheimer, Paul, trans. *A Pleasant Vintage of Till Eulenspiegel*. Middleton, CT: Wesleyan UP, 1973.

"Our History." *Alabama-Coushatta Tribe of Texas*, n.d., https://www.alabamacoushatta.com/about-us-our-history. Accessed 6 June 2022.

Paasonen, Susanne. "Pornification and the Mainstreaming of Sex." *Criminology and Social Justice. Oxford Research*

Encyclopedias, 26 Oct. 2016, https:// Doi.org/10.1093/acrefore/9780190264 079.013.159. Accessed 20 June 2022.

Pellowski, Anne. *The World of Storytelling*. New York: Bowker, 1977.

Perry, Ben Edwin, ed. and trans. "The Ground-Swallow and the Fox." In *Babrius and Phaedrus*. Cambridge, MA: Harvard UP, 1965. 415–417.

Postman, Neil. *The Disappearance of Childhood*. New York: Delacorte, 1982.

Sawyer, Ruth. *The Way of the Storyteller*. 1942. New York: Viking, 1962.

"Seminole Nation of Oklahoma." *Southern Plans Tribal Health Board*, https:// www.spthb.org/about-us/who-weserve/seminole-nation-of-oklahoma. Accessed 16 June 2022.

"Seminole Tribal Extension," 2022, https://tribalextension.org/project/ seminole. Accessed 16 June 2022.

Sharma, Jayanta Kar. "Oral Storytelling and Its Techniques." *International Journal of English Language, Literature, and Humanities* 4.2 (Feb. 2006): 269–281.

Shuck-Hall, Sheri Marie. "AlabamaCoushatta in Alabama." *Encyclopedia of Alabama*, 19 Jan. 2017, https:// encyclopediaofalabama.org/h-2352. Accessed 5 May 2022.

_____. *Journey to the West: The Alabama and Coushatta Indians*. Norman: U of OK Press, 2008.

Sirmans, M. Eugene. *Colonial South Carolina: A Political History, 1663–1763*. Chapel Hill: U of NC Press, 1966.

Speck, Frank G. *Catawba Texts*. New York: Columbia UP, 1934.

_____, and L.G. Carr. "Catawba Folk Tales from Chief Sam Blue." *The Journal of American Folklore* 60.235 (Jan.-Mar. 1947): 79–84.

Stuart, Claudio. "Creek Indians." *New Georgia Encyclopedia*, 25 Aug. 2020, https://www.georgiaencyclopedia.org/ articles/history-archaeology/creekindians. Accessed 2 Feb. 2022.

Swanton, John R. *Indian Tribes of North America*. Washington, D.C.: Smithsonian Institution, Bureau of American Ethnology, Bulletin 145, 1952.

_____. *Myths and Tales of the Southeast-*

Bibliography

ern Indians. Washington, D.C.: Smithsonian Institution, Bureau of American Ethnology, Bulletin 88, 1929.

Vacca, Richard T., Jo Anne L. Vacca, and Maryann Mraz. *Content Area Reading: Literacy and Learning Across the Curriculum.* 10th ed. Boston: Pearson, 2011.

Waldrep, Christopher. "French-Natchez War." *Mississippi Encyclopedia,* 14 April 2018, https://mississippi

encyclopedia.org/entries/french-natchez-war/. Accessed 16 May 2022.

Wasserman, Adam. *A People's History of Florida, 1513–1876: How Africans, Seminoles and Lower Class Whites Shaped the Sunshine State.* 4th ed. N.p.: n.p., 2010.

Young, Terrell A., and Phyllis M. Ferguson. "From Anansi to Zomo: Trickster Tales in the Classroom." *The Reading Teacher* 48.6 (Mar. 1995): 490–503.

Index

Index